Go Fi

An Introduction
to Figures of Speech
in the Bible

Julia Hans

Merrimack Media

Cambridge, Massachusetts

Library of Congress Control Number: 2015948406
ISBN 9781939166838

Copyright © 2016 Julia Hans
All rights reserved. No part of this book may be reproduced or transmitted in
any form or by any means, electronic or mechanical, including photocopying,
recording, without permissions in writing from the copyright owner.

Published by Merrimack Media, Cambridge, Massachusetts
January, 2016

COPYRIGHT

Unless otherwise indicated, all Scripture quotations are from The Holy Bible, King James Version. Cambridge: Cambridge UP: n.d.

The Original Aramaic New Testament in Plain English—with Psalms & Proverbs Copyright © 2007; 8th edition Copyright © 2013 All rights reserved.

Douay-Rheims Bible (1899 American Edition) is in the public domain.

The Holy Bible, English Standard Version® (ESV®) Copyright © 2001 by Crossway,a publishing ministry of Good News Publishers. All rights reserved. ESV Text Edition: 2011

Holman Christian Standard Bible ® Copyright © 1999, 2000, 2002, 2003, 2009 by Holman Bible Publishers. Used with permission by Holman Bible Publishers, Nashville, Tennessee. All rights reserved.

Scripture taken from the Holy Bible: International Standard Version®. Copyright © 1996-forever by The ISV Foundation. ALL RIGHTS RESERVED INTERNATIONALLY. Used by permission.

Scripture taken from the NEW AMERICAN STANDARD BIBLE®, Copyright © 1960,1962,1963,1968,1971,1972,1973,1975,1977,1995 by The Lockman Foundation. Used by permission.

Scripture quoted by permission. Quotations designated (NET) are from the NET Bible® copyright ©1996-2006 by Biblical Studies Press, L.L.C. http://netbible.com All rights reserved.

THE HOLY BIBLE, NEW INTERNATIONAL VERSION®, NIV® Copyright © 1973, 1978, 1984, 2011 by Biblica, Inc.® Used by permission. All rights reserved worldwide.

Holy Bible, New Living Translation copyright © 1996, 2004, 2007, 2013 by Tyndale House Foundation. Used by permission of Tyndale House Publishers Inc., Carol Stream, Illinois 60188. All rights reserved. New Living, NLT, and the New Living Translation logo are registered trademarks of Tyndale House Publishers. Weymouth New Testament in Modern Speech, Third Edition: 1913. Public Domain.

Robert Young, The Holy Bible, Consisting of the Old and New Covenants; Translated according to the Letter and Idioms of the Original Languages. Edinburgh: George Adam Young & Co., 1863. Revised edition 1887. Third edition 1898.

DEDICATION
To Ravi

TABLE OF CONTENTS

TABLE OF CONTENTS

PREFACE

Thy word is a lamp unto my feet and a light unto my path. (Psalm 119:105)

PREFACE

How I Came to Write this Book

I had just completed course work for a Master's Degree in English and was preparing to write a proposal for my thesis paper. I wanted to write on the significance of figures of speech used in the Pauline Epistles, something I had been interested in for years. The department chair applauded my idea, and I had the enthusiastic support of a classics professor who agreed to serve as my advisor. Now all I had to do was take a semester of New Testament Greek, which I did that spring. Everything was in place. I wrote my proposal, submitted it to the graduate committee, and waited.

My proposal was rejected.

The committee cited two reasons: first, my proposed topic was "too theological" for an English department; and second, there were not enough primary or secondary sources on the topic. The first reason was debatable. Why did the English department offer a course "Bible as Literature" if the topic was too theological? But I couldn't argue with the second. While there are plenty of books written about figures of speech in secular literature, particularly classical and Renaissance writings, and while there are dozens of reference books that define figures of speech, there is scant scholarship about figures of speech that occur in the Bible. And by scant, I mean one, E. W. Bullinger's *Figures of Speech Used in the Bible Explained and Illustrated* published in 1898. Disappointed, I chose another topic for my master's thesis—American satire, a topic I would later develop for my doctoral dissertation. Meanwhile, I tucked away the proposal on figures of speech in the Pauline Epistles and got on with my work.

Twelve years have passed since then, but I continued to study figures of speech in the Bible. As I studied, I could see the need for a book that might serve as an introduction to this field, something that would be useful to the general reader as well as to students of the Bible who know some Hebrew or Greek. *Go Figure! An Introduction to Figures of Speech in the Bible* is the result of those off-again, on-again years of study. My intent was to write an introduction to this vast topic and to make the field accessible to the modern reader, something that might serve as a springboard to the much more scholarly work done by Bullinger. What started out as a potential topic for a master's thesis turned into a small reference book on figures of speech used in the Bible. Go figure!

Why an Introductory book?

I thought an introductory book would be helpful because the one reference book dedicated to this topic can be difficult and intimidating to use. Without equivocation *Figures of Speech Used in the Bible Explained and Illustrated* remains the gold standard in the field. Bullinger, a nineteenth-century English scholar and Anglican clergyman, painstakingly classifies 217 figures of speech and provides more than 8000 Scripture references in his erudite, 1100-page volume. Like many scholars of his generation, Bullinger works in Hebrew, Greek, and Latin and moves seamlessly from one language to the other throughout his book. Consider his definition of *idiom:*

> *Id-i-ō´-ma.* Greek, ἰδίωμα, *a peculiarity*, from ἴδιος (*idios*), *one's own*, and ἰδιωτισμός (*id-i-o-tis´-mos*), *the common manner of speaking*. Whence the Latin name for the figure IDIOTISMUS (819).

Here Bullinger supplies the transliterated Greek, followed by the Greek word with a brief translation and etymology, then an English definition, ending with the Latin equivalent. If the reader is unfamiliar with Hebrew, Greek, or Latin, such a definition might be difficult to understand.

Figures of Speech Used in the Bible Explained and Illustrated can also be difficult to use today because of its classical nomenclature, Roman numerals, complex classification system, and technical terminology. (Note: The digital version has converted all of the Roman numerals to Arabic numbers.) Consider Bullinger's definition of *heterosis* of the tenses (past for the present): "The past tense expresses what is either imperfect or perfect, or what is a gentle imperative, or a fixed determination, or a continuation of the action or state" (517). Readers unfamiliar with grammatical terms would be hard pressed to understand this definition. And does anyone know what CXVIII is without using an online Roman numeral converter? I don't. So while Bullinger's work is an indispensible reference book, it can be difficult to use for readers who are unfamiliar with Roman numerals, classical languages, and grammatical technicalities.

Go Figure! An Introduction to Figures of Speech in the Bible is designed to serve as a way in to this important field. With examples drawn from popular and general culture, the book is written with today's reader in mind. It covers thirty-two major figures, provides comprehensive yet easy to understand definitions, and then gives examples (more than 500 in all) from general culture and from the Bible. Students who wish to go further in their study might consult the endnotes and bibliography, which are filled with added information and technical details. In addition, students may access a free, regularly updated database that lists occurrences of hundreds of different figures of speech used in the Bible. (Visit http://www.baystatebiblefellowship. org and click on the "Figures of Speech" tab.)

Why Study Figures of Speech?

1 Peter 1:23-25
Being born again, not of corruptible seed, but of incorruptible, by the word of God, which liveth and abideth for ever.
For all flesh *is* as grass, and all the glory of man as the flower of grass. The grass withereth, and the flower thereof falleth away:
But the word of the Lord endureth for ever. And this is the word which by the gospel is preached unto you.

Verse 24 contains a figure of comparison, simile (see chapter 21), where man's flesh and man's glory are compared to grass and to the flowers of grass. Grass and its flowers wither and fade away, but the Word of God lives and abides forever. In other words, the Bible is not another great book of literature; it is God's Word, which lives and abides forever. Therefore, we study figures of speech in the Bible so that we may understand the Word of God and thereby get to know its Author.

2 Peter 1:20-21
Knowing this first, that no prophecy of the scripture is of any private interpretation.
For the prophecy came not in old time by the will of man: but holy men of God spake *as they were* moved by the Holy Ghost.

We see from these verses that the Scriptures did not come by the will of man, meaning that men like Joshua, Moses, and Luke did not decide what words and accounts would go into the Bible. These men wrote as they were moved by the Holy Spirit ("Holy Ghost" in the KJV). This same truth is expressed figuratively in another verse:

2 Timothy 3:16
All scripture *is* given by inspiration of God, and is profitable for doctrine, for reproof, for correction, for instruction in righteousness:

The words "given by inspiration of God" are one Greek word, *theopneustos,* meaning God-breathed. This is the figure of speech *anthropopatheia* (see chapter 17) where God is portrayed as having human characteristics, in this case, the ability to breathe. Therefore we study figures of speech in the Bible because it may help us to better understand and to appreciate God's Word, which is God-breathed. Because the Scriptures did not come by the will of man and because all Scripture is inspired by God, it follows that the figures of speech that occur in its pages are also by divine design. We study figures so that we can understand what the Scriptures say and not miss out on any of its truths or meanings.

Finally, because Semitic languages like Hebrew and Aramaic are highly figurative, it is vital to be able to recognize figures of speech if we want to gain an accurate knowledge of the Scriptures. The Scriptures exhort us to study the Word of God and to rightly divide it:

2 Timothy 2:15
Study to show thyself approved unto God, a workman that needeth not to be ashamed, rightly dividing the Word of truth.

We study figures of speech because it is a tool that helps us to rightly divide the Word of Truth. While knowledge of figures of speech might help us to understand the Scriptures more, it is only *one tool* that might be used when seeking to rightly divide the Word of Truth. Scriptures are interpreted and understood in light of the remote and immediate context, in light of biblical customs and biblical usage of language, in light of specific words used in the verse, in light of a word's or words' previous usage, and in light of other considerations. For an excellent yet succinct guide to studying the Bible, the reader is referred to "A Basis for Scripture Study" in *Scripture Consulting: Select Studies* by Walter J. Cummins (see bibliography).

Acknowledgements

I have had the privilege of working with a number of people on this project and wish to thank the following individuals for their prayer, encouragement, and contributions. For their steadfast interest in and support of this project, I thank Mohinder and Dharampal Hans who helped to make the publication of this book possible. Many thanks go to Raj Hans for faithfully praying for the book. To my children Michael, Kristin, and Abigail I owe a debt of gratitude for their prayers and encouragement. My appreciation also goes to my sister, Nancy Hoffman, and mother, Claudia Dunbar, for their support year after year. What a tremendous blessing it is to have such a loving family.

For a few years I had the privilege of overseeing a small research group that provided me with insights into many aspects of figures of speech. I wish to thank the participants of that group, David Bergey, John Crouch, Greg Earle, and Amanda Reilly, for their assistance. To Abby Armstrong for designing the database, and to Eileen and Cliff LoVerme for reviewing a few chapters early on, I offer my thanks. Special thanks indeed goes to Oonagh Buchanan and Ray Myers who read through the manuscript and provided me with valuable feedback. Thank you for your labor of love. And of course the individual I owe the most thanks is my husband, Ravi. It is not hyperbole to say that without his love and patient encouragement, this book would not have been written. Rav, you have always been an Ephesians 3:20 kind of guy, and I'm so thankful we are heirs together of the grace of life.

Finally, all thanks and praise goes to God my Heavenly Father, the Ancient of Days, *L'Eternel* for His boundless mercy, kindness, patience, and grace. May I say, with the psalmist, "Great is the LORD, and greatly to be praised; and his greatness is unsearchable " (Psalm 145:3).

Like any student of God's Word who holds the Scriptures in the highest regard, I have approached this work with as much care, attention, and ability as I can muster. However, being human, I realize that error and mistakes will creep in. Whatever lack occurs in these pages is the sole responsibility of the author.

Unless otherwise noted, all English verses are taken from the King James or Authorized Version of the Bible. All quotes from *Figures of Speech Used in the Bible Explained and Illustrated* are from the Tenth Print Edition, Baker Books. This book is formatted according to 2011 MLA publishing standards.

INTRODUCTION

Thy word is a lamp unto my feet and a light unto my path. (Psalm 119:105)

So What are Figures of Speech Anyway?

Most writing, whether fiction, poetry, drama, or non-fiction makes use of figurative language for many reasons: to emphasize a point, to dramatize a setting, to imbue a passage with some sort of mood or tone, to make a passage more interesting or entertaining, and so on. Technically speaking, figures of speech are either departures from normal rules of speech or language, or they express a truth in an unusual or nonliteral way. Vilant Macbeth defines figurative language as "a word or words thrown into a peculiar form. A word is used figuratively when it is brought forward in a form, construction, or application different from its first or its simplest form, construction, or application" (xl). In other words, language is figurative when there is a departure from normal rules of grammar or syntax, or when the meaning of the word is not literal.

Most rhetoricians classify figures into two groups: figures of grammar and figures of thought.

> 1. Figures of Grammar
> 2. Figures of Thought

Figures of grammar are those that depart from rules of grammar or syntax. Bullinger writes, "All language is governed by law. But in order to increase the power of a word, or the force of an expression, these laws are designedly departed from, and words and sentences are thrown into, and used in, new forms, or *figures*" (v). For example, *polysyndeton* is a figure of grammar that uses repeated conjunctions more than ordinary usage would require. (Normal rules of grammar indicate that a conjunction comes between the last two nouns in a series, not between each noun.) And so an overabundance of "ands" in a sentence or verse may be the figure of speech *polysyndeton*. Consider the following verse:

> **Joshua 7:24** (emphasis added)
> And Joshua, and all Israel with him, took Achan the son of Zerah, **and** the silver, **and** the garment, **and** the wedge of **gold**, **and** his sons, **and** his daughters, **and** his oxen, **and** his asses, **and**

his sheep, **and** his tent, **and** all that he had: **and** they brought them unto the valley of Achor.

In this verse, eleven nouns (or noun phrases) are linked together by the conjunction "and." This abundant use of the word "and" in this sentence constitutes the figure *polysyndeton*, a figure of grammar that uses conjunctions beyond the grammatical norm. This figure draws emphasis to each item enumerated.

Figures of thought occur when what is stated is not literally true to fact or true to its natural meaning. We use these types of figures every day. I could say "I'm tired," but instead I say "I'm worn out." The dancer isn't merely talented; you can't hold a candle to her. And the ambitious executive isn't decisive; he takes the bull by the horns. This is figurative language, not true to fact but true in meaning. Now let's consider an example of a figure of thought in the Bible:

John 21:25
And there are also many other things which Jesus did, the which, if they should be written every one, I suppose that even the world itself could not contain the books that should be written. Amen.

Are the words literal here, that there would not be enough room in the world to hold all the books that should be written about the many other things that Jesus did? No, this is the figure of speech *hyperbole*, or exaggeration. In this verse, the figure is used to emphasize the significance of the "many other things" that Jesus did that were not written down.

Figures of speech, whether of grammar or of thought, enliven language and give it emphasis; they deepen expression, heighten the drama of communication, and give it freshness, vitality, and variety.

So, how do we know if a verse or passage or word in the Bible is figurative or literal? Let's consider something E. W. Bullinger writes as a way to answer this question:

. . .whenever and wherever possible, the words of Scripture are to be understood *literally*, but when a statement appears to be contrary to our experience, or to known fact, or revealed truth; or seems to be at variance with the general teaching of

the Scriptures, then we may reasonably expect that some figure
is employed. (xv)

Basically Bullinger is saying that whenever and wherever possible, the words
of the Bible are to be understood literally. Sometimes, though, the words are
figurative. When a statement appears to be

- contrary to our experience
- contrary to known fact, or revealed truth
- at variance with the general teaching of the Scriptures,

then we may reasonably expect that a figure or figures occurs. These
guidelines are helpful to keep in mind as we endeavor to understand and to
identify figurative language in the Bible.

Some figures, like many figures of repetition, are relatively easy to spot. You
can see the repetition right in the text. (One can imagine that these figures
were also quite apparent when the Scriptures were read aloud.) For instance,
note how the word "praise" is repeated in the following verses:

> **Psalm 148:1-4** (emphasis added)
> **Praise** ye the LORD.
> **Praise** ye the LORD from the heavens:
> **praise** him in the heights.
> **Praise** ye him, all his angels: **praise** ye him, all his hosts.
> **Praise** ye him, sun and moon: **praise** him, all ye stars of light.
> **Praise** him, ye heavens of heavens, and ye waters that *be* above
> the heavens.

This is the figure of speech *anaphora*, a figure of grammar that occurs when
a word is repeated at the beginning of successive sentences, phrases, or
clauses. In these four verses the word "praise" occurs eight times at the
beginning of eight successive clauses. Figures of repetition like *anaphora*
tend to be easier to identify than figures of thought because you can see the
words repeated.

Figures of thought can be more difficult to identify, however, and usually
require a careful consideration of the context. Consider these words spoken
to Rebekah by her family just before she was about to leave them to
marry Isaac:

Genesis 24:60

And they blessed Rebekah, and said unto her, Thou *art* our sister, be thou *the mother* of thousands of millions, and let thy seed possess the gate of those which hate them.

The phrase "be thou the mother of thousands of millions" is not literal; it is a figurative expression, either an idiom or hyperbole. In the context, Rebekah's family sends her off with a blessing, "be thou the mother of thousands of millions." This is a figurative way of saying, "may you be happy and prosperous." Motherhood was highly valued in the lands and times of the Bible, and so to be the mother of many children would be considered a blessing. Figures of thought like idiom and hyperbole can be more difficult to identify in the Scriptures than figures of grammar, and they require a careful consideration of the context in order to appreciate their meaning.

> Generally speaking, language is figurative when rules governing language are violated or when the words cannot be taken literally or are not true to fact.

Benefits of Studying Figurative Language

Identifying figures of speech in the Bible can benefit the reader in a number of ways. First, it can help to avoid misunderstandings when reading. Let's consider a record where Jesus Christ uses figurative language, and his disciples take him literally.

John 11:7-14

Then after that saith he to *his* disciples, Let us go into Judaea again.

His disciples say unto him, Master, the Jews of late sought to stone thee; and goest thou thither again?

Jesus answered, Are there not twelve hours in the day? If any man walk in the day, he stumbleth not, because he seeth the light of this world.

But if a man walk in the night, he stumbleth, because there is no light in him.

These things said he: and after that he saith unto them, Our friend Lazarus sleepeth; but I go, that I may awake him out of sleep.

Then said his disciples, Lord, if he sleep, he shall do well.
Howbeit Jesus spake of his death: but they thought that he had
spoken of taking of rest in sleep.
Then said Jesus unto them plainly, Lazarus is dead.

After receiving word that his friend Lazarus had died, Jesus responds, "Our friend Lazarus sleepeth; but I go, that I may awake him out of sleep." Here, Jesus is using *euphemismos* (euphemism), a figure that exchanges a harsh or unpleasant expression with a more pleasant one. We have many euphemisms in English: passed away for dead; made redundant for being let go from a job; collateral damage for accidental fatalities; and so on. Jesus Christ knows that Lazarus is dead but says, "Lazarus sleepeth." His disciples take him literally. They respond by saying that, quite logically, if he's sick, sleep will do him some good. Finally, Jesus Christ has to spell it out for them: "Lazarus is dead." In this record, Jesus Christ uses figurative language, but his disciples take him literally. Misunderstanding ensues. And so, understanding figures can help us to avoid misunderstanding when we read the Scriptures.

Second, identifying figures of speech in the Bible might help uncover hidden meaning or added emphasis. In his book *Key to the Book of Psalms*, Thomas Boys suggests that many figures are overlooked in an "ordinary reading" of the Bible and that this oversight may result in a loss of "sense or import" of a passage (22). In other words, failure to recognize a figure may result in failure to understand the emphasis or force in a particular passage. Consider the repetition of the word "faith" (*pistis* in Greek) in the following passage:

Hebrews 11:3-31 (emphasis added)
Through faith (***pistis***) we understand that the worlds were framed by the word of God, so that things which are seen were not made of things which do appear.
By faith (***pistis***) Abel offered unto God a more excellent sacrifice than Cain, by which he obtained witness that he was righteous, God testifying of his gifts: and by it he being dead yet speaketh.
By faith (***pistis***) Enoch was translated that he should not see death; and was not found, because God had translated him: for before his translation he had this testimony, that he pleased God.
But without faith (***pistis***) *it is* impossible to please *him*: for he that cometh to God must believe that he is, and *that* he is a rewarder of them that diligently seek him.

By faith (**pistis**) Noah, being warned of God of things not seen as yet, moved with fear, prepared an ark to the saving of his house; by the which he condemned the world, and became heir of the righteousness which is by faith.

By faith (**pistis**) Abraham, when he was called to go out into a place which he should after receive for an inheritance, obeyed; and he went out, not knowing whither he went.

By faith (**pistis**) he sojourned in the land of promise, as *in* a strange country, dwelling in tabernacles with Isaac and Jacob, the heirs with him of the same promise:

For he looked for a city which hath foundations, whose builder and maker is God.

Through faith (**pistis**) also Sara herself received strength to conceive seed, and was delivered of a child when she was past age, because she judged him faithful who had promised.

Therefore sprang there even of one, and him as good as dead, *so many* as the stars of the sky in multitude, and as the sand which is by the sea shore innumerable.

These all died in faith, (**pistis**) not having received the promises, but having seen them afar off, and were persuaded of *them*, and embraced *them*, and confessed that they were strangers and pilgrims on the earth.

For they that say such things declare plainly that they seek a country.

And truly, if they had been mindful of that *country* from whence they came out, they might have had opportunity to have returned.

But now they desire a better *country*, that is, an heavenly: wherefore God is not ashamed to be called their God: for he hath prepared for them a city.

By faith (**pistis**) Abraham, when he was tried, offered up Isaac: and he that had received the promises offered up his only begotten *son*,

Of whom it was said, That in Isaac shall thy seed be called:

Accounting that God was able to raise *him* up, even from the dead; from whence also he received him in a figure.

By faith (**pistis**) Isaac blessed Jacob and Esau concerning things to come.

By faith (**pistis**) Jacob, when he was a dying, blessed both the sons of Joseph; and worshipped, *leaning* upon the top of his staff.

By faith (*pistis*) Joseph, when he died, made mention of the departing of the children of Israel; and gave commandment concerning his bones.

By faith (*pistis*) Moses, when he was born, was hid three months of his parents, because they saw *he was* a proper child; and they were not afraid of the king's commandment.

By faith (*pistis*) Moses, when he was come to years, refused to be called the son of Pharaoh's daughter;

Choosing rather to suffer affliction with the people of God, than to enjoy the pleasures of sin for a season;

Esteeming the reproach of Christ greater riches than the treasures in Egypt: for he had respect unto the recompence of the reward.

By faith (*pistis*) he forsook Egypt, not fearing the wrath of the king: for he endured, as seeing him who is invisible.

Through faith (*pistis*) he kept the passover, and the sprinkling of blood, lest he that destroyed the firstborn should touch them.

By faith (*pistis*) they passed through the Red sea as by dry *land*: which the Egyptians assaying to do were drowned.

By faith (*pistis*) the walls of Jericho fell down, after they were compassed about seven days.

By faith (*pistis*) the harlot Rahab perished not with them that believed not, when she had received the spies with peace.

In this passage, the Greek word *pistis* occurs twenty times at the beginning of numerous clauses in close proximity making this the figure *anaphora*. Even though the King James Version inconsistently translates *pistis* (alternately "by faith" and "through faith"), it is the same word in the Greek. This figure emphasizes the repeated word *pistis* and that it is by faith or by believing that the aforementioned great and wondrous things occurred, as opposed to intellectual ability, moral rectitude, intense effort, and so forth. In this example, the force of the repetition is clear.

In other examples, the emphasis is subtler.

Ephesians 1:3 (emphasis added)
Blessed be the God and Father of our Lord Jesus Christ, who hath **blessed** us with all spiritual **blessings** in heavenly *places* in Christ:

In this example, the word "bless" occurs three times but in different forms: adjective, verb, and noun. This constitutes the figure of speech *polyptoton*, where a word is repeated in different inflections (see chapter 7). In this verse, the figure emphasizes the blessings we have in Christ.

All writing has natural places of emphasis, rendered either through diction (words), syntax (arrangement), or other rhetorical patterns or designs. Figures of speech usually (but not always) bring emphasis to a particular point or idea. And like all of God's Word, these figures occur in the Scriptures by divine design and therefore merit our attention. Recognizing figures of speech, then, helps us to appreciate a particular point of emphasis that may occur in the Scriptures.

A third benefit to identifying figures of speech in the Bible is that it allows the reader to gain an appreciation of the beauty and accuracy of God's Word. We often marvel at the intricate detail of God's creation in nature or at the perfection of the human body, which is "fearfully and wonderfully made" (Psalm 139:14). Yet the Scriptures are God-breathed and are therefore filled with linguistic beauty and perfection. Scholars often marvel at how writers like John Milton or William Shakespeare use figurative language in such complex and varied ways, and yet few marvel at how precisely and marvelously figures are used in the Holy Scriptures. There is no comparison! Without putting too fine a point on it, we might say that a third benefit to studying figures of speech in the Bible is that it allows us to appreciate the accuracy and beauty and divine design of God's Word.

> Studying figures of speech might help us:
> 1. To distinguish between literal and figurative meaning
> 2. To uncover hidden or obscured significance and emphasis
> 3. To appreciate the beauty of the Scriptures

Misconceptions about Figures of Speech

Myths about figurative language abound. The most common misconception is that all figurative language is metaphoric. If we say something that isn't literally true, we quickly add, "Oh, I was just speaking metaphorically." But *metaphor* is only one figure of comparison. When a poet compares a lover to a rose or calls a ruffian a beast or somehow expresses a truth in a non-literal way, the assumption is that the poet is using *metaphor*. Not necessarily. She might be using *hypocatastasis* or *simile* or *metonymy* or even *hyperbole*. So, it's important to first recognize that not all figurative language is metaphoric and that not all comparisons are *metaphors*.

Another misconception is that if words are figurative, they aren't true and that figurative language somehow weakens meaning. Quite the opposite is the case. In *A Poet's Guide to Poetry*, Mary Kinzie describes figures as "classical devices of rhetoric and grammar for arresting the attention and steering the audience" (413). While figures aren't true to fact, they are true to meaning. And because they arrest our attention, they are more potent, in a sense, than literal statements of fact. Far from weakening language, figures enliven language. Let's see how this plays out by considering a short passage by Charles Dickens, a masterful writer of figurative language:

> The ancient tower of a church, whose gruff old bell was always peeping slyly down at Scrooge out of a gothic window in the wall, became invisible, and struck the hours and quarters in the clouds, with tremulous vibrations afterwards, as if its teeth were chattering in its frozen head up there. (*A Christmas Carol*: Stave 1)

Perhaps the reader doesn't realize it, but what makes this description so lively is its use of figurative language. Dickens packs four figures into one sentence. Twice he uses *personification*: the bell is called "gruff" and it "peeps slyly down at Scrooge." He uses *metaphor* when the tower is compared to a frozen head; and he uses *simile* when the tolling of the bell is compared to the sound of teeth chattering. A compelling writer and storyteller, Dickens takes something as commonplace as a bell tower and animates it with figurative language, making it vivid and entertaining. He uses figurative language to draw the reader into Scrooge's world and help him feel how cold and harsh it is. Through figurative language, Dickens gives high drama to an otherwise mundane reality—a clock tower sounding on the half and quarter hours. Rather than weaken the meaning of language, figures of speech add force to language. If this is true in general literature, why wouldn't it be true in God's Word?

A third misconception about figurative language is that when it comes to the Bible, figures somehow erode the veracity of the Scriptures. Strict literalists might argue that if we consider a passage to be figurative, we are somehow saying that a passage isn't true. But is this the case? Figures of speech used in the Bible often emphasize truths; they may express truths in a non-literal way; and they frequently give force and feeling to language. Figurative language used in the Bible may not be literally true, but it is true nonetheless. So just because language is figurative doesn't mean it isn't true to meaning.

How Do Figures Bring Emphasis?

In literature, figures serve many functions. Here is a partial list, complied from numerous sources, of how figures function in writing:

- Add emphasis
- Intensify feeling
- Diminish impact
- Arrest attention
- Appeal to emotion
- Cite authority
- Add ornamentation
- Bolster an argument
- Add aesthetic flourish
- Add zest or impact
- Reflect vernacular speech
- Dramatize feeling
- Serve as a mnemonic device
- Achieve a desired auditory quality
- Achieve a desired cadence or rhythm
- Serve a social function within a group
- Add comic value

Myths about figures of speech	Truths about figures of speech
• All figures are metaphors	• All figures are not metaphors
• Figures weaken language	• Figures intensify language
• Figures in the Bible erode veracity	• Figures in the Bible express truths non-literally

One of the ways that a figure may function in the Scriptures is that it may draw attention to a passage, or a phrase, or a group of words. But how does one determine what a figure emphasizes? In large part, that depends on the *nature* or *characteristic* of the figure and upon the context in which the figure occurs. Let's consider the figure *asyndeton*, a figure that lists words or phrases together without using conjunctions.

Mark 7:21-23

For from within, out of the heart of men, proceed evil thoughts, adulteries, fornications, murders, thefts, covetousness, wickedness, deceit, lasciviousness, an evil eye, blasphemy, pride, foolishness: All these evil things come from within and defile the man.

Note how there is no conjunction between the last two words in this list of vices. *Asyndeton* marks out this passage by putting emphasis on what comes at the end, causing the reader to hasten through the list of vices and focus on the end matter—evil things come from within and defile a man. Understanding the figure, the reader realizes that the emphasis lies on the end matter, and not on each individual word in the passage.

Now let's take a look at the figure *polysyndeton*, which uses conjunctions beyond the grammatical norm.

Romans 9:4 (emphasis added)

Who are Israelites; to whom *pertaineth* the adoption, **and** the glory, **and** the covenants, **and** the giving of the law, **and** the service *of God*, **and** the promises;

In this verse, the conjunction ("and") is repeated five times, drawing attention to each item in the list. What's more, when we also consider the context of this verse, we learn that the Apostle Paul is speaking about his fellow Israelites. Noting the characteristic of the figure and keeping the context in mind, we understand that this *polysyndeton* draws attention to all the matters listed here and that they pertain, specifically, to Israel. (For more detailed discussion about how figures function in the Scriptures, please see Appendix 3: FAQs, particularly questions 5 and 6.)

How a figure conveys emphasis:
- By its unique characteristic
- By considering the context

What's in this book

Go Figure! A Introduction to Figures of Speech in the Bible is written to help students gain entry to the complex field of figurative language used in the Bible. Without a doubt, the definitive book on the subject of figures is E. W. Bullinger's *Figures of Speech Used in the Bible Explained and Illustrated.* At nearly 1000 pages, this erudite reference book covers more than 200 figures of speech, some with up to forty variations. *Go Figure!* narrows the field (32 figures) and simplifies the approach. The following criteria were used in selecting each of the thirty-two figures:

- The figure occurs with relative frequency in the Bible.
- The figure's definition and usage is fairly simple to understand.
- The figure is fairly recognizable in an English translation.
- No knowledge of Biblical languages and grammar is necessary in order to understand this figure.

If the figure met all or most of these requirements, then it made the list. If not, then I passed it by. For instance, *heterosis* isn't in the line-up even though this figure occurs frequently in the Bible because identifying this figure requires some knowledge of Hebrew and Greek grammar. Similarly, figures like *epitrope* (admission) or *apologue* (fable) aren't included because even though they are simple to understand, they don't occur frequently in the Bible. The 32 figures chosen provide a solid foundation for further study.

How the Book is organized

Go Figure! is a arranged in eight sections by topic:

1. FIGURES OF REPETITION
2. FIGURES OF OVERSTATEMENT AND UNDERSTATEMENT
3. FIGURES OF OMISSION
4. FIGURES USING HUMAN ATTRIBUTES
5. FIGURES OF EXCHANGE
6. FIGURES OF COMPARISON
7. RHETORICAL QUESTIONS
8. IDIOMS AND OTHER FAMILIAR FIGURES

I chose to arrange this book topically as an aid to understanding. Grouping figures of repetition together helps students remember that repetition is a key characteristic of these figures. Similarly, thinking about simile, metaphor, *hypocatastasis*, parable, and allegory as figures of comparison helps to remind us that these figures rest on some sort of comparison. So while this material could be adequately organized in any number of ways, I chose a topical arrangement because I thought it would help students understand and remember the figures.

Each section opens with a short introduction and then divides into chapters, with one chapter devoted to a single figure. In his work, Bullinger catalogues figures with extreme specificity separating figures into categories, subcategories, and sub-subcategories often to dizzying effect. In the interest of keeping things simple, however, I use only the occasional subdivision. For example, here's how the first section is organized:

Section 1: FIGURES OF REPETITION
        Chapter 1:   Anaphora
        Chapter 2:   Polysyndeton
                   a) "and"
                   b) other conjunctions
        Chapter 3:   Epistrophe
        Chapter 4:   Epanalepsis
        Chapter 5:   Anadiplosis
        Chapter 6:   Epizeuxis
        Chapter 7:   Polyptoton
        Chapter 8:   Synonymia
        Chapter 9:   Repetitio
        Chapter 10:   Pleonasm

Each chapter offers a detailed and comprehensive definition of the figure followed by numerous examples from general culture and from the Bible. Tips are included when applicable, and copious endnotes are provided for those who wish to investigate the field further.

The book also includes three appendices. The first, an original essay titled "Beautiful Feet: A Look at Seven Figures of Speech in Romans 10:8-15" is given as an example of how the study of figures of speech might inform a teaching. Appendix 2 includes an annotated bibliography of select print and digital resources that I found to be particularly helpful in my study of figurative language in the Bible. Appendix 3 includes answers to frequently asked questions about figures of speech. Finally, a Scripture index is provided for ease of reference.

Methodology

Names

The first obstacle encountered when assembling this material was determining which names to use. Classical or contemporary? Transliterated Greek or English? Choosing which names to use poses a unique problem for English readers because these names exist in Greek, Latin, English, and other languages; and, these names change over time or are known by multiple names. In *Go Figure!* the classical names (transliterated Greek or Latin) are used, followed by an English equivalent. These classical names are used for continuity: scholars across a spectrum of disciplines still refer to figures by these classical names, and so if a student wishes to further her study of a particular figure, she will be familiar with the term used by scholars today. Because these names can be difficult to pronounce, however, a pronunciation key is provided. When pronunciation of a term varies (usually between British and American English), *Go Figure!* follows the American pronunciation provided by the *Oxford English Dictionary*. Finally, a page reference to F*igures of Speech Used in the Bible Explained and Illustrated* (1968, Baker) is provided in each chapter heading so that students may easily reference Bullinger's book.

Readers can expect a chapter heading to look something like this:

Chapter 3

Epistrophe

(repeated sentence endings) 241

e-PIS-tro-fee

> *Epistrophe* is the repetition of the same word or words at the end of successive sentences, phrases, or clauses.

Here, the classical name is given, with short definition, page reference to *Figures of Speech Used in the Bible Explained and Illustrated* followed by a pronunciation key. Then a short definition follows.

When deciding on the names of figures, a second problem arises. Because language is fluid, names of some figures change over time. For instance, what is the name of the figure of understatement that uses a negative to express the positive in a high degree? Depending on the source, the answer might be *tapeinosis* or *litotes* or *meiosis*. E. W. Bullinger and Vilant Macbeth, both writing in the nineteenth century, equate *meiosis* and *litotes*. Bullinger considers *tapeinosis* or *antenantiosis* to be a figure of understatement that uses the negative to express the positive in a high degree, not *litotes*. But according to the *The Oxford English Dictionary (OED)*, the term *tapeinosis* is an obsolete term. Amongst twentieth-century scholars, there is wide consensus that *litotes* is a figure of understatement using the negative to express the positive in a high degree (see: Joseph, Lanham, Espy, *Silva Rhetorica*). Further, the *OED* defines *litotes* as, "A figure of speech, in which an affirmative is expressed by the negative of the contrary." So modern sources agree that a figure of understatement that uses a negative to express the positive in a high degree is *litotes*. In a case like this, I use the more modern term and note its older equivalent.

In my research, I consulted numerous sources from different disciplines and from different centuries. Sometimes sources were in agreement about a particular name, with variations in spelling. Sometimes they differed widely. Often I have encountered a clash of the centuries where older sources like Bullinger and Vilant Macbeth are in agreement; whereas, newer sources like Lanham and Espy concur with one another. When faced with this type of dilemma, I look to the *Oxford English Dictionary* to act as umpire. This authoritative source traces the meaning of a word throughout the centuries, and so one can see how a word might change over time. In the end, I have always tried to choose the term that I felt would be of most use to students today, especially those who wish to continue their study of this field. Hanging on to an obsolete term, for instance, would not be of much use to those wishing to further their study. At the same time, I have been careful to note the obsolete term or alternative names in the endnotes recognizing this is a fluid enterprise. I break my own rule, though, when it comes to the figure *hypocatastasis*. After much deliberation, I decided to keep the older name because even though most modern scholars consider this figure to be a type of metaphor, I believe there is some accuracy lost when we conflate these two figures. Interestingly, although the *OED* considers this term to be obsolete, online sources are starting to bring this term back to life. (For a full discussion of why I retained this name, please see chapter 23.)

Finally, readers will notice that I have relegated the academic debate—at times hairy and contentious—to the endnotes. There students will find enough detail that if they wish, they may research these inconsistencies themselves.

Definitions

If naming the figures was a challenge, deriving definitions was a monumental task. As one can imagine, there is little consensus about the definition of any one figure of speech. One challenge in writing this book has been sifting through the morass of opinion and theory about definitions of specific figures of speech. In the years spent researching this field, I have learned that generally speaking, the older the scholarship, the more precise and detailed the definition. There is a tendency in modern scholarship to conflate meaning and to blur or to erase distinctions, even to the point of error. I have also noticed that there are slight (and sometimes glaring) differences in definitions amongst literary scholars, classicists, rhetoricians, and linguists. Each field has its own theoretical framework, terminology, and intellectual bias, and so there is, quite understandably, differences amongst these disciplines when it comes to definitions of specific figures. The meaning of metaphor, for instance, varies widely between literary scholars and linguists. A literary scholar might adopt a more narrow definition while a linguist, a broader one; or, vice-versa. (In fact, whole books have been written about the meaning and significance of metaphor, and several academic camps have assembled around the divergent meanings of this one figure; so to write a short, succinct definition of metaphor is not without its challenges.) While there is undoubtedly merit and value in taking a linguistic approach to figurative language, and while I have consulted books by linguists on this topic, because I am trained in literary theory and history and know literary apparatus, I have naturally favored a literary view of language.

When it comes to writing a definition, I always start with *Figures of Speech Used in the Bible Explained and Illustrated* and then consult respectable literary sources like Vilant Macbeth, Espy, and Joseph. Next, I check general and specialized encyclopedias and handbooks on rhetoric such as those edited by Enos, Lanham, Quinn, and Sloane. I may consult works on a single figure like Jon Winokur's *The Big Book of Irony (2007)* or Benjaim Keach's *Tropologia: A Key to Open Scripture Metaphor in Four Books (1858)*, or I may consult a general work such as Sylvia Adamson's *Renaissance Figures of Speech (2007)* if it sheds light on a particular figure. Finally, I check credible online sources like Silva Rhetorica, Daily Trope, and RhetFig. At this point, I start to see overlap and the clash of centuries mentioned earlier. In the end, I have to make a judgment call and have tried to write definitions that were both easy to understand yet detailed enough to retain historic accuracy. In his book *The New Testament: Its Background, Growth, and Content* Bruce Metzger writes, "The chief danger, as every writer who has attempted to popularize research knows, is that, in making the complex clear, one may also make it appear simple, or, in making the debatable plain, one may also make it appear certain" (14). Indeed, while I have striven to make this book clear and simple, in no way do I mean to portray this field as non-debatable and clear as crystal.

Examples: General Culture

Now comes the easy part. After deciding on a name and writing a definition, I give examples of the figure as it occurs in general culture. By general culture, I mean early and modern literature, past and present popular culture including advertising slogans and television shows, song lyrics from secular and Christian songwriters, speeches, aphorisms both common and obscure, and from many other sources. While I have attempted to include a variety of examples from different generations and cultures, my examples are, admittedly, overwhelmingly American. This is more a result of convenience than it is of a desire to convey an American bias. Not only do I live in the United States, my graduate studies focused on twentieth-century American literature and culture, especially humor and satire. So if my examples seem to favor comedians or satirists, it's because these are the works I know best. However, as the collaborative aspect of this project grows, I hope to receive contributions from readers across the globe, thereby adding to the diversity of examples.

Examples: From the Scriptures

After giving examples from general culture, I next provide examples of the figure as it occurs in the Scriptures. The biblical examples used in this book are from the King James Version of the Bible. These examples come from my own research, from *Figures of Speech Used in the Bible Explained and Illustrated*, *The Might and Mirth of Literature*, and other sources. The selection process was pretty simple: I went for the low-hanging fruit, a metaphor or idiom meaning things that are relatively easy to grasp. If a figure like *anaphora* was pretty easy to see in the KJV, then I might select it for inclusion in *Go Figure!* If, however, the *anaphora* was hidden in the English translation, then I might have passed it by, or include it with explanatory notes.

And that leads me to an important point: Because these figures occur in the biblical languages, not in English, their occurrence needs to be verified in the Hebrew or Greek. Each biblical example in *Go Figure!* has been verified, to the best of my ability, in the Hebrew or Greek, meaning that I have checked interlinears, lexicons, and other research tools. On occasion, I offer another English translation if the figure was translated more than in the KJV. For example, because the figure *polyptoton* is not reflected in the KJV, I offer several other versions or translations that do reflect the figure:

Genesis 2:17b (KJV)
But of the tree of the knowledge of good and evil, thou shalt not eat of it: for in the day that thou eatest thereof thou shalt surely die.

Note how the *polyptoton* is not reflected in this version. Now note how the figure is reflected in several other English translations:

Genesis 2:17 (Young's Literal Translation) (emphasis added)
and of the tree of knowledge of good and evil, thou dost not eat of it, for in the day of thine eating of it—**dying thou dost die**.'

Genesis 2:17 (Douay-Rheims) (emphasis added)
But of the tree of knowledge of good and evil, thou shalt not eat. for in what day soever thou shalt eat of it, thou shalt **die the death**.

In these two versions, the *polyptoton* is translated. So when a figure is not clear in the KJV, I sometimes offer a different English translation if it helps to make the figure clearer to the reader.

Readers will undoubtedly notice that there is not much explanation or interpretation given in *Go Figure!* Because this is an introductory book on the topic, the exposition of the Scriptures has been kept to a minimum. Where possible, I have avoided controversial passages and have given just enough exposition so that students may understand how a figure might function in a particular passage. I have avoided turning this book into an expository treatise on the significance of figures in the Bible, which is not the focus of this book. When it comes to explaining the significance of a figure, as much as possible, I have endeavored to follow the admonition given in Ecclesiastes 5:2b "let thy words be few."

Unique Features of this book

- Topical arrangement
- Expanded definitions
- Research from various disciplines spanning several generations
- Popular culture examples
- Examples from the Scriptures
- Annotated bibliography
- Link to Figures of Speech Database

Figures of Speech Database: A Collaborative Effort

Identifying all the figures of speech used in the Bible would take several lifetimes. As research in this field continues, I expect that new figures will be identified and added to the online database, which lists hundreds of occurrences of figures of speech in the Bible not listed in *Go Figure!* To access the database, go to our website, www.baystatebiblefellowship.org. Click on the "Figures of Speech" tab and then scroll down to the link labeled "database." If you wish to contribute, please fill out the form found on our website, and your submission will be considered. This free database will be updated twice annually. Those wishing to receive notifications of these updates may send an email request to baystatebible@comcast.net

How To Use this Book

This is a small reference book that may be used in several ways. You may read one chapter to become familiar with a particular figure of speech. Using the examples provided, you might then note the figure in the margins of your Bible. The more familiar you are with the name and characteristic of the figure, the more likely you are to spot other occurrences on your own. Second, you might use this as a reference tool by consulting the index at the back of the book. There you will find the occurrence of every figure listed in this book, arranged in canonical order. Finally, you might use this book as a springboard for further study: the endnotes and bibliography are provided with this further study in mind. And don't forget to consult the database regularly.

Psalm 119:105

Thy word *is* a lamp unto my feet and a light unto my path.

Psalm 119:105 is the theme verse for this book. In it, the psalmist uses a lovely metaphor to compare God's Word to instruments that provide light—a lamp and a light. What a privilege it is to have the light of God's Word available to us today. I pray that this work may help students better understand and appreciate God's matchless Word, and that in the process, they might grow closer to God, who has been so kind and so gracious throughout the centuries to make Himself known in His Word.

SECTION 1
FIGURES OF REPETITION

FIGURES OF REPETITION

Repetition is one of the oldest, most basic literary devices and a fundamental tool of instruction. Today speechwriters, journalists, and other writers use repetition when they want to drive home a point or add drama or force to their writing. Figures of repetition are often the easiest figures to identify because you can literally *see* these figures in a text. Consider the repetition in these lines by Martin Luther King, Jr.:

> So let freedom ring from the prodigious hilltops of New Hampshire.
> Let freedom ring from the mighty mountains of New York.
> Let freedom ring from the heightening Alleghenies of Pennsylvania.
> Let freedom ring from the snow-capped Rockies of Colorado.
> Let freedom ring from the curvaceous peaks of California.
> But not only that, let freedom, ring from Stone Mountain of Georgia.
> Let freedom ring from Lookout Mountain of Tennessee.
> Let freedom ring from every hill and molehill of Mississippi.
> From every mountainside, let freedom ring.

The clause "let freedom ring" is repeated nine times in nine sentences. Now note how the phrase "it was" is repeated throughout the opening line from *A Tale of Two Cities:*

> It was the best of times, it was the worst of times, it was the age of wisdom, it was the age of foolishness, it was the epoch of belief, it was the epoch of incredulity, it was the season of Light, it was the season of Darkness, it was the spring of hope, it was the winter of despair, we had everything before us, we had nothing before us, we were all going direct to Heaven, we were all going direct the other way?

Now let's look an example of repetition in the Scriptures:

Matthew 5:3-11
Blessed *are* the poor in spirit: for theirs is the kingdom of heaven.
Blessed *are* they that mourn: for they shall be comforted.
Blessed *are* the meek: for they shall inherit the earth.
Blessed *are* they which do hunger and thirst after righteousness: for they shall be filled.
Blessed *are* the merciful: for they shall obtain mercy.

Blessed *are* the pure in heart: for they shall see God.
Blessed *are* the peacemakers: for they shall be called the children of God.
Blessed *are* they which are persecuted for righteousness' sake: for theirs is the kingdom of heaven.
Blessed *are* ye, when men shall revile you, and persecute you, and shall say all manner of evil against you falsely, for my sake.

Here, the word "blessed" (*makarios* in Greek) occurs nine times in nine sentences. In each of these examples, the figure of speech draws attention to the words that are repeated. And that's generally true for figures of repetition: they emphasize the word or words that are repeated.

Figures of repetition are grammatical figures that occur when a word or phrase is repeated beyond the norm or if a word or phrase is repeated in a distinguishable pattern. Rather than lump all figures of repetition into one general category however, rhetoricians have categorized these figures according to their specific characteristics and patterns. In *Figures of Used in the Bible Explained and Illustrated*, for example, E. W. Bullinger lists more than 40 figures of repetition, some with numerous variations. *Go Figure!* covers ten common and easily identifiable figures of repetition. The figures in this section are repetitions of a word or words rather than repetition of whole clauses or sentences.

Chapter 1

Anaphora

(like sentence beginnings) 199

an-AFF-o-ra

> *Anaphora* is the repetition of the same word or words at the beginning of successive sentences, phrases, or clauses.

It's not enough for words to be repeated: in order for it to be *anaphora*, the repetition must come at the *beginning* of a sentence, phrase, or clause; and those sentences, phrases, or clauses must come in close succession.

Anaphora can bring emphasis in several ways. Like most figures of repetition, *anaphora* may emphasize the word or phrase that is repeated. But *anaphora* might also emphasize the parallel or antithetical relationship between the sentence, phrase, or clause that is linked by the repeated word. Finally, *anaphora* is sometimes used as a rhetorical device to bring the reader along to an end point or climax. In that case, the emphasis in *anaphora* lies on the end matter. Context helps to determine how the figure might bring emphasis.

FROM GENERAL CULTURE

Example 1 (emphasis added)
She was not quite what you would call refined. **She was** not quite what you would call unrefined. **She was** the kind of person that keeps a parrot. (Mark Twain)

In the first example, the words "she was" are repeated at the beginning of successive phrases in order to emphasize the subject—Twain's unidentified woman. The repetition also serves to lead the reader to Twain's humorous climax, or punch line about the parrot.

> **Example 2** (emphasis added)
> **I'd be** packin' my bags when I need to stay
> **I'd be** chasin' every breeze that blows my way
> **I'd be** building my kingdom just to watch it fade away
> It's true (tobyMac, "Me Without You")

Song lyrics use lots of figures of repetition. In this example, the phrase "I'd be" draws attention to where the singer would be without God.

> **Example 3** (emphasis added)
> **Every** breath you take
> **Every** move you make
> **Every** bond you break
> **Every** step you take
> I'll be watching you
>
> **Every** single day
> **Every** word you say
> **Every** game you play
> **Every** night you stay
> I'll be watching you. (The Police, "Every Breath You Take")

Repeating the word "every" eight times at the beginning of eight successive sentences certainly draws attention to this word.

> **Example 4** (emphasis added)
> **With** malice toward none, **with** charity for all, **with** firmness
> in the right as God gives us to see the right. (Abraham Lincoln,
> "Second Inaugural Address")

This is one example where the emphasis is not necessarily on the repeated word. Instead, the word "with" joins the phrases together indicating that the three subjects are parallel in significance. In his closing remarks to a war-torn nation, Lincoln suggests that these three phrases are of equal importance to the nation's wellbeing.

FROM THE SCRIPTURES

Example 1
2 Corinthians 11:26 (emphasis added)
In journeyings often, *in* **perils** of waters, *in* **perils** of robbers, *in* **perils** by *mine own* countrymen, *in* **perils** by the heathen, *in* **perils** in the city, *in* **perils** in the wilderness, *in* **perils** in the sea, *in* **perils** among false brethren;

With the word "peril" occurring eight times in successive phrases, this is a textbook example of *anaphora*. The figure here stresses the perils Paul faced as a minister of Christ.

Example 2
Psalm 115:12-13 (emphasis added)
The Lord hath been mindful of us: **he will bless** *us*; **he will bless** the house of Israel; **he will bless** the house of Aaron.
He will bless them that fear the Lord, *both* small and great.

The figure emphasizes that God is the One that blesses. As the Psalmist records, God will bless the house of Israel, the house of Aaron, and those that fear Him.

Example 3
Philippians 3:2 (emphasis added)
Beware of dogs, **beware** of evil workers, **beware** of the concision.

The repetition of the word "beware" at the beginning of three sentences makes this an *anaphora*. In the context, the Apostle Paul warns the Philippians to beware of those who have confidence in their flesh to bring about their own righteousness. The repetition of this warning would certainly have arrested their attention.

Example 4
Jeremiah 5:17 (emphasis added)
And **they shall eat up** thine harvest, and thy bread, *which* thy sons and thy daughters should eat: **they shall eat up** thy flocks and thine herds: **they shall eat up** thy vines and thy fig trees:

they shall impoverish thy fenced cities, wherein thou trustedst, with the sword.

In this verse, the repeated words "they shall eat up" occur at the beginning of three successive sentences. This *anaphora* emphasizes the surety of pending devastation. But note how this figure also links the subjects together: Israel's enemies will consume food from the ground, food provided by animals, and food from trees and vines.

Example 5
Philippians 2:1-2 (emphasis added)
If *there be* therefore **any** consolation in Christ, **if any** comfort of love, **if any** fellowship of the Spirit, **if any** bowels and mercies, Fulfil ye my joy, that ye be likeminded, having the same love, *being of* one accord, of one mind.

Here's an example where the *anaphora* is not that obvious in the KJV but is clearer in the Greek where the phrase *ei tis* begins four successive clauses. In this example, the figure is used as a rhetorical device to bring the reader along to an end point or climax, which is stated in verse two.

Note how the NIV translates the *anaphora*:

Philippians 2:1-2 (NIV) (emphasis added)
Therefore, **if there is any** encouragement in the Messiah, **if there is any** comfort of love, **if there is any** fellowship in the Spirit, **if there is any** compassion and sympathy, then make my joy complete by being like-minded, having the same love, being one in spirit and of one mind.

This translation places the repeated words at the beginning of each phrase making the *anaphora* more obvious than in the KJV.

> *Anaphora* is the repetition of the same word or words at the beginning of successive sentences, phrases, or clauses.

Chapter 2
Polysyndeton

(repeated conjunctions) 208

pol-ee-SIN-de-ton

> *Polysyndeton* repeats a conjunction more than ordinary usage would require.

In English, as in Greek, grammar rules normally indicate that a conjunction occurs between the last two words (or word groups) in a series.[1] For instance, note the use of the conjunction "and" in the following sentence (emphasis added):

> The tiny amusement park consisted of a roller coast, a Ferris wheel, some bumper cars, **and** a merry-go-round.

In this example, there are four items in the series, so the conjunction comes between the last two nouns. *Polysyndeton* breaks that rule by placing a conjunction between each noun. If the sentence were rewritten using the figure, the sentence would read as follows (emphasis added):

> The tiny amusement park consisted of a roller coast **and** a Ferris wheel **and** some bumper cars **and** a merry-go-round.

The figure adds the conjunction "and" between each noun, bringing emphasis to each word in the series. Generally speaking, *polysyndeton* emphasizes **each individual item** in a series rather than the list as a whole. Perhaps subconsciously, the repeated "and" slows the reader down in order to consider each object and to weigh each matter in the list.

Writing about secular literature, some scholars say that this figure is used to achieve a certain rhythm to writing by giving a steady cadence to a passage, where words in a series are moved along at the same powerful pace, resulting in a "measured deliberateness" (Joseph 59). Others assert that *polysyndeton* draws attention not only to each item in a series but also to the fact that the items are "roughly equal members" (Quinn 11).

1. Repeated "and"

FROM GENERAL CULTURE

Example 1 (emphasis added)
As a medic, Rat Kiley carried a canvas satchel filled with morphine **and** plasma **and** malaria tablets **and** surgical tape **and** comic books **and** all the things a medic must carry, including M&M's for especially bad wounds, for a total weight of nearly 20 pounds. (Tim O'Brien, *The Things They Carried*)

In this list, the repeated "and" between words gives emphasis to each item.

Example 2 (emphasis added)
There were frowzy fields, **and** cow-houses, **and** dunghills, **and** dustheaps, **and** ditches, **and** gardens, **and** summer-houses, **and** carpet-beating grounds, at the very door of the Railway. Little tumuli of oyster shells in the oyster season, **and** of lobster shells in the lobster season, **and** of broken crockery **and** faded cabbage leaves in all seasons, encroached upon its high places. (Charles Dickens, *Dombey and Son*)

In this rich description, Dickens uses *polysyndeton* to draw attention to each image and perhaps to emphasize how crowded the scene was with the many items mentioned.

Example 3 (emphasis added)
By seven o'clock the orchestra has arrived, no thin five-piece affair, but a whole pitful of oboes **and** trombones **and** saxophones **and** viols **and** cornets and piccolos, **and** low and high drums. . . . The bar is in full swing, and floating rounds of cocktails permeate the garden outside, until the air is alive with chatter **and** laughter, **and** casual innuendo **and** introductions forgotten

on the spot, **and** enthusiastic meetings between women who never knew each other's names. (F. Scott Fitzgerald, The Great Gatsby)

In this description of a party scene, Fitzgerald uses *polysyndeton* in a list of musical instruments and then in a list of types of speech.

 # FROM THE SCRIPTURES

Example 1
Ephesians 4:31 (emphasis added)
Let all bitterness, **and** (*kai*) wrath, **and** (*kai*) anger, **and** (*kai*) clamour, **and** (*kai*) evil speaking, be put away from you, with all malice:

In this example, the word "and" (in the Greek, *kai*) occurs four times between five nouns drawing emphasis to each item enumerated and how believers are to put away all of these things.

Example 2
Luke 7:38 (emphasis added)
And stood at his feet behind *him* weeping, **and** (*kai*) began to wash his feet with tears, **and** (*kai*) did wipe *them* with the hairs of her head, **and** (*kai*) kissed his feet **and** (*kai*) anointed *them* with the ointment.

In this verse, five phrases are linked together by the conjunction "and." This figure emphasizes the woman's actions calling attention to each loving gesture. (Note how the Lord later commends the woman's actions. re: Luke 7:44-50)

Example 3
Romans 9:4 (emphasis added)
Who are Israelites; to whom *pertaineth* the adoption, **and** (*kai*) the glory, **and** (*kai*) the covenants, **and** (*kai*) the giving of the law, **and** (*kai*) the service of God, **and** (*kai*) the promises;

In this verse, the conjunction "and" occurs three times drawing attention to each item in the list. When we consider the context of this verse, we learn that the Apostle Paul is speaking about his fellow Israelites. This figure of speech draws attention to all the matters listed here and that they pertain, specifically, to Israel.

Example 4
1 Corinthians 4:11-12 (emphasis added)
Even unto this present hour we both hunger, **and** (*kai*) thirst, **and** (*kai*) are naked, **and** (*kai*) are buffeted, **and** (*kai*) have no certain dwellingplace;
And (*kai*) labour, working with our own hands: being reviled, we bless; being persecuted, we suffer it;

In this passage, the figure draws attention to each of the actions the Apostle Paul and others endured for the sake of the gospel.

Example 5
1 Corinthians 14:3 (emphasis added)
But he that prophesieth speaketh unto men *to* edification, **and** (*kai*) exhortation, **and** (*kai*) comfort.

The figure here emphasizes the benefits of prophecy spoken in the church.

2. Other Repeated Conjunctions like "or" and "nor"

Polysyndeton repeats a conjunction more than ordinary usage would require.

In Greek, the most common occurrence of *polysyndeton* involves the repetition of the word *kai*, generally translated "and" in English. However, this figure occurs with other conjunctions such as "but," "or," and "nor."[2] Because these words are conjunctions (or more technically disjunctive conjunctions), when they are repeated beyond the norms of grammar, they function the same way any other *polysyndeton* might: they emphasize each word or phrase in a series.

FROM GENERAL CULTURE

Example 1 (emphasis added)
Neither snow **nor** rain **nor** heat **nor** gloom of night stays these couriers from the swift completion of their appointed rounds.

This saying is associated with The United States Postal Service, taken from an inscription on the James Farley Post Office in New York City. With the repeated conjunction "nor," the emphasis is that the delivery of the mail will not be hindered, no matter what the weather condition.

Example 2 (emphasis added)
Happiness is neither virtue **nor** pleasure **nor** this thing **nor** that but simply growth.
We are happy when we are growing. (John Butler Yeats, Letter to Miss Grierson, June 2, 1909)

Stating it in the negative, Yeats describes what happiness is not. The repeated conjunction "nor" emphasizes that happiness, according to the writer, is not any of the things listed in this sentence.

 # FROM THE SCRIPTURES

Example 1
Romans 8:35 (emphasis added)
Who shall separate us from the love of God? shall tribulation or (ē) distress, or (ē) persecution, or (ē) famine, or (ē) nakedness, or (ē) peril, or (ē) sword?

In this example, "or" (ē in Greek) occurs six times in this short series, making it the figure *polysyndeton*.[3] It brings emphasis to each word in the group, causing the reader to stop and to consider whether any of these dreadful conditions might separate the born-again believer from God's love. (The answer comes later in verses 38 and 39).

Example 2
Romans 8:38-39 (emphasis added)
I am persuaded that **neither** (*oute*) death, **nor** (*oute*) life, **nor** (*oute*) angels, **nor** (*oute*) principalities, **nor** (*oute*) powers, **nor** (*oute*) things present, **nor** (*oute*) things to come, **nor** (*oute*) height, **nor** (*oute*) depth, **nor** (*oute*) any other creature shall be able to separate us from the love of God, which is in Christ Jesus our Lord.

The repeated "nor" (*oute* in Greek) emphasizes each word listed, drawing attention to the truth that none of these things, despite their power and reach, can separate the born-again believer from the love of God, which is in Christ Jesus our Lord.[4]

Example 3
1 Thessalonians 2:6 (emphasis added)
Nor (*oute*) of men sought we glory, **neither** (*oute*) of you, **nor** (*oute*) yet of others, when we might have been burdensome, as the apostles of Christ.

In the Greek, *oute* occurs three times in this verse, although it is translated inconsistently in the KJV. The *polysyndeton* draws the reader's attention to each item in this list. In the context, we read that Paul and company did not seek the glory of people—not men, nor the Corinthians, nor other people. The figure here makes this emphatic.

Example 4
1 Corinthians 5:11
(emphasis added)
But now I have written unto you not to keep company, if any man that is called a brother be [either] ($\bar{e}$) a fornicator, **or** ($\bar{e}$) covetous, **or** ($\bar{e}$) an idolator, **or** ($\bar{e}$) a railer, **or** ($\bar{e}$) a drunkard, **or** ($\bar{e}$) an extortioner; with such an one no not to eat.

In this example, the repetition of the Greek word $\bar{e}$ makes this *polysyndeton*. The figure draws the reader's attention to each item in the list, making the admonition emphatic. The Apostle Paul admonishes the Corinthians not to keep company (to associate with) nor to eat with any brother who is any of the things listed in this verse.

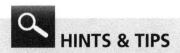

HINTS & TIPS

According to many sources, in *Koine* Greek, sentences are often joined by a connecting particle or conjunction such as *kai* (and). Consider the Gospel of Mark, sections of the Book of Acts, or the Book of Revelation, for example, where many verses start with the word "and." Because *polysyndeton* uses conjunctions like "and" in an unusual way, we don't normally consider the first "and" in a sentence (translated from Greek) when identifying this figure in the Scriptures. Generally speaking, starting a sentence with the conjunction "and" (*kai*) is not unusual for *Koine* Greek but is actually normative.

Polysyndeton repeats a conjunction more than ordinary usage would require.

Chapter 3

Epistrophe

(repeated sentence endings) 241

e-PIS-tro-fee

> *Epistrophe* is the repetition of the same word or words at the end of successive sentences, phrases, or clauses.

When looking for this figure, it's important to remember that the repeated word(s) occur at the end of successive sentences, phrases, or clauses.[5] In most cases, the figure emphasizes the repeated word or words.

FROM GENERAL CULTURE

Example 1 (emphasis added)
If you did know to whom I gave **the ring**,
If you did know for whom I gave **the ring**
And would conceive for what I gave **the ring**
And how unwillingly I left **the ring**,
When nought would be accepted but **the ring**,
You would abate the strength of your displeasure.
If you had known the virtue of **the ring**,
Or half her worthiness that gave **the ring**,
Or your own honour to contain **the ring**,
You would not then have parted with **the ring**.
(*The Merchant of Venice*, Act 5, scene 1)

With the words "the ring" occurring at the end of nine lines, is there any question what Shakespeare wishes to emphasize in this passage?

Example 2 (emphasis added)
No matter how lost you are, you're not that far, **you're not too far**
No matter how hurt you are, you're not that far, **you're not too far**
No matter how wrong you are, you're not that far, **you're not too far**
No matter who you are, you're not that far, **you're not too**
Far from forgiveness
(TobyMac, "Ask for forgiveness")

Song lyrics make frequent use of *epistrophe*, as we can see in this example. Note how the figure emphasizes the encouraging message being communicated, that no matter what a person has done or experienced, he or she is never too far to receive God's forgiveness.

Example 3 (emphasis added)
"…and that government of **the people**, by **the people**, for **the people** shall not perish from the earth." (Abraham Lincoln, "The Gettysburg Address," Nov. 19, 1863)

In this example, Lincoln emphasizes that the American republic is of, by, and for *the people* as opposed to a government that is of, by, and for something else. Repeating the phrase "the people" drives home Lincoln's point about this form of government.

 ## FROM THE SCRIPTURES

Example 1
Galatians 1:8-9 (emphasis added)
But though we, or an angel from heaven, preach any other gospel unto you than that which we have preached unto you, **let him be accursed**.
As we said before, so say I now again, If any *man* preach any other gospel unto you than that ye have received, **let him be accursed**.

The sentence "let him be accursed" is repeated at the end of two successive sentences making this the figure of speech *epistrophe*. In the context, the Apostle Paul addresses those who preach a gospel that is different from the gospel of God concerning His son Jesus Christ. And the figure makes Paul's message emphatic—they are to be accursed.

Example 2
Psalm 136:1-7 (emphasis added)
O give thanks unto the Lord; for he is good; **for his mercy *endureth* forever**.
O give thanks unto the God of gods; **for his mercy *endureth* forever.**
O give thanks to the Lord of lords; **for his mercy *endureth* forever**.
To him who alone doeth great wonders; **for his mercy *endureth* forever**.
To him that by wisdom made the heaves; **for his mercy *endureth* forever**.
To him that stretched out the earth above the waters; **for his mercy *endureth* forever**.
To him that made great lights: **for his mercy *endureth* for ever**:

Seven verses are given here by way of example, but every verse in Psalm 136 ends with the phrase "for his mercy endureth forever," making prominent God's mercy and that it endures forever.

Example 3
2 Corinthians 11:22 (emphasis added)
Are they Hebrews? **so *am* I**. Are they Israelites? **so *am* I**. Are they the seed of Abraham? **So *am* I**.

In this short verse, the phrase "so am I" occurs three times at the end of three successive questions. This figure makes Paul's response emphatic. If he had asked the questions and then answered with "so am I" only once, then that answer would not have been emphasized. However, Paul repeats his answer ("so am I") after each question to emphasize his response. How significant this is in light of the accusations that were continually heaped upon the Apostle Paul.

Example 4
Deuteronomy 27:15-26 (emphasis added)

Cursed *be* the man that maketh *any* graven or molten image, an abomination unto the Lord, the work of the hands of the craftsman, and putteth *it* in *a* secret *place*. **And all the people shall answer and say, Amen.**

Cursed *be* he that setteth light by his father or his mother. **And all the people shall say, Amen.**

Cursed *be* he that removeth his neighbour's landmark. **And all the people shall say, Amen.**

Cursed *be* he that maketh the blind to wander out of the way. **And all the people shall say, Amen.**

Cursed *be* he that perverteth the judgment of the stranger, fatherless, and widow. **And all the people shall say, Amen.**

Cursed *be* he that lieth with his father's wife; because he uncovereth his father's skirt. **And all the people shall say, Amen.**

Cursed *be* he that lieth with any manner of beast. **And all the people shall say, Amen.**

Cursed *be* he that lieth with his sister, the daughter of his father, or the daughter of his mother. **And all the people shall say, Amen.**

Cursed *be* he that lieth with his mother in law. **And all the people shall say, Amen.**

Cursed *be* he that smiteth his neighbour secretly. **And all the people shall say, Amen.**

Cursed *be* he that taketh reward to slay an innocent person. **And all the people shall say, Amen.**

Cursed *be* he that confirmeth not *all* the words of this law to do them. **And all the people shall say, Amen.**

With the words "and all the people shall say, amen" occurring twelve times at the end of twelve successive sentences (verse 15 reads "answer and say"), this is a clear example of the figure *epistrophe*. "Amen" means "verily" or "truly," and the repetition of this word in this passage draws attention to the veracity and solemnity of the curses listed as well as drawing attention to the phrase "and all the people shall say." (Note: the repetition of the words "cursed be he" at the beginning of each sentence in this passage constitutes the figure *anaphora*.)

Example 5
Revelation 22:11 (emphasis added)
He that is unjust, let him be unjust **still**: and he which is filthy, let him be filthy **still**: and he that is righteous, let him be righteous **still**: and he that is holy, let him be holy **still**.

While there are several other figures of repetition in this verse, note the *epistrophe* where the word "still" occurs four times at the end of four successive sentences.

> *Epistrophe* is the repetition of the same word or words at the end of successive sentences, phrases, or clauses.

Chapter 4

Epanalepsis

(like sentence beginning and end) 245

ep-an-a-LEP-sis

> *Epanalepsis* is the repetition of the same word or words at the beginning and end of a sentence, phrase, or clause.

Because the repetition comes at the beginning and end of a sentence, this figure has an encircling effect. The emphasis would be on the repeated word and on the completeness of the encircling thought.[6]

FROM GENERAL CULTURE

Example 1 (emphasis added)
"**Common** sense is not so **common**." (–Voltaire)

Used here, the figure has an ironic, connotation. Rather than write, "common sense isn't prevalent," he repeats the word "common" to draw attention to the central irony of his thought, that common sense is actually quite rare.

Example 2 (emphasis added)
"**Nothing** can be created out of **nothing**." (–Lucretius)

With the word "nothing" occurring at the beginning and end of this short sentence, the writer draws attention to the repeated word.

Example 3 (emphasis added)
"**Next time** there won't be a **next time**." (common saying)

In this common expression, the writer cleverly emphasizes the finality of a situation. Rather than say, "next time you won't have more chances," the figure *epanalepsis* is used to draw attention to the fact that there aren't going to be other opportunities.

 FROM THE SCRIPTURES

Example 1
Philippians 4:4 (emphasis added)
Rejoice in the Lord always: *and* again I say, **Rejoice**.

In this short sentence, the Apostle Paul uses the word "rejoice" to encircle his admonition. In the context, the figure doesn't emphasize "in the Lord" but that the Philippians were to *rejoice* in the Lord.

Example 2
Romans 8:24b (emphasis added)
Hope that is seen is not **hope**; for what a man seeth, why doth he yet hope for?

Similar to the example from Lucretius printed above, this instance of *epanalepsis* makes emphatic the repeated word "hope."

Example 3
Psalm 27:14 (emphasis added)
Wait on the Lord: be of good courage, and he shall strengthen thine heart: **wait, I say, on the Lord**.

Repeating the phrase "wait on the Lord" lends completeness to this verse. In between the bookends "wait on the Lord" is an admonition ("be of good courage") and a promise ("he shall strengthen thine heart"). The repeated phrase emphasizes the admonition to "wait on the Lord."

Example 4
Ecclesiastes 1:2 (emphasis added)
Vanity of vanities, saith the Preacher, vanity of vanities; all *is* **vanity**.

The figure is used to here to draw our attention to the subject matter of the opening of Ecclesiastes, that "all is vanity." (Note that the phrase "vanity of vanities" is a *polyptoton*.)

> **Example 5**
> **James 2:14-16** (emphasis added)
> **What *doth it* profit,** my brethren, though a man say he hath faith, and have not works? can faith save him?
> If a brother or sister be naked, and destitute of daily food,
> And one of you say unto them, Depart in peace, be *ye* warmed and filled; notwithstanding ye give them not those things which are needful to the body; **what *doth it* profit?**

The same question, "what profit?" starts and ends this passage, making this the figure *epanalepsis*. As such, it calls the reader's attention to the question asked and to the details mentioned in between the repeated question.

Epanalepsis is the repetition of the same word or words at the beginning and end of a sentence, phrase, or clause.

Chapter 5

Andiplosis

(repeated word at end of sentence, beginning of next) 251

an-a-di-PLO-sis

> *Anadiplosis* is the repetition of the same word or words at the end of one sentence, phrase, or clause and at the beginning of the next.

This figure is also known as the "rhetorical echo" for the way in which it immediately repeats a sound. Occasionally, a conjunction comes between this repetition but has no effect on the figure.[7]

FROM GENERAL CULTURE

Example 1 (emphasis added)
"The land of **my fathers. My fathers** can have it."
(Dylan Thomas on Wales)

Here *anadiplosis* is used humorously. The repeated phrase "my fathers" draws attention to Thomas's displeasure with his ancestral country.

Example 2 (emphasis added)
Death, as the Psalmist saith, is certain to **all; all** shall die.
(*Henry the Fourth* 3.2.41)

In this example, *anadiplosis* draws attention to the repeated word ("all") and the idea that all shall die. Perhaps Shakespeare was not aware that all shall not die! (1 Thess. 4:15-17)

> **Example 3** (emphasis added)
> With **death, death** must be recompensed;
> On **mischief, mischief** must be heaped. – Ovid

In this example, Ovid makes use of *anadiplosis* in both lines.

FROM THE SCRIPTURES

Example 1
Psalm 121:1-2 (emphasis added)
I will lift up mine eyes unto the hills, from whence cometh **my help**.
My help *cometh* from the LORD, which made heaven and earth.

Here the phrase "my help" occurs at the end of one and the beginning of the next sentence, underscoring how that the psalmist's help comes from the Lord.[8]

Example 2
Genesis 31:6-7 (emphasis added)
Ye know that with all my power I have served **your father**: and **your father** hath deceived me, and changed my wages ten times; but God suffered him not to hurt me.

The repetition of the words "your father" emphasizes that it was Leah and Rachel's father who dealt deceitfully with Jacob. (Note: the conjunction "and" does not affect the figure in this instance.)

Example 3
Romans 9:30
What shall we say then? That the Gentiles, which followed not after righteousness, have attained to righteousness, even the righteousness which is of faith.

Here's an example of the figure not appearing in an English translation like the KJV. In the Greek, the word righteousness (*dikaiosune*) occurs at the end of one phrase and at the beginning of the next. It would therefore read: "What shall we say then? That the Gentiles which followed not after righteousness have attained to **righteousness; righteousness** which is of faith." How beautifully this figure draws our attention to this word!

Example 4
Romans 12:3 (emphasis added)

For I say, through the grace given unto me, to every man that is among you, not to think of *himself* more highly than he ought **to think**; but **to think** soberly, according as God hath dealt to every man the measure of faith.

Here the verb "to think" occurs at the end of one sentence and at the beginning of the next, albeit with the conjunction "but" between the two infinitives. This figure draws attention to the verb "to think." Seeing as the context of this chapter is the renewing of the mind, it follows that the emphasis here would be on thinking.

Example 5
2 Corinthians 9:6

But this I *say*, He which soweth sparingly shall reap also sparingly; and he which soweth bountifully shall reap also bountifully.

There is a double *anadiplosis* in this verse although it is not apparent in the KJV. In the Greek, the word "sparingly" (*pheidomenos*) occurs at the end of one clause and at the beginning of the next. Likewise, the word "bountifully" (Greek *euolgia*) occurs at the end of one clause and at the beginning of the next. Noting the *anadiplosis*, the verse might therefore read: "But I say, he which sows sparingly, sparingly shall he reap also. And he that sows bountifully, bountifully shall he reap." The dramatic figure draws the reader's attention to the truth that one reaps as one sows, whether sparingly or bountifully. Note how the figure is retained in another English translation:

2 Corinthians 9:6 (YLT) (emphasis added)

And this: He who is sowing **sparingly, sparingly** also shall reap; and he who is sowing **in blessings, in blessings** also shall reap;

This translation places the repeated words back to back making the *anadiplosis* more obvious than in the KJV.

Example 6
Romans 8:17 (emphasis added)
And if children, then **heirs; heirs** of God, and joint-heirs with Christ; if so be that we suffer with *him*, that we may be also glorified together.

The repetition of the word "heirs" at the end of one phrase and at the beginning of the next phrase draws attention to the truth that believers are heirs of God.

> *Anadiplosis* is the repetition of the same word or words at the end of one sentence, phrase, or clause and at the beginning of the next.

Chapter 6
Epizeuxis

(repeated word back-to-back) 189

e-pi-ZOOK-sis

Epizeuxis repeats the same word with no other words between.

Many scholars say that this is a particularly powerful figure and that it is one commonly used in oral cultures.[9]

FROM GENERAL CULTURE

Example 1 (emphasis added)
Keeping **time, time, time**,
In a sort of Runic rhyme,
To the tintinnabulation that so musically wells
From the **bells bells bells bells bells bells.** (Edgar Allan Poe, "The Raven")

In the well-known poem, the writer uses *epizeuxis* perhaps in an attempt to mimic the rhythmic sound of a bell tolling.

Example 2 (emphasis added)
O **dark, dark, dark** amid the blaze of noon. (John Milton, "Samson Agonistes")

The poet John Milton, author of *Paradise Lost*, makes frequent use of this figure. Here, the word "dark" occurs three times in a row, drawing emphasis to the darkness.

Example 3 (emphasis added)
Out, out brief candle. (*Macbeth*. 5.5.23)

This line, taken from one of Shakespeare's soliloquies, makes use of *epizeuxis* to dramatize the despair of the speaker.

Example 4 (emphasis added)
"the only people for me are the mad ones, the ones who are mad to live, mad to talk, mad to be saved, desirous of everything at the same time, the ones who never yawn or say a commonplace thing, but **burn, burn, burn** like fabulous yellow roman candles exploding like spiders across the stars." (Jack Kerouac, *On the Road*)

This is one of the most famous passages from *On the Road* where Kerouac uses an *epizeuxis* ("burn, burn, burn") to draw attention to the kind of people he admires, those with energy and brilliance.

 FROM THE SCRIPTURES

Example 1
Isaiah 51:9 (emphasis added)
Awake, awake, put on strength, O arm of the Lord; awake, as in the ancient days, in the generations of old. *Art* thou not it that hath cut Rahab, *and* wounded the dragon?

The prophet Isaiah, by revelation, uses the figure *epizeuxis* to draw attention to the request for God to awake or act for His people.

Example 2
2 Samuel 18:33 (emphasis added)
And the king was much moved, and went up to the chamber over the gate, and wept: and as he went, thus he said, O my son Absalom, **my son, my son** Absalom! would God I had died for thee, O Absalom, **my son, my son**!

King David has just received news that his son, Absalom, has been killed while endeavoring to usurp David's throne. In his anguish, David repeats the phrase "my son" twice, emphasizing his grief. The figure also emphasizes that David had lost his *son*, and not just a soldier or a close friend. How poignant this figure is in the context. How powerfully it conveys David's grief over the loss of his beloved son, even though Absalom had betrayed him.

Example 3
Genesis 22:11 (emphasis added)
And the angel of the LORD called unto him out of heaven, and said, **Abraham, Abraham**: and he said, Here *am I*.

There are seven occurrences in the Scriptures of *epizeuxis* where a person's name is repeated, including this one in Genesis 22:11.10 Bullinger writes, "when thus used, the figure calls special attention to the occasion or to the person, and to some solemn moment of importance in the action, or of significance in the words" (190). The other occurrences include:

Genesis 46:2 (emphasis added)
And God spake unto Israel in the visions of the night, and said, **Jacob, Jacob**. And he said, Here *am* I.

Exodus 3:4 (emphasis added)
And when hen the LORD saw that he turned aside to see, God called unto him out of the midst of the bush, and said, **Moses, Moses**. And he said, Here *am* I.

1 Samuel 3:10 (emphasis added)
And he LORD came, and stood, and called as at other times, **Samuel, Samuel**. Then Samuel answered, Speak; for thy servant heareth.

Luke 10:41 (emphasis added)
And Jesus answered and said unto her, **Martha, Martha**, thou art careful and troubled about many things:

Luke 22:31 (emphasis added)
And the Lord said, **Simon, Simon**, behold, Satan hath desired *to have* you, that he may sift *you* as wheat:

Acts 9:4 (emphasis added)
And he fell to the earth, and heard a voice saying unto him, **Saul, Saul**, why persecutest thou me?

Sometimes in an English Bible like the KJV, the figure is obscured as in the following examples:

Example 4
1 Samuel 2:3
Talk no more so exceeding proudly; let *not* arrogancy come out of your mouth: for the LORD *is* a God of knowledge, and by him actions are weighed.

In the Hebrew, it reads, "Talk no more proudly proudly (*gaboah*)(*gaboah*)."

Example 5
Isaiah 26:3
Thou wilt keep *him* in perfect peace, *whose* mind *is* stayed on *thee*: because he trusteth in thee.

In the Hebrew, it reads, "Thou will keep him in peace peace (*shalom*) (*shalom*)." What a beautiful way to emphasize that God will keep a person in peace when his or her mind is stayed on Him because he or she trusts in Him.

HINTS & TIPS

Sometimes a figure is lost in translation (re: Isaiah 26:3), so it's important to check the original languages when seeking to identify this, or any figure of speech.

Example 6
Ecclesiastes 7:24
That which is far off, and exceeding deep, who can find it out?

In the Hebrew, it reads, "That which is far off and deep deep (*amoq*) (*amoq*)"

A note on the phrase "verily, verily"

John 1:51 (emphasis added)
And he saith unto him, **Verily, verily**, I say unto you, Hereafter ye shall see heaven open, and the angels of God ascending and descending upon the Son of man.

Some scholars believe that the phrase "verily, verily" is an idiomatic expression while others argue that the repetition of the same word back-to-back constitutes the figure *epizeuxis*. It is interesting that this phrase occurs only in the Gospel of John.[11] Whether an idiom or a figure of repetition, "verily, verily" is used for emphasis, drawing attention to a most solemn declaration or pronouncement.

> *Epizeuxis* repeats the same word with no other words between.

Chapter 7

Polyptoton

(repeated inflections) 267

po-lip-TO-ton

> *Polyptoton* is the repetition of the same root word but in a different form, also known as an inflection.

An inflection is any change in the form of a word, usually the ending.[12] Noun inflections include changes in case, gender, and number. Verb inflections include changes in tense, mood, person, number, case, and gender. Typically *polyptoton* occurs when a noun is repeated in a different case, gender, or number or when a verb is repeated in a different tense or mood. However, *polyptoton* can occur with verbs, nouns, pronouns, adjectives or any combination thereof.

Here are a few familiar examples:

- "**Choosy** mothers **choose** JIF." The root word "choose" is used first as an adjective ("choosy") and then as a verb ("choose").
- "The things you **own** end up **owning** you." Here two different tenses ("own" and "owning") of the same root word are used.
- "He was a **man** amongst **men**." In this example, the singular and plural of the same root word is used.

The phrase "a Hebrew of the Hebrews" is a *polyptoton* because a noun is repeated in the singular and then in the plural. A few biblical examples of this type include "king of kings," "lord of lords," "holy of holies," "a servant of servants," "vanity of vanities" and others. (See *Figures of Speech Used in the Bible Explained and Illustrated*, p. 283-284).

What might *polyptoton* emphasize? Like other figures of repetition, this figure typically emphasizes the repeated root word. For example, a "man among men" emphasizes the person's manliness. At the same time, this expression also connotes that the man is exemplary amongst other men. It's another way to express something in a superlative degree.

FROM GENERAL CULTURE

Example 1 (emphasis added)
Always on a trail of another female
Well, well they say my papa was a player
Somebody's **honesty is honest** in me baby
Somehow in college Greek letters made me cuter
All the time online I still couldn't compute it. (Lecrae, "Runners")

In these song lyrics, the rapper Lecrae makes use of a *polyptoton* in the third line where he writes, "somebody's honesty is honest in me baby." The figure provides auditory dimension to the lyrics while also emphasizing the concept of honesty.

Example 2 (emphasis added)
Let me not to the marriage of true minds
Admit impediments. Love is not love
Which **alters** when it **alteration** finds,
Or bends with the **remover** to **remove**
(Shakespeare, Sonnet 116, l. 1-4)

Shakespeare evidently had a fondness for this figure because it occurs frequently in his poetry. In Sonnet 116, he uses a verb-noun pairing (alters-alteration) and a noun-verb pairing (remover-remove). The *polyptoton* has a witty, play-on-word effect while also emphasizing the key ideas.

Example 3 (emphasis added)
Few men speak **humbly** of **humility, chastely** of **chastity, skeptically** of **skepticism**. (Blaise Pascal)

In this example, the seventeenth-century French philosopher Blaise Pascal uses three adverb-noun pairings to draw attention to his ironic observations about human nature.

 # FROM THE SCRIPTURES

Example 1
Ephesians 1:3 (emphasis added)
Blessed (*eulogetos*) be the God and Father of our Lord Jesus Christ, who hath **blessed** (*eulogeo*) us with all spiritual **blessings** (*eulogia*) in heavenly *places* in Christ:

In this example, the word "bless" appears as an adjective, verb, and noun respectively making emphatic the blessings that are in Christ.

Example 2
2 Timothy 3:13 (emphasis added)
But evil men and seducers shall wax worse and worse, **deceiving**, and being **deceived**.

In the Greek, the same root word (*planao*) is used, translated here "deceiving" (*planotes*) and "deceived" (*planomenoi*).

Example 3
Psalm 145:3 (emphasis added)
Great *is* the LORD, and greatly to be praised; and his **greatness** *is* unsearchable.

In the Hebrew, the words translated here "great" (*gadol*) and "greatness" (*gedullah*) have the same root word (*gadol*). (Note: the word "greatly" is a different Hebrew word.) What a beautify way to magnify God's greatness!

Example 4
Genesis 2:17
But of the tree of the knowledge of good and evil, thou shalt not eat of it: for in the day that thou eatest thereof thou shalt surely die.

Here is an example of *polyptoton* that is not seen in an English translation like the KJV. In the Hebrew, the word "die" is repeated in two verb forms—infinitive and imperfect, respectively.[13] Noting the figure of speech, here's how the verse might read:

> **Genesis 2:17** (emphasis added)
> But of the tree of the knowledge of good and evil, thou shalt not eat of it: for in the day that thou eatest thereof **dying** (*muwth*) **thou shalt die** (*muwth*).

The *polyptoton* makes emphatic the outcome of disobeying God's commandment regarding eating from the tree of knowledge of good and evil. In this context, the outcome for such disobedience was death, made emphatic by the figure of speech. Now note how other translations retain the figure:

> **Genesis 2:17 (YLT)** (emphasis added)
> And of the tree of knowledge of good and evil, thou dost not eat of it, for in the day of thine eating of it—**dying thou dost die**.'

> **Genesis 2:17 (Douay-Rheims)** (emphasis added)
> But of the tree of knowledge of good and evil, thou shalt not eat. for in what day soever thou shalt eat of it, thou shalt **die the death**.

These translations make the *polyptoton* more apparent than in the KJV.

Example 5
Galatians 1:11

> But I certify you, brethren, that the gospel (*euangelion*) which was preached (*euangelizo*) of me is not after man.

Here is another example of a *polyptoton* that is hidden in an English Bible like the KJV. In this verse, both the noun (*euangelion*) and the verb (*euangelizo*) are used. In the context, the Apostle Paul is addressing the Galatian's belief in "another gospel" (v.6) and not the gospel of Christ (v. 7), which Paul had preached to them. It is interesting to note how frequently derivations of the word "gospel" occur in this first chapter of the Epistle to the Galatians. Such repetition arrests our attention to the subject matter being addressed.

Polyptoton is the repetition of the same root word but in a different form, also known as an inflection.

GO FIGURE!

Chapter 8

Synonymia

(repeated synonyms) 324

si-no-NI-mee-a

Synonymia is the repetition of synonyms in close proximity.

Synonyms are words that have the same meaning or are very closely related in meaning but are different in sound and origin. For example, in English "close" and "shut" are synonyms. Although these words differ etymologically, they convey an equivalent meaning and are synonyms. Likewise, when we refer to "the Bible" or "God's Word" or "the Scriptures" we refer to the same book. These are synonyms. The figure of speech *synonymia* brings emphasis through amplification, explanation, or clarification.[14] It is used to enhance the force of a passage or to call attention through repetition.

FROM GENERAL CULTURE

Example 1 (emphasis added)
His **metabolic processes are now history**! He's **off the twig**! He's **kicked the bucket**, he's **shuffled off his mortal coil**, **rung down the curtain**, and **joined the choir invisible!** This is an **ex**-parrot! (*Monty Python*, "Dead Parrot" sketch)

Humor makes use of many figures of speech including *synonymia*. In this Monty Python sketch, the speaker is emphatically arguing that the parrot for sale in the pet shop is not living but is dead. He uses seven synonyms for "dead" including some English idioms: "metabolic processes are now history," "off the twig," "kicked the bucket," "shuffled off his mortal coil," "rung down the curtain," "joined the choir invisible," and "ex-parrot."

> **Example 2** (emphasis added)
> We are **the odd**,
> **The outcast**,
> **The peculiar**,
> **The Strangers**.
> And they say you don't fit in
> But I say, God exactly God created us to be anomalies
> The system didn't plan for this. (Lecrae, "Anomaly")

In these song lyrics, Lecrae makes use of the figure *synonymia* by using the words "odd," "outcast," "peculiar," and "stranger" in close proximity.

> **Example 3** (emphasis added)
> "You **blocks**, you **stones**, you worse than **senseless things**!"
> (*Julius Caesar* 1.1.35)

Emphasizing the obstinacy of those he is addressing, the speaker here uses three synonyms to make his point.

FROM THE SCRIPTURES

Example 1
Exodus 1:7 (emphasis added)
And the children of Israel were **fruitful**, and **increased**, and **multiplied**.

The words "fruitful," "increased," and "multiplied" are synonyms. Used in close proximity, they constitute the figure of speech *synonymia*, calling attention to the fecundity of the Israelites. (Note also the *polysyndeton*.)

Example 2
2 Corinthians 6:14 (emphasis added)
Be ye not unequally yoked together with unbelievers: for what

fellowship hath righteousness with unrighteousness? and
what **communion** hath light with darkness?

In the Greek, the words "fellowship" (*metoche*) and "communion" (*koinonia*)
are synonyms; both words mean partnership or association. In the context,
Paul admonishes the Corinthians not to be unequally joined together
with unbelievers. Then he asks a question using two synonyms that mean
essentially the same thing. Together, these two synonyms draw attention
to the partnership Christian believers ought to have but that it is not to be
with unbelievers.

Example 3
Colossians 1:16 (emphasis added)
For by him were all things created, that are in heaven, and that
are in earth, visible and invisible, whether *they be* **thrones**,
or **dominions**, or **principalities**, or **powers**: all things were
created by him, and for him:

The Greek words for "thrones," (*metonymy* for rulers or those in authority),
"dominions," "principalities," and "powers" may all be considered synonyms
for rulers or those in authority.

Example 4
2 Corinthians 9:12 (emphasis added)
For the **ministry** of this **service** is not only supplying the needs
of the saints, but is also overflowing in many acts of thanksgiving
to God.

In the Greek, the words "ministry" (*diakonia*) and service (*leitourgia*) are synonyms.
Used together, they emphasize the service being addressed in this passage.

Example 5
Proverbs 4:14-15 (emphasis added)
Enter not into the path of the wicked, and **go not in** the way
of evil *men*.
Avoid it, **pass not by** it, **turn from** it, and **pass away**.

In order to emphasize the necessity of turning away from all evil and from
evil people, the figure of speech *synonymia* is used in these verses where

six verbs with similar meanings are used to convey and to emphasize one central truth.

> *Synonymia* is the repetition of synonyms in close proximity.

Chapter 9

Repetitio

(irregular repetition) 263

re-pe-TI-shee-o

> *Repetitio* is the repetition of the same word or words irregularly in the same passage.

In *Go Figure!* the term "irregular" is used to mean that there is no readily identifiable or set pattern of repetition such as seen in *anaphora*, *epistrophe*, *epizuexis*, or other grammatical figures of repetition. In other words, as we read the Scriptures, we sometimes notice an unusual repetition of a word in a passage, but the repetition doesn't follow a particular pattern. For example, note the repetition of the word "themselves" in the following verse:

2 Corinthians 10:12 (emphasis added)
For we dare not make ourselves of the number, or compare ourselves with some that commend **themselves**: but they measuring **themselves** by **themselves** and comparing **themselves** among **themselves** are not wise.

In this verse the English word "themselves" occurs five times, translated from the same Greek word *heautou*. Although there is no distinguishable pattern of repetition here, the word is repeated beyond the norm and therefore might be considered to be a figure of repetition. This is an example of *repetitio* where a notable repetition of the same word occurs in the same verse or passage. And, if we consider the context—Paul was writing about others who were praising themselves—we see that this figure calls attention to the idea that these people were using *themselves* as standards of judgment and of praise, and that their focus was on *themselves*, rather than on God.

Similarly, the phrase "son of man" occurs frequently (more than 90 times) in the book of Ezekiel yet does not follow a set pattern of repetition. According to Bullinger, this phrase is used to highlight the contrast between Ezekiel and the celestial beings. Like many other figures of repetition, *repetitio* draws attention to or makes emphatic the repeated word or words.

FROM GENERAL CULTURE

Example 1 (emphasis added)
"...the only people for me are the **mad** ones, the ones who are **mad** to live, **mad** to talk, **mad** to be saved, desirous of everything at the same time, the ones who never yawn or say a commonplace thing, but burn, burn, burn like fabulous yellow roman candles exploding like spiders across the stars." (Jack Kerouac, *On the Road*)

In this short passage, Kerouac repeats the same word ("mad") in various places. For "Beat" writers like Kerouac, this word had taken on new meaning and occurs frequently in his writing. Because there is no readily identifiable pattern, this repetition might be considered *repetitio*.

Example 2 (emphasis added)
"In the **fall** the war was always there, but we did not go to it any more. It was cold in the **fall** in Milan and the dark came very early. Then the electric lights came on, and it was pleasant along the streets looking in the windows. There was much game hanging outside the shops, and the snow powdered in the fur of the foxes and the **wind** blew their tails. The deer hung stiff and heavy and empty, and small birds blew in the **wind** and the **wind** turned their feathers. It was a cold **fall** and the **wind** came down from the mountains."—Ernest Hemingway

Known for his simple style and carefully crafted sentences, Hemingway here makes use of repetition of the words "fall" and "wind." Note how there is no pattern to the repetition.

Example 3 (emphasis added)
You cleaned up my soul and
Gave me **new** life—I'm so brand **new**
And that's all that matters
I-I ain't love you first, but you first loved me
In my heart I cursed you, but you set me free
I gave you no reason to give me **new** seasons, to give **new** life,
new breathing
(Lecrae, "Tell the World")

The repetition of the word "new" in these song lyrics underscores that word.

 # FROM THE SCRIPTURES

Example 1
Matthew 10:40 (emphasis added)
He that **receiveth** you **receiveth** me, and he that **receiveth** me **receiveth** him that sent me.

The word "receiveth" (from the same Greek word *dechomai*) occurs four times in one verse, drawing emphasis to this word.

Example 2
1 Corinthians 9:12-18 (emphasis added)
If others be partakers of *this* power over you, *are* not we rather? Nevertheless we have not used this power; but suffer all things, lest we should hinder the **gospel** of Christ.
Do ye not know that they which minister about holy things live *of the things* of the temple? and they which wait at the altar are partakers with the altar?
Even so hath the Lord ordained that they which preach the **gospel** should live of the **gospel**.
But I have used none of these things: neither have I written these things, that it should be so done unto me: for *it were* better for me to die, than that any man should make my glorying void.
For though I preach the **gospel**, I have nothing to glory of: for necessity is laid upon me; yea, woe is unto me, if I preach not the **gospel**!

For if I do this thing willingly, I have a reward: but if against my will, a dispensation *of the gospel* is committed unto me.
What is my reward then? *Verily* that, when I preach the **gospel**, I may make the **gospel** of Christ without charge, that I abuse not my power in the **gospel**.

In the passage the same word translated here as "gospel" (from the same Greek root *euaggelion*) occurs seven times. Is there any doubt what is emphasized in this passage?

Example 3
Colossians 2:6-13 (emphasis added)
As ye have therefore received Christ Jesus the Lord, *so* walk ye **in him**:
Rooted and built up **in him**, and stablished in the faith, as ye have been taught, abounding therein with thanksgiving.
Beware lest any man spoil you through philosophy and vain deceit, after the tradition of men, after the rudiments of the world, and not after Christ.
For **in him** dwelleth all the fulness of the Godhead bodily.
And ye are complete **in him**, which is the head of all principality and power:
In whom [or him] also ye are circumcised with the circumcision made without hands, in putting off the body of the sins of the flesh by the circumcision of Christ:
Buried **with him** in baptism, wherein also ye are risen **with *him*** through the faith of the operation of God, who hath raised him from the dead.
And you, being dead in your sins and the uncircumcision of your flesh, hath hequickened together **with him**, having forgiven you all trespasses;

In this passage, the same phrase "in him" occurs five times and the same phrase "with him" occurs three times. In the context, the believer is admonished to walk in him (v.6), meaning in Christ Jesus the Lord. With the repetition of the phrases "in him" and "with him" the reader's attention is arrested. This repetition emphasizes that these new birth realities are in Christ Jesus the Lord.

Example 4
Revelation 8:7-12 (emphasis added)

The first angel sounded, and there followed hail and fire mingled with blood, and they were cast upon the earth: and the **third part** (*triton*) of trees was burnt up, and all green grass was burnt up.

And the second angel sounded, and as it were a great mountain burning with

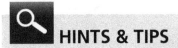

HINTS & TIPS

1. Repetitio may occur in a sentence but it's more likely to occur in a longer passage.
2. Look for a pattern: if there is none, then it's a likely candidate for this figure.
3. Consider the context: does the repetition of the word or words fit with the context?.

fire was cast into the sea: and the **third part** (*triton*) of the sea became blood;

And the **third part** (*triton*) of the creatures which were in the sea, and had life, died; and the third part (triton) of the ships were destroyed.

And the **third** (*tritos*) angel sounded, and there fell a great star from heaven, burning as it were a lamp, and it fell upon the **third part** (*triton*) of the rivers, and upon the fountains of waters;

And the name of the star is called Wormwood: and the **third part** (*triton*) of the waters became wormwood; and many men died of the waters, because they were made bitter.

And the fourth angel sounded, and the **third part** (*triton*) of the sun was smitten, and the **third part** (*triton*) of the moon, and the **third part** (*triton*) of the stars; so as the **third part** (*triton*) of them was darkened, and the day shone not for a **third part** (*triton*) of it, and the night likewise.

Note how often the Greek word *triton* (meaning "third") occurs in this passage![15]

> *Repetitio* is the repetition of the same word or words irregularly in the same passage.

Chapter 10
Pleonasm

(apparent redundancy) 405

PLEE-o-naz-um

> *Pleonasm* is using more words than is semantically necessary.

Writing styles differ from culture to culture. While we in modern American society value short, succinct writing (with lots of images and bullet points), Victorian writers preferred long, circuitous writing styles dense with detail and description. Compare your basic Tom Clancy novel to one by Charles Dickens, and you'll see what I mean.

When it comes to the languages of the Bible, especially Semitic languages like Hebrew and Aramaic, the style (by our standards) is highly redundant. They use more words than is necessary for grammar or for meaning, and they tend to say the same thing in two different ways. Consider the following verse:

Genesis 25:8
Then Abraham gave up the ghost, and died in a good old age, an old man, and full of *years*; and was gathered to his people.

There's quite a lot of redundancy in this one verse. First, to give up the ghost and to die is the same thing. Then, to say Abraham was "in a good old age," and "old man," and "full of years" means the same thing, expressed in three different ways. In modern English vernacular, we might write something like, "Abraham died, being quite old." But Semitic writing style prefers to express things with redundancy.

We know that all Scripture is given by inspiration of God (2 Timothy 3:16) and that the words of the Lord are "pure words; *as* silver tried in a furnace of earth, purified seven times" (Psalm 12:6). So <u>none</u> of the words in the Bible are superfluous or needlessly repetitious. When we talk about the figure of speech *pleonasm* (from the Latin meaning "surplus"), we mean when more words are used than are necessary for grammar or for meaning.

To compound matters, there is an overlap between idiomatic expressions and *pleonasm*.

For example, "sons of men" and "children of men" are both pleonastic and idiomatic.

> **Ephesians 3:5** (emphasis added)
> Which in other ages was not made known unto the **sons of men**.

> **Psalm 36:7** (emphasis added)
> How excellent *is* thy lovingkindness, O God! Therefore the **children of men** put their trust under the shadow of thy wings.

The phrase "sons of men" doesn't literally mean only the male offspring ("sons") of adult males ("men"). It is an idiomatic and pleonastic way of saying "people." Similarly, the phrase "children of men" doesn't mean the young offspring of adult males; it means "people." This phrase is both an idiom and a *pleonasm*. "Answered and said" is another example of a pleonastic idiom.

It's unclear whether or not these expressions bring emphasis to a passage; a consideration of the context would help to make that determination. Pleonastic writing is intrinsic to the Scriptures and is a beautiful mode of expression worth noting.

So when does this redundancy become a figure of speech? That can be difficult to pin down, but in *Go Figure!* the figure of speech *pleonasm* (from the Latin meaning "surplus") involves saying the same thing in different ways, often in positive and negative terms. "I will keep my grandmother's lace tablecloth and not discard it" is an example of saying the same thing in a positive and then negative way. Now here's a biblical example of this type of *pleonasm*:

Deuteronomy 33:6 (emphasis added)
Let Reuben **live** and **not die**; and let *not* his men be few.

To live and to not die is the same thing, isn't it? This is an example of a *pleonasm* that is a figure of speech.

FROM GENERAL CULTURE

Example 1
My fellow countrymen, I speak to you as coequals, knowing you are deserving of the honest truth. And let me warn you in advance, my subject matter concerns a serious crisis caused by an event in my past history: the execution style killing of a security guard on a delivery truck. At that particular point in time, I found myself in a deep depression, making mental errors, which seemed as though they might threaten my future plans. I am not over-exaggerating. (George Carlin, "Count the Superfluous Redundant Pleonastic Tautologies.")

Carlin uses redundancy for comic effect but also as a way to drive home his point: many common expressions are needlessly redundant. Can you identify all of them?[16]

Example 2
"It's déjà vu all over again." (Yogi Berra)

This expression became popular because of its comic redundancy. The French phrase deja vu means "already seen," so to say "already seen over again" is redundant. Whether Berra used this figure intentionally or not is up for debate. (It's interesting that another popular *pleonasm* is attributed to Berra: "You can see a lot just by looking.")

Writing teachers (like me) are always on the lookout for redundancy in our students' work. Here are a few that crop up on a regular basis:

The future lies ahead of us.
I thought in my mind that the coach should replace the goalie.
The reason why she left her job was clear.
I myself went to Mexico for spring break.

FROM THE SCRIPTURES

Example 1
Genesis 40:23 (emphasis added)
Yet **did not** the chief butler **remember** Joseph, but **forgat** him.

In this record, Joseph makes a request to his fellow prisoner, the chief butler: "But think on me when it shall be well with thee, and shew kindness, I pray thee, unto me, and make mention of me unto Pharaoh, and bring me out of this house" (Genesis 40:14). Once restored to his royal position, however, the chief butler forgets to mention Joseph to Pharaoh. The poignancy of this situation is emphasized by the figure *pleonasm*. How wonderful that God did not forget Joseph! (Acts 7:9-10)

Example 2
Romans 12:14 (emphasis added)
Bless them which persecute you; **bless**, and **curse not**.

The admonition here is made emphatic through the figure *pleonasm*. Not only is the word "bless" repeated, its opposite "curse not" is also stated. Is there any doubt what the figure draws attention to in this verse?

Example 3
1 John 1:5 (emphasis added)
This then is the message which we have heard of him, and declare unto you, that God is **light**, and in him is **no darkness** at all.

In this declaration about God, a *pleonasm* is used to draw attention to the nature of God, that He is light and that there is no darkness in Him at all.

Example 4
Deuteronomy 32:6a (emphasis added)
Do ye thus requite the LORD, O **foolish** people and **unwise**?

To describe people as foolish and unwise is to say the same thing in two different ways, positively and negatively. In this verse the *pleonasm* draws our attention to the foolishness of the people being addressed.

Pleonasm is using more words than is semantically necessary.

Notes

1.Bullinger defines this figure as "the repetition of the word 'and' at the beginning of successive clauses" (208). However, many scholars adopt a broader definition of this figure and consider the unusual repetition of *any* conjunction to be *polysyndeton*.

2. According to older sources like Bullinger and Vilant Macbeth *paradiostole* is a figure of speech with repeated disjunctives occurring outside the normal rules of grammar. This includes the phrase "neither . . . nor" and the disjunctives "or" and "nor." However, recent sources define *paradiostole* as a figure of thought, not a figure of grammar. For example, Lanham and Espy define the figure as "a putting together of dissimilar things" (107, 193). Sister Miriam Joseph defines *paradistole* as "a figure, which extenuates in order to flatter or soothe" (152). The Silva Rhetorica also defines paradiostole as a figure of thought: "A figure by which one extenuates something in order to flatter or soothe, or by which one refers to a vice as a virtue." Perhaps the meaning of this word has changed over time, or perhaps there are two different meanings of this word. Whatever the case, today most rhetoricians consider the repetition of disjunctive conjunctions to be *polysyndeton*, not *paradiostole*.

3. The word "or" is the Greek word *ē*, which is a particle, but Thayer also defines it as a "disjunctive conjunction."

4. The word "nor" is the Greek word *oute*, which is an adverb, but Thayer also defines it as an "adjunctive negative conjunction."

5. Some scholars refer to this figure as *epiphora* or *antistrophe*. A combination of *anaphora* and *epistrophe* is also frequently referred to as the figure *symploce*. See 1 Corinthians 12:4-6 for an example of *symploce*.

6. There is some discrepancy about the naming of this figure. Bullinger defines *epanalepsis* as "the repetition of the same word after a break, or parenthesis" (206) and adds that "the use of an *epanalespsis* to mark off a whole passage is called an inclusion" (89) with an example given from James 2:14 where the phrase "what doth it profit" begins and ends the sentence. Bullinger refers to this figure as *epanadiplosis*, an obsolete term. Others define *epanalepsis* as the repetition of the same word or words at the beginning of a sentence, phrase, or clause, and do not list or define ep*anadiplosis* (Lanham,Quinn, Espy, Enos, Joseph). Because ep*anadiplosis* seems to be an obsolete term, I have opted to use the more current name for this figure.

7. A repeated *anadiplosis* is sometimes referred to as the figure climax. In this book, I do not distinguish between *anadiplosis* and *climax* because one is a repetition of the other. However, students are referred to *Figures of Speech Used in the Bible Explained and Illustrated* (256-259) if they would like a further explanation of the figure *climax*.

8. According to several sources, the second clause in verse one should be a question: "From whence cometh my help?" Rather than look to idols that were typically placed on hills, the psalmist declares that he will look to God for his help.

9. There is some discrepancy about the naming of this figure and whether or not a word may occur between the repeated words. Bullinger asserts that the repetition of the same word in immediate succession is the figure *geminatio* and that *epixuesis* occurs when the repeated word is separated by one or more intervening words, but then his examples do not support that definition. Quinn and others (Joseph, Espy) write that if a word interrupts the immediate repetition, then this is the figure *diacope* as in "words, words, mere words" (qtd. in Quinn 82). Lanham and more recent scholars defines *epizeuxis* as the "emphatic repetition of a word with no other words between" (71) and then gives *geminatio* as an alternative name. This is one example of the challenge in naming and defining figures of speech; it also reflects how definitions change over time as well as the tendency for contemporary scholars to conflate alternate names rather than retain a surgeon-like precision, as did their Victorian counterparts. For the most part, I have chosen the more modern term over the antiquated or obsolete term so that interested students may find these terms should they care to do more research.

10. Similar examples include "Lord, Lord" (Matt. 7:21, 22. Luke 6:46; 13:25), "Jerusalem, Jerusalem" (Matt. 23:37. Luke 13:34), and "Eli, Eli" (Mark 15:34. Matt. 27:46. Ps. 22:1).

11. See John 1:51; 3: 3,5,11; 5: 19,24,25; 6:26,32,47,53; 8:34,51,58; 10: 1,7; 12:24; 13:16,20,21,38; 14:12; 16:20,23; 21:18.

12. There is some discrepancy about the naming of this figure. See also the figure *paregmenon*, which Bullinger defines as "the repetition of words derived from the same root" (304).

13. Several interlinear texts indicate that the word "dying" and "die" is the same word transliterated *muwth*. However, the first occurrence of the word is in the infinitive absolute form while the second occurrence of *muwth* is a verb in the second person masculine singular form. In this example, the *polyptoton* intensifies the second person masculine singular verb "to die."

14. This figure is also known as interpretatio, nominis communio, synonymy, the figure of store, the interpreter.

15. See *A Journey Through the Acts and Epistles: The Authorized King James Version with Notes and a Working Translation*, Vol. 2 (n. page 217). Taking this into account, the word "third" occurs thirteen times in this passage.

16. 1) fellow countrymen, 2) coequals, 3) honest truth, 4) warn you in advance, 5) subject matter 6) serious crisis, 7) past history, 8) execution style killing, 9) security guard 10) delivery truck 11) deep depression 12) that particular point in time, 13) I myself, 14) future plans, 15) over-exaggerating

SECTION 2
FIGURES OF UNDERSTATEMENT
AND OVERSTATEMENT

FIGURES OF UNDERSTATEMENT AND OVERSTATEMENT

Figures of understatement and overstatement covered in this book include *litotes, meiosis, and hyperbole*. With understatement (*litotes, meiosis*), less is said than is meant; with overstatement (*hyperbole*), more is said than is meant. Related to irony, these figures express an idea in a non-literal way. With understatement (*litotes, meiosis*), the strength of the statement is downplayed or minimized. British humor is especially noted for its use of understatement, as we can see in this excerpt from the book *How to Be a Brit:*

> Understatement is still in the air. It is not just a specialty of the English sense of humour; it is a way of life. When gales uproot trees and sweep away roofs of houses, you should remark that it is 'a bit blowy.' . . . Yesterday, a man in charge of a home where 600 old people lived, which was found to be a fire risk where all the inhabitants might burn to death, admitted: 'I may have a problem.' (Mikes 212)

Describing a gale-force wind as a "bit blowy" and a perilous living condition as a possible "problem" are examples of understatement.

In modern Western culture, understatement and overstatement are the mainstays of comedy. While understatement typifies British comedy, overstatement (*hyperbole*) characterizes American comedy, as we can see in this excerpt from humor columnist Dave Barry:

> When we talk about fashion models, we are talking about mutated women, the results of cruel genetic experiments performed by fashion designers so lacking in any sense of human decency that they think nothing of putting their initials on your eyeglass lenses. These experiments have resulted in a breed of fashion models who are 8 and sometimes 10 feet tall, yet who weigh no more than an abridged dictionary. *(Greatest Hits 166)*

Describing fashion models as women who are "8 and sometimes 10 feet tall" is a classic example of *hyperbole*. This description draws attention to how tall most female models are but does so in an exaggerated way for two purposes: 1) to get a laugh and 2) to draw attention to the absurdly strict standards of the fashion industry. American humor abounds in overstatement just as British humor relies on understatement.

While understatement and overstatement are often used today in the context of humor, these figures are not used for that purpose in the Bible. In many cases, *hyperbole* in the Scriptures is used to express deep feelings such as anguish and distress or to put emphasis on the gravity of a situation. *Litotes* and *meiosis* in the Scriptures are often used to stress a point, and not for humorous effect. So while the examples provided from general culture tend to be funny, the examples from the Bible do not carry a humorous connotation. It's important to keep this distinction in mind as we consider figures of understatement and overstatement used in the Bible.

Chapter 11

Litotes

(understatement using the negative) 159

li-TO-tees

> *Litotes* is understatement using the negative to express the positive in a high degree.

Litotes is a figure of understatement where the negative is used to express the positive (or opposite) in a high degree.[1] For example, when something is simple we say, "It isn't rocket science." Rocket science of course is complex and difficult to understand. By saying it *isn't* rocket science, we mean that it isn't complex or difficult to understand but is just the opposite—very simple. Other familiar examples of *litotes* include:

> A cup of coffee would not be unwelcomed. (Meaning, it would be welcomed.)
> You won't be sorry! (Meaning, you will be pleased or satisfied.)
> I'm not a huge fan of vegetables. (Meaning, I hate vegetables.)
> It's not the best idea I've ever heard. (Meaning, it's a bad idea.)

Litotes is generally used for emphasis, but this figure may also be used as a form of indirection with the intention of weakening or softening a claim, typically to avoid the appearance of boasting. After completing a daring mission, the masked spy states, "'Not a bad day's work on the whole,...Not a bad day's work." (Baroness Emmuska Orczy, *The Scarlet Pimpernel*)

FROM GENERAL CULTURE

Example 1 (emphasis added)
"Are you also aware, Mrs. Bueller, that Ferris **does not have** what we consider to be **an exemplary attendance record?**"
(Ferris Bueller's Day Off, 1986)

In the movie, the character Ferris Bueller is chronically absent from school. Rather than say that Ferris is often absent, the principal uses the negative ("does not have an exemplary attendance record") to express the opposite in a high degree. In this example, the figure of speech is used for comic effect and to draw attention to Bueller's chronic delinquency.

Example 2 (emphasis added)
"The captain's horn-book informed him that these people were cannibals, so that our position **was not a little alarming**."
(J. Hudson Taylor)

In this account of one of his sea voyages to China, the missionary J. Hudson Taylor records that how during a storm, his boat had come close to crashing on the coast of northern New Guinea, a location inhabited by cannibals. Taylor records the unique danger of this situation using *litotes*. Rather than write, "it was very frightening," Taylor uses understatement, "not a little alarming." Anyone familiar with Taylor's memoirs knows that understatement is a distinguishing characteristic of his writing, no doubt a reflection of the man's humility. Perhaps Taylor uses *litotes* in this instance to soften the severity of the situation, especially since Taylor had great trust in God amidst these types of perilous circumstances.

Example 3 (emphasis added)
"I **cannot say** that I think **you are very generous** to the ladies; for, whilst you are proclaiming peace and good-will to men, emancipating all nations, you insist upon retaining an absolute power over wives." (Abigail Adams, letter to John Adams, May 7, 1776)

In this well known excerpt from a letter written to her husband, Abigail Adams uses *litotes* as a way to soften her statement. She uses the negative ("I cannot say you are very generous") to express the opposite in a high degree. In this example, *litotes* tones down the criticism, making it a somewhat playful exchange between wife and husband. At the same time, the figure draws attention to a weighty matter—equality for women.

 # FROM THE SCRIPTURES

In the Scriptures, a consideration of the context will help to determine where, how, and if *litotes* might be used to bring emphasis.

Example 1
Acts 20:7-12 (emphasis added)
And upon the first day of the week, when the disciples came together to break bread, Paul preached unto them, ready to depart on the morrow; and continued his speech until midnight. And there were many lights in the upper chamber, where they were gathered together.

And there sat in a window a certain young man named Eutychus, being fallen into a deep sleep: and as Paul was long preaching, he sunk down with sleep, and fell down from the third loft, and was taken up dead.

And Paul went down, and fell on him, and embracing *him* said, Trouble not yourselves; for his life is in him.

When he therefore was come up again, and had broken bread, and eaten, and talked a long while, even till break of day, so he departed.

And they brought the young man alive, and were **not a little comforted.**

In this record, Paul was preaching for a long time (until midnight, v. 7) when one of the young men in attendance, Eutychus, fell asleep. As Paul continued to preach, Eutychus fell into an even deeper sleep and fell from the third story (loft) and was "taken up dead." Later, when it is known that Eutychus was alive, they were "not a little comforted," another way of saying they were greatly comforted. The figure of speech *litotes* draws attention to the great comfort they felt knowing that Eutychus was alive. Note how some English Bibles render verse twelve:

Acts 20:12 (NIV)
The people took the young man home alive and were greatly comforted.

Acts 20:12 (NASB)
They took away the boy alive, and were greatly comforted.

Acts 20:12 (WEY)
They had taken the lad home alive, and were greatly comforted.

In these versions, the meaning the figure is given rather than a word-for-word translation.

Example 2
Acts 26:19 (emphasis added)
Whereupon, O king Agrippa, I was **not disobedient** unto the heavenly vision:

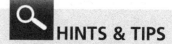

HINTS & TIPS

1. When determining if an expression might be the figure *litotes*, ask:
   a) Does the context warrant an emphatic stating?
   b) Is this expressing the opposite in a high degree?
   c) Can this be literally true? If not literally true, then it may be a good candidate for *litotes*.
2. The occurrence of a negative ("not") alone does not automatically constitute this figure.
3. Repeated phrases like "not ashamed" may be *litotes* in one instance but not in another.

While addressing King Agrippa, the Apostle Paul recounts the heavenly vision of the Lord Jesus while he was on the road to Damascus (re: Acts 9). Paul tells the king that he was "not disobedient" to this vision, meaning that he was extremely obedient to the vision. Stating it in the negative draws attention to the positive in a high degree.

Example 3
Acts 12:18 (emphasis added)
Now as soon as it was day, there was **no small stir** among the soldiers, what was become of Peter..

In this example, "no small stir" is a *litotes* used to emphasize the big commotion amongst the soldiers.
Note how other English versions translates this verse:

Acts 12:18 (ISV)
When morning came, there was a great commotion among the soldiers as to what had become of Peter.

Acts 12:18 (Aramaic Bible Plain English)
When it was morning, there was a great uproar among the
Soldiers about Shimeon: "What happened to him?"

In these versions, the meaning of the figure is given rather than a word-for-word translation.

Example 4
Acts 17:4, 12 (emphasis added)
And some of them believed, and consorted with Paul and Silas;
and of the devout Greeks a great multitude, and of the chief
women **not a few**.
Therefore many of them believed; also of honourable women
which were Greeks, and of men, **not a few**.

In these verses, the phrase "not a few" is a *litotes* meaning many. The figure draws attention to the truth that numerous of the chief women (v. 4) and men (v. 12) believed. Note how several English Bibles translate this figure:

Acts 17:4, 12 (NIV)
Some of the Jews were persuaded and joined Paul and Silas,
as did a large number of God-fearing Greeks and quite a few
prominent women.
As a result, many of them believed, as did also a number of
prominent Greek women and many Greek men.

Acts 17:4, 12 (NLT)
Some of the Jews who listened were persuaded and joined Paul
and Silas, along with many God-fearing Greek men and quite a
few prominent women.
As a result, many Jews believed, as did many of the prominent
Greek women and men.

In these versions, the meaning of the figure is given rather than a word-for-word translation.

Example 5 (emphasis added)
Acts 5:42
And daily in the temple, and in every house, they **ceased not** to
teach and preach Jesus Christ.

"Ceased not" is *litotes*. In the context of Acts 5 we see that the apostles had been put in prison and had been commanded by various religious leaders in Jerusalem not to speak in the name of Jesus Christ. The apostles were then rescued out of prison by an angel and were commanded by the angel to "go, stand, and speak in the temple to the people all the words of this life." They obeyed this command. The apostles were then brought before the Sanhedrin and the high priest and were sternly reminded that they had been forbidden to teach in the name of Jesus Christ. Peter responded, "We ought to obey God rather than men" (verse 29). The apostles were then beaten and commanded again not to speak in the name of Jesus. They were released, but they kept right on teaching and preaching Jesus Christ. The *litotes* in verse 42 makes emphatic their persistence in speaking about Jesus Christ, despite the prohibitions and punishments of antagonistic and powerful men. The figure makes emphatic their obedience to God rather than to men.

Note how the following English Bibles render this verse:

Acts 5:42 (NASB)
And every day, in the temple and from house to house, they kept right on teaching and preaching Jesus as the Christ.

Acts 5:42 (ISV)
Every day in the Temple and from house to house they kept teaching and proclaiming that Jesus is the Messiah.

These English Bibles give the meaning of the figure rather than a word-for-word translation.

> *Litotes* is understatement using the negative to express the positive in a high degree.

Chapter 12

Meiosis

(understatement) 155

my-O-sis

> The figure *meiosis* is understatement where less is said than
> is meant.

To describe subzero Arctic weather as "a bit chilly" is to use *meiosis*, or understatement. *Meiosis* differs from *litotes* in that it does not use the negative to convey understatement; it uses a form of diminution, or lessening.

- "It's just a flesh wound!"

One well-known example of *meiosis* involves a scene from the movie *Monty Python and the Holy Grail* where a knight has had his arm cut off in battle yet says, "It's just a flesh wound." Using *meiosis*, the knight tries to make his wound (amputated limb) appear less serious (flesh wound) than it really is. The radical incongruity between reality and understatement supplies the humor.

Meiosis might also be understood as a type of diminishing when one thing is diminished in order to increase another thing. E. W. Bullinger writes, "One thing is lowered in order to magnify and intensify something else by way of contrast. It is used for the purpose of emphasis; to call our attention, not to the smallness of the thing thus lessened but to the importance of that which is put in contrast with it" (155). This type of *meiosis* occurs in the following verse:

Genesis 18:27
And Abraham answered and said, Behold now, I have taken
upon me to speak unto the LORD, which *am but* dust and ashes:

When Abraham refers to himself as "but dust and ashes," he is using the
figure *meiosis*. The figure draws attention to the greatness and magnificence
of God compared to the relative insignificance of Abraham.[2]

Some scholars also say that *meiosis* may be used to express affection. For
instance, when the Apostle John refers in his epistles to his readers as "little
children," he may be using the figure *meiosis* to draw attention to his
affectionate care for the people he is addressing.[3] His addressees are not
literally young children, but he may be using this expression as a term of
endearment, like we might use the word "baby" or "babe" for someone
dear to us. Other writers suggest that that the expression "little children"
used in 1 John refers to young and immature believers in Christ. As such, the
meiosis is used not necessarily as a form of endearment but a figurative way
to describe immature believers in Christ.

FROM GENERAL CULTURE

Example 1
"I have to have this operation. It isn't very serious. I have this
tiny little tumor on the brain." (J. D. Salinger, *Catcher in the Rye*)

Of course, a brain tumor is extremely serious, but the character in this novel,
Holden Caufield, uses *meiosis* to make his point.

Example 2
"For my study abroad, I'm going across the pond to Oxford University!"

It's part of American English vernacular to refer to Great Britain as a country
"across the pond." In calling the Atlantic Ocean a "pond" we use *meiosis*
to draw attention to the close and amicable relationship that has historically
existed between the two countries by diminishing the geographic distance
between them. In American vernacular, the expression is used as a way to
express an affinity between the two countries.

Example 3
"Ladies and gentlemen, you may have noticed we were hit by
lightning." (Monday 31st March 2014)

According to the *Daily Mail,* a plane was struck by lightning during a flight from Amsterdam to Birmingham, England. Passengers reported seeing "a bright flash of light" and heard "booming noises" and a "massive bang" as one of the bolts struck the body of the plane. At one point, three bolts hit the plane at once. The pilot made the above announcement to the distressed passengers using *meiosis* ("may have noticed"). This use of understatement diminishes the severity of the incidence while bringing some levity to a doubtless tense situation.

 ## FROM THE SCRIPTURES

Example 1
I Corinthians 3:1 (emphasis added)
And I, brethren, could not speak unto you as unto spiritual, but
as unto carnal, *even* as unto **babes in Christ**.

To refer to the Corinthians as "babes in Christ" is to use the figure *meiosis* to draw attention to their current immature state regarding spiritual matters. The context reveals that Paul is addressing carnality amongst the Corinthians, which is contrasted to being spiritual. As such, the *meiosis* is not used here as a form of endearment but as a way to emphasize the immaturity and carnality of Paul's addressees. The World English Bible translates this phrase "babies in Christ," which is hardly a compliment.

Example 2
Ephesians 3:8 (emphasis added)
Unto me, who am **less than the least** of all saints is this grace given that
I should preach among the Gentiles the unsearchable riches of Christ.

In this verse, Paul refers to himself as "less than the least" of all saints as a way to draw attention to the grace he received concerning his apostleship to the Gentiles. Many verses in the Scriptures speak about the equality amongst the members of the Body of Christ where each member has received the same information that can be believed and where each member is equally needed. Therefore, this cannot be literal where Paul sees himself at the bottom of some meretricious hierarchy. Indeed, it is the figure *meiosis* used to draw attention to the grace that Paul recognized he received regarding his apostleship to the Gentiles.

Example 3
Romans 5:6 (emphasis added)
For when we were yet **without strength,** in due time Christ died for the ungodly.

The Greek word for "without strength" is *asthenes*, which means frail, sickly, or feeble. This might be considered an understatement, for in Ephesians 2:1 it declares "And you *hath he quickened*, who were dead in trespasses and sins." To refer to someone as frail, sickly, or feeble when one is dead is to use understatement. In this context, the *meiosis* emphasizes the utter weakness of those for whom Christ died.

Example 4
1 Samuel 24:14 (emphasis added)
After whom is the king of Israel come out? After whom dost thou pursue? After a **dead dog, after a flea**.

In the record, David confronts King Saul who is intent on killing him. As a way to emphasize that David is not a threat to King Saul, he calls himself a "dead dog" and a "flea." In Biblical culture, dogs were despised animals, so to call himself a dead dog is to dramatically and figuratively emphasize David's lowliness in comparison to the king. David also calls himself a "flea" the tiniest, least threatening of creatures. Using *meiosis*, David draws attention to his lowly position in contrast to the high, exalted position of the king. One can only imagine how this dramatic self-humbling might have assuaged Saul's hostility towards David.

Example 5
1 Samuel 25:41 (emphasis added)
And she arose, and bowed herself on *her* face to the earth, and said, Behold, *let* thine handmaid *be* **a servant to wash the feet of the servants** of my lord.

In this record, David has just sent servants to Abigail to inform her that she is to become his wife. Abigail responds using a beautiful understatement. As the widow of Nabal, a very wealthy man, Abigail would not have assumed the mundane task of washing a servant's feet. That task would have been relegated to someone well down the chain of command, so her response cannot be taken literally. In using this figure, Abigail emphatically expresses her humility before David, the Lord's anointed, something she does consistently in this record.

> The figure *meiosis* is understatement where less is said than is meant.

Chapter 13

Hyperbole

(exaggeration) 423

hi-PER-bo-lee

> *Hyperbole* is rhetorical exaggeration.

Hyperbole is the most used and best-loved figure in the entire world. Well, that's an exaggeration, or *hyperbole*, but the figure certainly is used extensively in popular and literary culture. Simply put, *hyperbole* is saying more than is literally meant. It is a figure of overstatement that uses exaggeration to convey meaning.

This figure might be used to emphasize feeling or to convey a dramatic effect or to call attention to something. Often, *hyperbole* is conveyed via comparisons like simile and metaphor. And of course *hyperbole* is a staple of comedy because most people find distortion funny. Below is a list of some common hyperbolic expressions found in American English. Note the frequent use of comparison.

- It was so quiet, you could hear a pin drop.
- I told her a million times not to forget her passport.
- That's about as interesting as watching paint dry.
- He would go to hell and back again for his troop.
- I'm sick to death of this song.
- They are so poor, they don't have two cents to rub together.
- He's got tons of money.

- She's as skinny as a toothpick.
- You could knock me over with a feather.

FROM GENERAL CULTURE

Example 1

I have never met a woman, no matter how attractive, who wasn't convinced, deep down inside, that she was a real woofer. Men tend to be just the opposite. A man can have a belly you could house a commercial aircraft in and a grand total of eight greasy strands of hair, which he grows real long and combs across the top of his head so that he looks, when viewed from above, like an egg in the grasp of a giant spider, plus this man can have B.O. to the point where he interferes with radio transmissions, and he will still be convinced that, in terms of attractiveness, he is borderline Don Johnson.[4] (Dave Barry, *Greatest Hits*)

This excerpt makes effective use of *hyperbole* for comic effect

Example 2

In her memoir *Bossypants*, Fey frequently uses *hyperbole*, usually to highlight absurdity:

> "When I was thirteen I spent a weekend at the beach in Wildwood, New Jersey, with my teenage cousins Janet and Lori. In the space of thirty-six hours, they taught me everything I know about womanhood." (Tina Fey, *Bossypants*)

While describing the details of her photo shoot for a woman's magazine, Fey uses *hyperbole* to criticize pampered celebrities:

> "While this is going on, someone gives you a manicure and a pedicure. At really fancy shoots, a celebrity fecalist will study your bowel movements and adjust your humours" (150).

Fey's cousins did not literally teach her everything she knows about womanhood, and celebrities don't literally have someone examine their fecal matter (one hopes.) In these two examples, Fey uses *hyperbole* to draw attention to absurd situations.

Example 3 (emphasis added)
Waiting on a **never ending** train at the crossing
Paying it no mind cause you just keep talking
We'll just imagine it's the good old days and take it slow.
(Reliant K, "Can't Complain")

Anyone who has waited at an intersection while a long cargo train slowly lumbers past knows that the first line of this song rings true. These song lyrics make use of *hyperbole* to intensify that feeling.

Example 4
#11: Bring wine or chocolate to everything. People love when guys do that. Not just because of the gift, but because it is endearing to imagine you standing in line at Trader Joe's before the party. (Mindy Kaling, *Is Everyone Hanging Out Without Me?*)

Does she really mean to bring wine or chocolate to everything? A funeral? You doctor's appointment? Kaling uses overstatement to underscore the point she is trying to make about civility.

 # FROM THE SCRIPTURES

Hyperbole used in the Bible usually draws attention to something by stating it in a non-literal, exaggerated way. Frequently (but not always) the figure is used for emphasis and to convey depth of emotion like human anguish, or to convey awe and amazement.

Example 1
Micah 6:7-8 (emphasis added)
Will the Lord be pleased with **thousands of rams**, *or* with **ten thousands of rivers of oil**? shall I give my firstborn *for* my transgression, the fruit of my body *for* the sin of my soul?
He hath shewed thee, O man, what *is* good; and what doth the Lord require of thee, but to do justly, and to love mercy, and to walk humbly with thy God?

The phrases "thousands of rams" and "ten thousands of rivers of oil" are beautiful examples of *hyperbole* used here to draw attention to the question posed. What the Lord requires is not stupendous sacrifice (like ten thousands of rivers of oil), but to do justly, to love mercy, and to walk humbly with Him.

Example 2
John 21:25 (emphasis added)
And there are also many other things which Jesus did, the which, if they should be written every one, I suppose that even the **world itself could not contain the books** that should be written. Amen.

In the Greek, the wording is "not even the world itself should have the space." This is an exaggerated, emphatic way of saying that Jesus did many other things that were not recorded by the Apostle John. Rather than state this literally, John uses a figure to draw attention to the number of things Jesus did that were not recorded. Also implied in this overstatement is the unparalleled significance of Jesus Christ's actions.

Example 3
Judges 20:16 (emphasis added)
Among all this people *there were* seven hundred chosen men left-handed; every one could sling stones **at an hair *breadth*** and not miss.

In the Hebrew, the word "breadth" is omitted, so the verse reads, "every one could sling stones at a hair and not miss." This is not literally true—these men didn't sling stones at an individual human hair. This is *hyperbole* used to draw attention to the men's impressive accuracy with slings. We have a similar expression today when we claim that the race was won "by a hair's breadth." We don't literally mean that the width of a hair separated the two runners. We mean that the race was so close that the winner won by a very small margin.

Example 4
Timothy 1:15-16 (emphasis added)
This *is* a faithful saying, and worthy of all acceptation, that Christ Jesus came into the world to save sinners; of **whom I am chief.** Howbeit for this cause I obtained mercy, that in me first Jesus Christ might shew forth all longsuffering, for a pattern to them which should hereafter believe on him to life everlasting.

In the Greek, the word chief is *protos*, which is in the superlative and might be translated as "chief," "first," or "principal." For Paul to refer to himself as the chief sinner is to use *hyperbole*, a figure of speech used to draw attention, in this context, to the longsuffering and mercy of Jesus Christ.

Example 5
Luke 14:26 (emphasis added)
If any *man* come to me, and **hate** not his father, and mother, and wife, and children, and brethren, and sisters, yea, and his own life also, he cannot be my disciple.

Would Jesus Christ have literally meant that the only way to become his disciple would be to hate one's family members and one's own lives? No, it is a figurative way of describing the requirements of discipleship. In the context we see that in order to be a disciple of Jesus Christ, one must put nothing else before the Lord Jesus Christ—not beloved family members or even one's self. Hatred of others is not the requirement. Using *hyperbole*, Jesus Christ dramatically emphasizes the commitment needed to become his disciple. Now let's consider the parallel record in Matthew:

Matthew 10:37
He that loveth father or mother more than me is not worthy of me: and he that loveth son or daughter more than me is not worthy of me.

Note how the same idea is conveyed literally in Matthew but figuratively in Luke.

Hyperbole is rhetorical exaggeration.

Notes

---

1. There is some discrepancy about the naming of this figure. E. W. Bullinger and Vilant Macbeth conflate the figure *meiosis* and *litotes* (155). Bullinger considers *tapeinosis* or *antenantiosis* to be a figure of understatement that uses the negative to express the positive in a high degree, not *litotes*. However, there is general consensus amongst modern scholars that *litotes* is a figure of understatement using the negative to express the positive in a high degree (see: Joseph, Lanham, Espy, *Silva Rhetorica*). Further, *The Oxford English Dictionary* defines *litotes* as, "A figure of speech, in which an affirmative is expressed by the negative of the contrary." According to the *OED*, the term *tapeinosis* is an obsolete term.
2. See also 1 Kings 16:2 and Psalm 113:7 for other examples of this type of *meiosis*.
3. According to Thayer's Greek Lexicon, this expression may also be a common idiom used by a teacher to refer to his pupils.
4. When Barry was writing, Don Johnson was a popular television actor known for his good looks and suave demeanor.

SECTION 3

FIGURES OF OMISSION

FIGURES OF OMISSION

Figures of omission occur when a word or words are purposefully left out of a sentence. When used in general literature, figures of omission achieve a hurried effect or brevity of style. But when these figures occur in the Bible, they often serve another purpose—to call attention to the words that remain.

While there are many types of figures of omission, this book covers only the two most commonly found in the Bible: *asyndeton* and *ellipsis*. *Asyndeton* occurs when there is an enumeration of things given without the use of conjunctions. Note the use of *asyndeton* in this quote from nineteenth-century art historian and writer Anna Jameson:

> "To trust religiously, to hope humbly, to desire nobly, to think rationally, to will resolutely, to work earnestly—may this be mine!"

Here Jameson makes effective use of the figure, which leads the reader to her emphatic end point—"may this be mine." We see a similar use of *asyndeton* in the following verse:

Luke 17:27
They did eat, they drank, they married wives, they were given in marriage, until the day that Noah entered into the ark, and the flood came and destroyed them all.

In this example, *asyndeton* hastens the reader to the end matter—that in the day that Noah entered the ark, the flood came and destroyed them all, despite their quotidian activities.

Another common figure of omission, *ellipsis*, occurs when a word or phrase is omitted but is readily supplied from the context. Many maxims, or short pithy sayings, use ellipses to achieve the desired brevity. Note the well-placed *ellipsis* in this aphorism from Benjamin Franklin: "Don't throw stones at your neighbors' if your own windows are glass." In this example the word "windows" is omitted from the first clause. The maxim, "Everybody's friend is nobody's" omits the word "friend" at the end of the sentence. By omitting the word "friend," the author achieves the brevity necessary for a maxim.

While in general literature *ellipses* may be used to achieve a certain style, or rhythm, or may be simply the result of inattentive craftsmanship, in the Bible *ellipsis* is typically used to draw emphasis to the words that remain in the text. E. W. Bullinger states it succinctly: "The omission arises not from want of thought, or lack of care, or from accident, but from design, in order that we may not stop to think, or lay stress on, the word omitted, but may dwell on the other words which are thus emphasized by the omission." (1)

Chapter 14

Asyndeton

(omission of conjunction) 137

a-SIN-de-ton

Asyndeton omits conjunctions between clauses.

The word *"asyndeton"* literally means without any conjunctions. This figure enumerates things without using conjunctions, primarily the connective "and."[1] Generally speaking, conjunctions occur between the last two nouns in a series or between a series of clauses, so a deviation from this norm constitutes a figure of speech. According to New Testament scholar David Alan Black, this lack of connectives is highly irregular for Koine (biblical) Greek. Black writes, "Most scholars agree that this feature is contrary to the spirit of the Greek language. Most Greek sentences are linked by a connecting particle, and, where *asyndeton* is found, it is generally used with rhetorical effect". As we will see from the biblical examples, this figure of speech tends to hasten the reader along to the emphatic end matter.

FROM GENERAL CULTURE

Example 1
"I came; I saw; I conquered." (Latin phrase)

Attributed to Julius Caesar, this Latin phrase (*veni, vidi, vici*) uses *asyndeton* as a way to emphasize how quickly conquest was made. So quickly, in fact, he did not even have time to insert a conjunction between three short clauses.

Example 2

For God's sake, let us sit upon the ground
And tell sad stories of the death of kings:
How some have been depos'd, some slain in war,
Some haunted by the ghosts they have depos'd,
Some poison'd by their wives, some sleeping kill'd:
All murder'd.   (*Richard II* 3.2.156)

In this passage *asyndeton* moves the reader along to the end point—that all the kings being discussed had been murdered.

Example 3

Razors pain you;
Rivers are damp;
Acids stain you;
And drugs cause cramp.
Guns aren't lawful;
Nooses give;
Gas smells awful;
You might as well live. ("Resumé," 1926, Dorothy Parker)

Known for her sharp wit and mordant sense of humor, Dorothy Parker here makes sly use of *asyndeton* in one of her best-known poems. Rather than use conjunctions between the clauses in lines 1-3 and lines 5-7, Parker relies on the semi-colon, a non-verbal connector. The result is to hasten the reader along to the darkly comic end matter: you might as well live. Readers familiar with Parker's writing recognize how aptly this sums up both her perspective on life and her sardonic sense of humor.

 # FROM THE SCRIPTURES

Example 1
1 Corinthians 13:13

And now abideth faith, hope, charity, these three; but the greatest of these *is* charity.

Because there is no conjunction between the word "hope" and the word "charity," this constitutes the figure *asyndeton* where the emphasis lies on the end matter—that the greatest of these is charity, the love of God.

Example 2
1 Corinthians 3:12-13
Now if any man build upon this foundation gold, silver, precious stones, wood, hay, stubble;
Every man's work shall be made manifest: for the day shall declare it, because it shall be revealed by fire; and the fire shall try every man's work of what sort it is.

A list of six possible foundations is enumerated in verse 12: gold, silver, precious stones, wood, hay, stubble. The *asyndeton* draws attention to the end matter, which follows in verse 13, that "every man's work shall be made manifest: for the day shall declare it."

Example 3
1 Corinthians 12:27-31
Now ye are the body of Christ, and members in particular.
And God hath set some in the church, first apostles, secondarily prophets, thirdly teachers, after that miracles, then gifts of healings, helps, governments, diversities of tongues.
Are all apostles? *are* all prophets? *are* all teachers? *are* all workers of miracles?
Have all the gifts of healing? do all speak with tongues? do all interpret?
But covet earnestly the best gifts: and yet shew I unto you a more excellent way.

This section of 1 Corinthians addresses the different ministries or functions that individuals in the Body of Christ might provide for the profit of the Church. Because there is a long list here without any conjunction, this constitutes the figure *asyndeton*. The emphasis in this instance would be on verse 31 and the "more excellent way" of the love of God, which the Apostle Paul, by revelation, addresses in chapter 13.

Example 4
Philippians 3:5-7
Circumcised the eighth day, of the stock of Israel, *of* the tribe of Benjamin, an Hebrew of the Hebrews; as touching the law, a Pharisee;
Concerning zeal, persecuting the church; touching the righteousness which is in the law, blameless.
But what things were gain to me, those I counted loss for Christ.

111

Here, Paul enumerates his religious credentials without using any conjunctions. The effect on the reader is to hasten through this list and to focus on the end matter: "But what things were gain to me, those I counted loss for Christ." In the context, Paul addresses those who might have confidence in the flesh to bring about their own righteousness. Paul then trots out a seemingly impeccable religious resumé. Yet the figure does not ask the reader to dwell on each item but to instead focus on the end statement—that all those things were counted loss for Christ. The next verses expand on this idea as Paul declares, "Yea doubtless, and I count all things but loss for the excellence of the knowledge of Christ Jesus my Lord: for whom I have suffered the loss of all things, and do count them but dung, that I may win Christ."

Example 5
Galatians 5:19-22
Now the works of the flesh are manifest, which are *these*; Adultery, fornication, uncleanness, lasciviousness, Idolatry, witchcraft, hatred, variance, emulations, wrath, strife, seditions, heresies, Envyings, murders, drunkenness, revellings, and such like: of the which I tell you before, as I have also told *you* in time past, that they which do such things shall not inherit the kingdom of God. But the fruit of the Spirit is love, joy, peace, longsuffering, gentleness, goodness, faith, meekness, temperance:against such there is no law.

The works of the flesh (17 characteristics) and the fruit of the spirit (nine characteristics) are listed without the use of any conjunctions. Therefore, the reader's attention would rest on the concluding statements given at the end of each enumeration: "they which do such things shall not inherit the kingdom of God," and "against such there is no law."

Asyndeton omits conjunctions between clauses.

Chapter 15
Ellipsis

(omission of a word or words) 3

ee-LIP-sis

> *Ellipsis* is the omission of a word or phrase easily supplied from the context.

A common figure of speech both in profane and sacred writing, *ellipsis* occurs when a word or words are omitted in a sentence that would otherwise be needed to make the sentence grammatically sound or to complete the thought. [2] The omitted words are easily supplied from the context. Rhetoricians classify many different types and subcategories of *ellipses* such as absolute and relative ellipses, complex ellipses of repetition, with many variations thereof. But because this is an introduction to figures of speech, this book covers only the simple *ellipsis* of a word or words.

In English, *ellipsis* of the verb is quite common. P.G. Wodehouse writes, "His brow was furrowed, his mouth peevish." Leaving out the verb "was" in the second clause lends an economy of speech to this witty description. *Ellipsis* of the adjective is also common in English. The familiar phrase, "The average person thinks he isn't" omits the adjective "average." *Ellipsis* is used frequently in advertising where brevity counts. An ambitious advertisement reads: "Yogurt improves your morale . . .releases your inhibitions . . .postpones death." The [. . .] indicate that the word "yogurt" is omitted, but it easily supplied from the context.

While *ellipsis* is often used today to achieve brevity or wit, in the Bible *ellipsis* is used to draw attention to the words that remain in the text. As Dona Hickey puts it, *ellipsis* encourages readers to "supply what isn't there by stressing heavily what is" (*Developing a Written Voice*).

In the KJV, *ellipses* are frequently supplied by italics, like in the following verse:

Romans 6:5
For if we have been planted together in the likeness of his death,
we shall be also *in the likeness* of *his* resurrection.

In other words, in the original Greek, the phrase "in the likeness of" is not repeated in the second part of this verse. For the most part, the KJV correctly supplies omitted words. But sometimes translators add an *ellipsis* where none exists or fail to note an *ellipsis* when one does exist in the original.[3] Therefore, care should be taken when seeking to verify this figure of speech.

While adding omitted words does help smooth out the reading style in English, it may also diminish the impact of the figure. Note how Romans 6:5 reads with the figure in place:

Romans 6:5 (words in italic omitted)
For if we have been planted together in the likeness of his death,
we shall be also of resurrection.

Admittedly, the English rendering here is awkward. But note how the *ellipsis* now draws our attention to the word "resurrection" in this verse.

FROM GENERAL CULTURE

Example 1
Telegram: "HOW OLD CARY GRANT?"
Response: "OLD CARY GRANT FINE. HOW YOU?"

This may be an urban legend, but this exchange between actor Cary Grant and and a newspaper editor who wanted to know Grant's age makes comic use of *ellipsis*. Telegrams were charged by the word, and so needless words would be omitted to save money. But in this case, Grant omits the verbs "is" and "are" not necessarily to save money but to make a joke. (Ben Zimmer, "Crash Blossoms." *The New York Times*, Jan. 27, 2010)

Example 2
"Superman debuted in 1938, Batman in 1939, Wonder Woman in 1941."
(Jill Lepore, "The Last Amazon." *The New Yorker*, September 22, 2014)

Ellipsis of the verb is common in English, as we see from this example where the word "debuted" is omitted, likely to draw attention to the years stated.

Example 3
"In proportion as he simplifies his life, the laws of the universe will appear less complex, and solitude will not be solitude, nor poverty poverty, nor weakness weakness."(Henry David Thoreau, *Walden*)

In this example, Thoreau uses an *ellipsis* of the verb. The figure draws attention to the words that remain while also achieving brevity of style.

 # FROM THE SCRIPTURES

Ellipsis not supplied in KJV

Example 1
Romans 2:6-8
Who will render to every man according to his deeds:
To them who by patient continuance in well doing seek for glory and honour and immortality, eternal life: But unto them that are contentious, and do not obey the truth, but obey unrighteousness, indignation and wrath,

There is an *ellipsis* of the verb in verses seven and eight ["He will render"], which is easily supplied from the context. Note how the figure now draws attention to the outcome of every man's deeds, and not to the One doing the rendering.

Example 2
Romans 5:3-5
And not only so, but we glory in tribulations also: knowing that tribulation worketh patience;
And patience, experience; and experience, hope:
And hope maketh not ashamed; because the love of God is shed abroad in our hearts by the Holy Ghost which is given unto us.

There is an *ellipsis* of the verb in verse four, ["worketh"] readily supplied from the context.

Example 3
1 Corinthians 15:53-54
For this corruptible must put on incorruption, and this mortal *must* put on immortality.
So when this corruptible shall have put on incorruption, and this mortal shall have put on immortality, then shall be brought to pass the saying that is written, Death is swallowed up in victory.

In these verses, there is an *ellipsis* of the noun ["body"] supplied from the context. Note how another English translation supplies the word "body" in these verses:

1 Corinthians 15:53-54 (NLT)
For our dying bodies must be transformed into bodies that will never die; our mortal bodies must be transformed into immortal bodies. Then, when our dying bodies have been transformed into bodies that will never die, this Scripture will be fulfilled: "Death is swallowed up in victory

This translation adds the word "body" to verses 53 and 54 even though the word does not occur in the Greek texts. The meaning may be clearer with these added words, but the addition somewhat detracts from the emphasis achieved by the figure of speech. The figure draws our attention to the words that remain.

Ellipsis correctly supplied in KJV

Example 1
1 Corinthians 15:45
And so it is written, The first man Adam was made a living soul the last Adam *was made* a quickening spirit.

In the Greek, there is an *ellipsis* of the verb ("was made") correctly supplied by the translators to convey the sense. The figure of speech draws emphasis to the truth that Jesus Christ, referred to here as the last Adam, was made a quickening (life giving) spirit in contrast to Adam, who was made a living soul.

Example 2
Psalm 7:11
God judgeth the righteous, and God is angry *with the wicked* every day.

If we don't consider the *ellipsis* in the second part of this verse, it would read, "God is angry every day." The translators here correctly supply the omitted words, which are determined from the context. The wicked are mentioned in verse nine of Psalm 7, "Oh let the wickedness of the wicked come to an end; but establish the just: for the righteous God trieth the hearts and reins." The *ellipsis* is supplied from that verse. In cases like this, the reader needs to look to the near context to understand what might be omitted.

Example 3
2 Corinthians 8:14
But by an equality, *that* now at this time your abundance *may be a supply* for their want, that their abundance also may be *a supply* for your want: that there may be equality:

HINTS & TIPS

In this example, the words in italics are correctly supplied so that the English reads more clearly. But consider this verse with the *ellipsis* in place:

2 Corinthians 8:14
But by an equality, now at this time your abundance for their want, that their abundance also may be for your want: that there may be equality:

1. In the KJV, omitted words supplied by the translators are usually given in italic type. However, not all added words occur in italic print, and not all *ellipses* are noted correctly. This requires checking with an interlinear or other research tool to verify what words might actually have been omitted in the Biblical languages.

2. Check the immediate and near context to determine what word or phrase is omitted.

Certainly this is awkwardly worded in English. But stated this way, our attention is drawn to the relationship between "abundance" and "want," words that are repeated in this verse, along with the word "equality." When we look at this verse with the *ellipsis* in place, the emphasis becomes more apparent largely because the repetition becomes clearer. Here, the Corinthian believers are reminded that God desires there to be equality amongst believers regarding having their physical needs met. Those who have abundance might share with those who lack, knowing that should the tables turn, they might be on the receiving end of another believer's generosity. Keeping the figures of speech in mind (*ellipsis* and repetition), the reciprocity amongst believers regarding physical wants and abundance is highlighted.

> *Ellipsis* is the omission of a word or phrase easily supplied from the context.

Notes

1. This figure is known by other names including *asyntheton, dialysis, dialyton, solutum, dissolution, epitrochasmos, percursio.*
2. This figure is sometimes also referred to as *brachylogia, eclipsis,* or default.
3. In some cases the King James Version offers false *ellipses*, meaning that italics are inserted where no omission occurs in the Hebrew or Greek. The topic of false *ellipses* is outside the scope of this book, but readers are referred to *Figures of Speech Used in the Bible Explained and Illustrated* (p. 115-127) to read more about this subject.

SECTION 4
FIGURES USING HUMAN ATTRIBUTES

FIGURES USING HUMAN ATTRIBUTES

The figure of speech *prosopopoeia* or personification is giving human characteristics to non-sentient beings (like animals), to inanimate object (like rocks), or to abstract ideas (like wisdom). Some common examples include:

- Referring to the United States as "Uncle Sam"
- Opportunity knocks
- Wind whistling through the trees
- That Ferrari has a lot of guts.

Personification is used extensively in advertising. In the slogan, "Oreo: Milk's favorite cookie," milk is depicted as showing favoritism or partiality. No doubt the advertisers would like consumers to show the same favoritism and buy their cookie. Visual personification in advertising is commonplace. Think of the chatty Geico gecko, the Energizer bunny, acrobatic *M and M's* diving into a candy dish, Gatorade bottles wearing boxing gloves, and so on.

In the Scriptures, animals, trees, rocks, mountains, and other inanimate things or non-sentient beings are personified. Abstract ideas like wisdom are also personified in the Scriptures. Why this figure is used or how it brings emphasis to a particular passage might be determined by considering the context.

Anthropopatheia is similar to personification in that it also uses human characteristics in a figurative way, but *anthropopatheia* deals specifically with the depiction of God as having human attributes, qualities, or characteristics. Consider what the following verse declares about the nature of God:

John 4:24 (ESV)
God is spirit, and those who worship him must worship in spirit and truth.

Because God is spirit and not a human, to refer to God by using human or physical attributes is to employ the figure of speech *anthropopatheia*. In the Bible, God is referred to as having human body parts including eyes, hands, feet, nostrils, hands, a mouth, a soul, arms, fingers, bowels, ears, and so forth.

Psalm 16:11
Thou wilt shew me the path of life: in thy presence *is* fulness of joy; at thy right hand *there are* pleasures for evermore.

Psalm 31: 2
Bow down thine ear to me; deliver me speedily: be thou my strong rock, for an house of defence to save me.

In the first example, God is described as having a right hand. In the second, God is depicted as having ears. This type of *anthropopatheia*, attributing human body parts to God, occurs frequently in the Scriptures.

Another type of *anthropopatheia* includes attributing human affections (like sorrow and grief) and feelings (like anger and vengeance) to God. For example, when God is described as rejoicing (Psalm 104:31) or as grieving (Genesis 6:6) or as hating (Psalm 5:5), these are examples of *anthropopatheia*. Bullinger explains that human feelings or emotions are attributed to God, "not that He has such feelings; but, in infinite condescension, . . . in order to enable us to comprehend Him" (882). *Anthropopatheia* also occurs when God is described as having or owning possessions such as a throne or riches.

Chapter 16

Prosopopeia

(personification) 861

pro-so-po-PEE-a

> *Prosopopeia* attributes human characteristics or abilities to non-sentient beings, inanimate objects, or abstract ideas.

Prosopopeia, or personification, is a figure of speech where human characteristics or abilities are attributed to non-sentient being, inanimate objects, or abstract ideas. What effect does this figure produce? Aside from grabbing our attention by stating something in a non-literal manner, personification also attracts the reader because we can all relate to human experience. Rather than describe something in abstract terms, a writer may use personification as a way draw the reader into something familiar—human emotions, human activities, and human characteristics. Some scholars believe that personification acts as a starting point to understanding, a way to connect with the reader at a most fundamental level.

FROM GENERAL CULTURE

Example 1 (emphasis added)
"It **slumbers** between broad prairies, **kissing** the long meadow grass, and **bathes** the overhanging boughs of elder bushes or willows or the roots of elms or ash-trees and clumps of maples" (Nathaniel Hawthorne, *The Old Manse*)

Popular in the early nineteenth-century, American literary Romanticism makes frequent use personification where elements of nature are given human characteristics. In this example, Hawthorne depicts streams as having the ability to slumber, to kiss, and to bathe. Perhaps the desired effect is to give nature preternatural life.

Example 2 (emphasis added)
"The woods are **getting ready to sleep**—they are not yet asleep but they are **disrobing** and are **having** all sorts of little bed-time **conferences** and **whisperings** and **good-nights**."
(L. M. Montgomery, *The Green Gables Letters*)

Here Canadian novelist Lucy Maude Montgomery makes use of personification in a similar fashion but for a different reason than Hawthorne. Reading the entire passage, one sees that the woods are portrayed as children preparing to go to sleep: they are disrobing, having little conferences, whispering, and saying goodnight. A children's novelist, Montgomery was writing to young readers, and so this personification of children getting ready for bed would certainly resonate with her readers. The figure also gives the passage a whimsical effect not uncommon in children's literature.

Example 3 (emphasis added)
New York City is the most fatally fascinating thing in America. She **sits** like a great witch at the gate of the country, **showing** her alluring white **face and hiding** her crooked **hands and feet** under the folds of her **wide garments**—constantly **enticing** thousands from far within, and tempting those who come from across the seas to go no farther. And all these become the victims of her **caprice**. Some she at once **crushes** beneath her cruel **feet**; others she **condemns** to a fate like that of galley slaves; a few she **favors** and **fondles**, **riding** them high on the bubbles of fortune; then with a sudden **breath** she **blows** the bubbles out and **laughs** mockingly as she **watches** them fall.
(James Weldon Johnson, *Autobiography of an Ex-Colored Man*)

In this passage Johnson personifies New York City as a woman. (He uses simile, not personification, to compare the city to a witch.) The personified language is noted in bold print—the city has a face, hands, feet, and takes on human abilities like sitting, showing, enticing, and so forth. Here, the personification is fraught with political implication where the city is portrayed as a white woman whose behavior is capricious and destructive. Perhaps Johnson, whose *Autobiography* was written in 1912 and then republished in 1927, makes extensive use of personification in this passage to draw attention to the human cost of racism in the city at that time.

We can see from these literary examples that personification might be used for different purposes: to animate nature, to add whimsy, to convey sociopolitical opinion.

 FROM THE SCRIPTURES

Example 1
Isaiah 49:13 (emphasis added)
Sing, O heavens; and **be joyful**, O earth; and **break forth into singing**, O mountains; for the Lord hath comforted his people, and will have mercy upon his afflicted.

The book of Isaiah has many occurrences of personification. In this verse, the prophet tells the heavens to sing, the earth to be joyful, and the mountains to break out in song. Isaiah isn't literally commanding these things to take on human abilities like singing and being joyful; rather, he uses personification to emphatically express the joy in knowing that the Lord has comforted His people and that He will have mercy on His afflicted. To spontaneously burst into song truly is a demonstration of joy. How beautifully and powerfully this joy is expressed through personification. How it draws attention to the wonderful blessing of God's comfort and God's mercy.

Example 2
Job 28:22 (emphasis added)
Destruction and death **say**, We have heard the fame thereof with our ears.

This is a different type of personification than the one occurring in Isaiah 49:13, for here, abstract ideas (destruction, death) are given the ability of human speech ("say"). The figure draws attention to the power and awe of wisdom, which is spoken of in verse 20. Significantly, the book of Job, a record filled with human anguish, has many occurrences of personification. The figure seems to be well suited to convey depth of emotion.

Example 3

1 Corinthians 12:15-16 (emphasis added)

If the foot shall **say**, Because I am not the hand, I am not of the body; is it therefore not of the body?

And if the ear shall **say**, Because I am not the eye, I am not of the body; is it therefore not of the body?

Perhaps this was intended to be a humorous use of personification: would the Corinthians believers have found it funny to think about hands and feet and ears speaking to one another? Possibly. There does seem to be some comic absurdity in these verses. Whether or not it is used humorously, personification nonetheless draws attention to the absurdity of members in the Body of Christ thinking disparagingly of themselves or others rather than thinking of believers as having equal importance in the Body of Christ.

Example 4

Genesis 4:10 (emphasis added)

And he said, What hast thou done? the voice of thy brother's blood **crieth** unto me from the ground.

In the context, Cain has just murdered his brother, Abel. God asks Cain what he has done, and then God remarks that Abel's blood "cries unto Him" from the ground. What a chilling use of personification! How vividly and powerfully it expresses the grim reality of Abel's murder and of God's knowledge of this heinous act.

Example 5

Psalm 77:16 (emphasis added)

The waters **saw** thee, O God, the waters **saw** thee; they **were afraid**: the depths also **were troubled**.

Notice how the NIV gives the personification a little more forcefully than the KJV:

Psalm 77:16 (NIV) (emphasis added)

The waters **saw** you God, the waters **saw** you and **writhed**; the very depths were **convulsed**.

TWO MODES USED TO CONVEY PERSONIFICATION

In narrative, there are several ways to convey personification, but most commonly the figure occurs through description and direct speech. These two narrative modes occur in Proverbs 8 where the abstract concept, wisdom, is personified as a woman. Wisdom is portrayed as having human abilities (like sitting, standing, crying):

Proverbs 8:1-3
Doth not wisdom cry? and understanding put forth her voice?
She standeth in the top of high places, by the way in the places of the paths.
She crieth at the gates, at the entry of the city, at the coming in at the doors.

Personification in these three verses is conveyed via description. In the rest of the chapter, wisdom (personified) is portrayed as speaking directly. Verses 4-36 record the direct speech of wisdom. Here are four verses by way of example:

Proverbs 8:4-8
Unto you, O men, I call; and my voice *is* to the sons of man.
O ye simple, understand wisdom: and, ye fools, be ye of an understanding heart.
Hear; for I will speak of excellent things; and the opening of my lips *shall be* right things.
For my mouth shall speak truth; and wickedness is an abomination to my lips.
All the words of my mouth *are* in righteousness; *there is* nothing froward or perverse in them.

In some English translations, this direct speech is set off by quotation marks, signaling to the reader that direct speech occurs. Note how in the English Standard Version the quotation marks begin in verse four and continue through to verse 36. Verses 4-8 are given here by way of example, but readers should note that the quotation marks continue through the rest of the chapter:

Proverbs 8: 4-8 (ESV)
"To you, O men, I call,
and my cry is to the children of man.
O simple ones, learn prudence;
O fools, learn sense.
Hear, for I will speak noble things,
and from my lips will come what is right,
for my mouth will utter truth;
wickedness is an abomination to my lips.
All the words of my mouth are righteous;
there is nothing twisted or crooked in them."

Placing quotation marks around these words helps to highlight the personification in this chapter.

What effect might this figure have? The Scriptures could have listed the characteristics of wisdom in abstract terminology; but by using personification, the reader's attention is surely arrested. The direct speech adds a layer of complexity and power to this passage. What a marvelous, memorable way to convey the depth and value of godly wisdom. (It is also worth noting how "wisdom" is not hidden as illustrated in this passage, for she "cries" in public places that are accessible to everyone.)

> *Prosopopeia* attributes human characteristics or abilities to non-sentient beings, inanimate objects, or abstract ideas.

Chapter 17
Anthropopatheia

(condescension) 871

an-thro-po-PAY-thee-a

> *Anthropopatheia* is a figure of speech that portrays God as having human qualities or human abilities.

The word *anthropopatheia* comes from *anthropos*, meaning man and *pathos*, meaning feelings or emotions. The Latin name for this figure is *condescensio*, or condescension in English. Benjamin Keach explains that this figure is known as condescension because "God in his holy word descends as it were, so low as our capacities, expressing his heavenly mysteries after the manner of men, which the Hebrews elegantly call the way of the sons of men" (40).[1] While *Figures of Speech Used in the Bible Explained and Illustrated* lists more than twenty different divisions of *anthropopatheia*, *Go Figure!* covers three types:

1. God is referred to as having body parts
2. God is attributed with having human feelings
3. God is attributed with having human actions[2]

GENERAL CULTURE

Example 1
In the epic poem *Paradise Lost*, Milton portrays God, angels, archangels, Satan, and devils as having human qualities and attributes.[3] In the

following excerpt from Book III, note how Milton portrays God via the figure *anthropopatheia*:

> Now had the almighty Father from above
> From the pure empyrean where he sits
> High throned above all height, bent down his eye (*Paradise Lost* III. l. 56-58).

In these lines, God is depicted as sitting on a throne (a human action) and as having eyes (a human body part). Later in this passage, Milton portrays God as giving a detailed defense for having created Adam and Eve:

> I formed them free and free they must remain
> Til they enthrall themselves. I else must change
> Their nature and revoke the high decree
> Unchangeable, eternal, which ordained
> Their freedom; they themselves ordained their fall.
> The first sort by their own suggestion fell,
> Self-tempted, self-depraved; man falls deceived
> By the other first; man therefore shall find grace,
> The other, none. In mercy and justice both,
> Through Heaven and earth, so shall my glory excel,
> But mercy first and last shall brightest shine." (*Paradise Lost* III. l. 124-134).

 **FROM THE SCRIPTURES**

1) Human body parts

Example 1
Psalm 89:15 (ESV) (emphasis added)
Blessed are the people who know the festal shout, who walk, O LORD, in the light of your **face**,

In this example, God is depicted as having a face ("countenance" in the KJV), a figurative way of meaning God's presence.

Example 2
Job 4:9 (emphasis added)
By the blast of God they perish, and by the breath of his **nostrils** are they consumed.

Here God is describing as having nostrils. In the context, Eliphaz the Temanite, implies that Job's miserable condition is due to his iniquity and wickedness (v. 8) and claims that God is angry with Job and has sent this devastation to Job. In the context, the "breath of his nostrils" signifies God's purported anger at Job's wickedness. What a dramatic and memorable way for Eliphaz to convey his opinion about Job's situation.

Example 3
Deuteronomy 8:3 (emphasis added)
And he humbled thee, and suffered thee to hunger, and fed thee with manna, which thou knewest not, neither did thy fathers know; that he might make thee know that man doth not live by bread only, but by every *word* that proceedeth out of the **mouth** of the Lord doth man live.

Here the figure is used to convey the words that come from God, drawing attention to the truth that man is to live not only by eating ("bread" is *metonymy* for food) but also by every word that originates from God.

2) Human feelings

Example 1
Ephesians 4:30 (emphasis added)
And **grieve** not the holy Spirit of God, whereby ye are sealed unto the day of redemption.

Here God is depicted as having the ability to grieve.

Example 2
Numbers 25:11 (emphasis added)
Phinehas, the son of Eleazar, the son of Aaron the priest, hath turned my **wrath** away from the children of Israel, while he was zealous for my sake among them, that I consumed not the children of Israel in my **jealousy**.

Here God is depicted as having two human emotions: wrath and jealousy.

Example 3
Ezekiel 5:13 (emphasis added)
Thus shall mine **anger** be accomplished, and I will cause my fury to rest upon them, and I will be **comforted**: and they shall know that I the LORD have spoken *it* in my **zeal**, when I have accomplished my **fury** in them.

In this verse, God is depicted as having four distinct human feelings: anger, comfort, zeal, and fury.

3) Human abilities

Example 1
Isaiah 7:18 (emphasis added)
And it shall come to pass in that day, *that* the LORD shall **hiss** for the fly that *is* in the uttermost part of the rivers of Egypt, and for the bee that *is* in the land of Assyria.

In this verse, God is portrayed as hissing, or as some English Bibles render it, as whistling. Both are human abilities.

Example 2
Genesis 18:20-21 (emphasis added)
And the LORD said, Because the cry of Sodom and Gomorrah is great, and because their sin is very grievous; I will **go down** now, and see whether they have done altogether according to the cry of it, which is come unto me; and if not, I will know.

In verse 21, God is depicted as having the human ability to descend to the cities of Sodom and Gomorrah.

Example 3
Psalm 14:2 (emphasis added)
The LORD **looked down** from heaven upon the children of men, to **see** if there were any that did understand, *and* seek God.

This verse portrays God as having the ability to look down from heaven and to see.

Example 4
Jeremiah 32:41 (emphasis added)
Yea, I will **rejoice** over them to do them good, and I will **plant** them in this land assuredly with my whole **heart** and with my whole **soul**.

This verse is noteworthy in that it includes three types of this figure: God is depicted here as having the human feeling of rejoicing, the human ability to plant, and the human body parts of heart and soul.

What a joy and privilege it is to get to know God, who has condescended to make Himself known to us through His Word.

> *Anthropopatheia* is a figure of speech that portrays God as having human qualities or human abilities.

Notes

----

1. Benjamin Keach considered the figure of speech *anthropopatheia* to be a type of metaphor (see pages 40-88).

2. Bullinger offers a more comprehensive definition of this figure indicating that *anthropopatheia* includes attributing to God the characteristics of animals, plants, or even non-living things (see page 894ff).

3. Readers will probably notice a lack of various examples from general culture in this chapter. While I did locate several examples of *anthropopathia* from profane literature, I did not wish to include them because I felt they did not portray God in a respectful or truthful light. My apologies for the gap in this chapter.

SECTION 5
FIGURES OF EXCHANGE

FIGURES OF EXCHANGE

In language, it's common to use one word to mean another as a type of transference or exchange of meaning. When this occurs with a noun, it is the figure *metonymy*, which literally means, "change of name or noun."[1] *Metonymy* occurs when one noun is substituted for a related noun. For example, when we say, "Boston won the Stanley Cup in 2011," we use *metonymy* where the name of the city is put for the NHL team, the Boston Bruins. When we refer to New York City's financial district as "Wall Street," we use *metonymy* where a street name is used for a district. Or when we say, "put your John Hancock on this document," we use *metonymy*, where one noun phrase ("John Hancock") is meant to indicate another noun phrase (one's own signature).

A double or compound *metonymy* is the figure *metalepsis*. "The pen is mightier than the sword" is a double *metonymy* where two words (pen, sword) are used in one sentence to mean two other related things (writer, military might). Another type of *metalepsis* occurs when one word is put for two other related words. The phrase "the blood of Jesus Christ" is a *metalepsis* because the word "blood" is put for two things: 1) Jesus Christ's shed blood, meaning his death. 2) all that Jesus Christ's death accomplished.[2]

Synecdoche is a figure of speech that also relies on an exchange of one word put in place of a related word. But with *synecdoche*, the relationship between the two nouns is typically more specific than in *metonymy*. In order for a figure to be *synecdoche*, the word used must be a part of a whole, or (less often) whole of a part. It's not enough for the words to be related; they must be in a specific relationship to one another, most typically part of a whole.

A common *synecdoche* occurs when body parts are used to suggest a whole person. "Those parents have a lot of mouths to feed" uses *synecdoche* where part ("mouth") is put for the whole, meaning the people in the family. When we refer to the section of an orchestra as the "strings," we use *synecdoche* where a part (strings) is put for the whole (all the string sections of an orchestra.) There are other types of *synecdoche* in the Bible, but the most common type is the part-put-for-whole variety.

In some cases, it's unclear if a figure is a *metonymy* or a *synecdoche*. Considering the context often helps to determine which figure it might be. And sometimes the same word like "belly" or "heart" might be either a *metonymy* or a *synecdoche*.

> **John 7:38** (emphasis added)
> He that believeth on me, as the scripture hath said, out of his **belly** shall flow rivers of living water.

In this verse, the word "belly" is a *metonymy* where the belly is put for the innermost part of the person. But the word "belly" might also be a *synecdoche*, where a body part is put for the whole person:

> **Romans 16:18** (emphasis added)
> For they that are such serve not our Lord Jesus Christ, but their own **belly**; and by good words and fair speeches deceive the hearts of the simple.

Here the "belly" is a *synecdoche* for the whole person. In other words, they serve themselves.

If you have trouble distinguishing between *metonymy* and *synecdoche*, don't worry. You're in good company! Scholars continuously argue about the differences between these two figures and often give contradictory examples and explanations of both. As rhetoric scholar Theresa Enos observes, "Because ancient rhetoricians lacked precise definitions for the tropes, the fine distinction between *metonymy* and the related figure *synecdoche* has remained unclear for centuries" (444).[3]

Perhaps it helps to think of it this way: *synecdoche* bears an internal relationship with the replaced subject while *metonymy* bears an external relationship with the replaced subject. It may also help to remember that even if you can't identify the exact figure, you can still appreciate that it is a figure of exchange where one word is put for another word.

Chapter 18

Metonymy

(a noun put for another related noun) 538

me-TON-i-mee

> *Metonymy* is a noun or name put for a related noun or name.

Metonymy is one of the most commonly occurring figures in the Bible. While most scholars agree that *metonymy* exists only with nouns, a few scholars, including Bullinger, make the case that other parts of speech might also be metonymic. *Go Figure!* only considers *metonymy* of nouns.

When we refer to a king as "the crown," we use *metonymy* where the crown is put for the monarch. When we call a government official a "suit," we use *metonymy* where the suit is put for the official, who normally wears this type of attire. In both cases, the word used is related to the word it evokes. A crown is related to a monarch, and a suit is related to a government official. *Metonymy* is founded on relationship and not on resemblance.

FROM GENERAL CULTURE

The following are familiar examples of *metonymy* from American English vernacular.

"The **chair** called the meeting to order even though few members were present."
Chair is put for the chairperson, the one leading the meeting.

"Many believe that the **press** slant the news to one political extreme or another."

Press (shortened from "printing press") is put for professionals working in news media.

"**Shakespeare** continues to be taught in American universities despite a decline in literacy rates."

Here the writer (Shakespeare) is put for his writings.

"Do the owners of this restaurant take **plastic**?"

Plastic is put for a credit card.

Here the material (plastic) is put for the thing (credit card) it is made of.

HINTS & TIPS

1. Because the word "*metonymy*" means change of name or change of noun, look for a noun when identifying this figure of speech.
2. The word used is in relationship to the word that is not used.
3. A noun may be used as a *metonymy* in one instance but a *synecdoche* in the next. It helps to consider the context to determine which figure it may be.
4. Not all metonymies carry emphasis.

In all of these examples, the word occurring is closely related to the word it is substituting.

FROM THE SCRIPTURES

Figures of Speech Used in the Bible Explained and Illustrated lists more than 100 subcategories of *metonymy* based on the relationship that exists between the two nouns (or two verbs). Much insight might be gained by studying Bullinger's detailed explanations and illustrations. However, for ease of study, this chapter organizes *metonymy* by subject matter.[4] Of course, these categories are not exhaustive and certainly are not meant to be definitive. The *metonymies* were chosen because they are relatively simple to understand and because they occur frequently in the Bible. And, the short list of Scripture references is meant to be a starting point. There are many more examples to be found in the Bible.

1. PARENTS, or ancestors are put for their descendants. In the following verses, the bolded word is a *metonymy* where the parent is put for his descendants.

Genesis 9:27 (emphasis added)
God shall enlarge **Japheth**, and he shall dwell in the tents of **Shem**; and Canaan shall be his servant.

Genesis 18:18 (emphasis added)
Seeing that **Abraham** shall surely become a great and mighty nation, and all the nations of the earth shall be blessed in him?

1 Kings 18:17 (emphasis added)
And it came to pass, when Ahab saw Elijah, that Ahab said unto him, *Art* thou he that troubleth **Israel**?

2. WRITER is put for his writing. In the following verses, "Moses" is put for what he wrote meaning the Pentateuch, the first five books of the Bible.

Luke 24:27 (emphasis added)
And beginning at **Moses** and all the prophets, he expounded unto them in all the scriptures the things concerning himself.

Acts 15:21 (emphasis added)
For **Moses** of old time hath in every city them that preach him, being read in the synagogues every sabbath day.

2 Corinthians 3:15 (emphasis added)
But even unto this day, when **Moses** is read, the vail is upon their heart.

3. PARTS of the mouth (mouth, lips, tongue, throat) are put for what is spoken, meanings words, language, speech.

Deuteronomy 17:6 (emphasis added)
At the **mouth** of two witnesses, or three witnesses, shall he that is worthy of death be put to death; *but* at the **mouth** of one witness he shall not be put to death.

It isn't the mouths of witnesses that determine if someone is or isn't worthy of death. It is the words spoken by those witnesses that make this determination.

Psalm 5:9 (emphasis added)
For *there* is no faithfulness in their **mouth**; their inward part *is* very wickedness; their **throat** *is* an open sepulchre; they flatter with their **tongue**.

In this verse, three *metonymies* exist where the word "mouth," "throat," and "tongue" all indicate words spoken.

The Book of Proverbs is filled with this type of *metonymy* where different organs of speech like the lips, mouth, or tongue are put for words issuing forth from those organs of speech. Here are but a few examples:

Proverbs 10:11 (emphasis added)
The **mouth** of a righteous *man* is a well of life: but violence covereth the **mouth** of the wicked.

Proverbs 10:20 (emphasis added)
The **tongue** of the just *is as* choice silver: the heart of the wicked *is* little worth.

Proverbs 12:19 (emphasis added)
The **lip** of truth shall be established forever: but a lying **tongue** *is* but for a moment.

4. HAND is put for people's actions.

Psalm 7:1-4 (emphasis added)
O Lord my God, in thee do I put my trust: save me from all them that persecute me, and deliver me:
Lest he tear my soul like a lion, rending *it* in pieces, while *there* is none to deliver.
O Lord my God, If I have done this; if there be iniquity in my **hands**;
If I have rewarded evil unto him that was at peace with me; (yea, I have delivered him that without cause is mine enemy:)

In verse three, the Psalmist does not mean that iniquity is literally in his hands but that it is in his actions.

Psalm 24:1-4 (emphasis added)
The earth *is* the Lord's, and the fulness thereof; the world, and they that dwell therein.
For he hath founded it upon the seas, and established it upon the floods.
Who shall ascend into the hill of the Lord? or who shall stand in his holy place?
He that hath clean **hands**, and a pure heart; who hath not lifted up his soul unto vanity, nor sworn deceitfully.

Here the word "hands" is a *metonymy* put for the person's actions.

5. SWORD is put for war or for slaughter.

Leviticus 26:6 (emphasis added)
And I will give peace in the land, and ye shall lie down, and none shall make *you* afraid: and I will rid evil beasts out of the land, neither shall the **sword** go through your land.

Jeremiah 14:12-16 (emphasis added)
When they fast, I will not hear their cry; and when they offer burnt offering and an oblation, I will not accept them: but I will consume them by the **sword**, and by the famine, and by the pestilence.
Then said I, Ah, Lord God! behold, the prophets say unto them, Ye shall not see the **sword**, neither shall ye have famine; but I will give you assured peace in this place.
Then the Lord said unto me, The prophets prophesy lies in my name: I sent them not, neither have I commanded them, neither spake unto them: they prophesy unto you a false vision and divination, and a thing of nought, and the deceit of their heart.
Therefore thus saith the Lord concerning the prophets that prophesy in my name, and I sent them not, yet they say,
Sword and famine shall not be in this land; By **sword** and famine shall those prophets be consumed.
And the people to whom they prophesy shall be cast out in the streets of Jerusalem because of the famine and the **sword**; and they shall have none to bury them, them, their wives, nor their sons, nor their daughters: for I will pour their wickedness upon them.

Romans 8:35 (emphasis added)
Who shall separate us from the love of Christ? *shall* tribulation, or distress, or persecution, or famine, or nakedness, or peril, or **sword**?

6. MATERIAL, such as silver, gold, iron, stone, wood, and so forth, is put for the thing made of or from it

Psalm 105:18 (emphasis added)
Whose feet they hurt with fetters: he was laid in **iron**:

Here iron is put for the thing made out of it, meaning the chains and fetters of prison.

Psalm 115:4 (emphasis added)
Their idols *are* **silver** and **gold**, the work of men's hands.

Failing to recognize the *metonymy*, we might think that the idol referred to here is money—silver and gold. But both the silver and the gold are put for the things made out of them, meaning silver and gold graven images, which are idols.

Jeremiah 3:9 (emphasis added)
And it came to pass through the lightness of her whoredom, that she defiled the land, and committed adultery with **stones** and with **stocks**.

There are two *metonymies* in this verse where "stone" is put for idols made out of stone, and "stocks" is put for idols made out of "stock," an antiquated English word meaning wood or timber.

7. HOUSE is put for the people in a household.

1 Chronicles 10:6 (emphasis added)
So Saul died, and his three sons, and all his **house** died together.

Isaiah 36:3 (emphasis added)
Then came forth unto him Eliakim, Hilkiah's son, which was over the **house**, and Shebna the scribe, and Joah, Asaph's son, the recorder.

Acts 10:2 (emphasis added)
A devout *man*, and one that feared God with all his **house**, which gave much alms to the people, and prayed to God alway.

1 Timothy 3:4 (emphasis added)
One that ruleth well his own **house**, having his children in subjection with all gravity;

Titus 1:11 (emphasis added)
Whose mouths must be stopped, who subvert whole **houses**, teaching things which they ought not, for filthy lucre's sake.

8. SEED is put for son or offspring.

Genesis 4:25 (emphasis added)
And Adam knew his wife again; and she bare a son, and called his name Seth: For God, *said she*, hath appointed me another **seed** instead of Abel, whom Cain slew.

Genesis 15:13 (emphasis added)
And he said unto Abram, Know of a surety that thy **seed** shall be a stranger in a land *that* is not theirs, and shall serve them; and they shall afflict them four hundred years;

Acts 7:6 (emphasis added)
And God spake on this wise, That his **seed** should sojourn in a strange land; and that they should bring them into bondage, and entreat *them* evil four hundred years.

9. WORLD is put for the inhabitants or portion of its inhabitants.

John 3:16 (emphasis added)
For God so loved the **world**, that he gave his only begotten Son, that whosoever believeth in him should not perish, but have everlasting life.

2 Corinthians 5:19 (emphasis added)
To wit, that God was in Christ, reconciling the **world** unto himself, not imputing their trespasses unto them; and hath committed unto us the word of reconciliation.

1 John 2:2 (emphasis added)
And he is the propitiation for our sins: and not for ours only, but also for *the sins of* the whole **world**.

1 John 5:19 (emphasis added)
And we know that we are of God, and the **whole** world lieth in wickedness.

1 John 3:1 (emphasis added)
Behold, what manner of love the Father hath bestowed upon us, that we should be called the sons of God: therefore the **world** knoweth us not, because it knew him not.

10. REGION, geographic location (including city) is put for its inhabitants.

Psalm 105:38 (emphasis added)
Egypt was glad when they departed: for the fear of them fell upon them.

Matthew 11:21 (emphasis added)
Woe unto thee, **Chorazin**! woe unto thee, **Bethsaida**! for if the mighty works, which were done in you, had been done in Tyre and Sidon, they would have repented long ago in sackcloth and ashes.

Matthew 23:37 (emphasis added)
O **Jerusalem**, **Jerusalem**, *thou* that killest the prophets, and stonest them which are sent unto thee, how often would I have gathered thy children together, even as a hen gathereth her chickens under *her* wings, and ye would not!

11. EARTH or LAND is put for inhabitants.

Genesis 6:11 (emphasis added)
The **earth** also was corrupt before God, and the earth was filled with violence.

Genesis 11:1 (emphasis added)
And the whole **earth** was of one language, and of one speech.

1 Samuel 14:29 (emphasis added)
Then said Jonathan, My father hath troubled the **land**: see, I pray you, how mine eyes have been enlightened, because I tasted a little of this honey.

Proverbs 28:2 (emphasis added)
For the transgression of a **land** many are the princes thereof:
but by a man of understanding and knowledge the state *thereof*
shall be prolonged.

12. HEAVEN is put for God.

Psalm 73:9 (emphasis added)
They set their mouth against the **heavens**, and their tongue
walketh through the earth.

Matthew 21:25 (emphasis added)
The baptism of John, whence was it? from **heaven**, or of men?
And they reasoned with themselves, saying, If we shall say, From
heaven; he will say unto us, Why did ye not then believe him?

John 3:27 (emphasis added)
John answered and said, A man can receive nothing, except it
be given him from **heaven**.

13. HEART is put for the function of the mind such as thoughts, affection,
emotion, desire, or purpose. (Note: the word "heart" can be a *metonymy*
or a *synecdoche*. A consideration of the context will help to determine
which figure exists in a verse of Scripture.)

Proverbs 23:12 (emphasis added)
Apply thine **heart** unto instruction, and thine ears to the words
of knowledge.

In this verse, "heart" is a *metonymy* for thoughts because instruction takes
place in the mind.

Proverbs 28:26 (emphasis added)
He that trusteth in his own **heart** is a fool: but whoso walketh
wisely, he shall be delivered.

Here the word "heart" is a *metonymy* either for one's thoughts or one's
emotions or desires.

2 Samuel 15:6 (emphasis added)
And on this manner did Absalom to all Israel that came to the

king for judgment: so Absalom stole the **hearts** of the men of Israel.

Absalom didn't literally take the blood-pumping organs out of Israelites' chests, but he did steal their affection and with it, their allegiance.

> **1 Chronicles 12:38** (emphasis added)
> All these men of war, that could keep rank, came with a perfect **heart** to Hebron, to make David king over all Israel: and all the rest also of Israel *were* of one **heart** to make David king.

In this example the word "heart" occurs twice. In the first occurrence, "heart" is a *metonymy* for thoughts or desires while the second "heart" is a *metonymy*, meaning purpose. Note how other versions translate this verse:

> **1 Chronicles 12:38 (NIV)** (emphasis added)
> All these were fighting men who volunteered to serve in the ranks. They came to Hebron **fully determined** to make David king over all Israel. All the rest of the Israelites were also **of one mind** to make David king.

> **1 Chronicles 12:38 (ISV)** (emphasis added)
> All these warriors arrived in battle order at Hebron, **fully intending** to establish David as king over all Israel. Furthermore, all of the rest of Israel **were united in their intent** to make David king.

In these Bible versions, the meaning of the figure is given rather than a word-for-word translation.

14. UNITS of time (such as day, hour, year) are put for things done in it or existing in it.

> **Psalm 37:13** (emphasis added)
> The Lord shall laugh at him: for he seeth that his **day** is coming.

In the context, the "day" refers to the judgment that is coming. Note how the following version translates the *metonymy*:

> **Psalm 37:13 (NLT)** (emphasis added)
> But the Lord just laughs, for he sees their day of judgment coming.

In this translation, a specific time period ("day of judgment") is given rather than the word "day."

Ezekiel 21:29 (emphasis added)
Whiles they see vanity unto thee, whiles they divine a lie unto thee, to bring thee upon the necks of *them that are* slain, of the wicked, whose **day** is come, when their iniquity *shall have* an end.

The context again indicates that what is coming is the judgment of the wicked.

Mark 14:35 (emphasis added)
And he went forward a little, and fell on the ground, and prayed that, if it were possible, the **hour** might pass from him.

Here, Jesus Christ is not praying that a certain time span will pass but that the suffering that is imminent would pass.

John 12:27 (emphasis added)
Now is my soul troubled; and what shall I say? Father, save me from this **hour**: but for this cause came I unto this **hour**.

Again, "hour" is not a specific span of time but a *metonymy* for the things that will take place including the imminent trial and suffering Jesus Christ would endure.

Ephesians 5:16 (emphasis added)
Redeeming the time, because the **days** are evil.

It isn't the seven days of the week that are evil but the evil deeds done in those days.

15. PASSOVER put for the lamb sacrificed during the Passover Feast or for the meal itself. (The first two examples are *metonymy* for the lamb; the second two examples are *metonymy* for the meal.)

Exodus 12:21 (emphasis added)
Then Moses called for all the elders of Israel, and said unto them, Draw out and take you a lamb according to your families, and kill the **passover**.

2 Chronicles 30:17 (emphasis added)
For *there were* many in the congregation that were not sanctified: therefore the Levites had the charge of the killing of the **passovers** for every one *that was* not clean, to sanctify *them* unto the LORD.

Matthew 26:17 (emphasis added)
Now the first *day* of the *feast* of unleavened bread the disciples came to Jesus, saying unto him, Where wilt thou that we prepare for thee to eat the **passover**?

Mark 14:14 (emphasis added)
And wheresoever he shall go in, say ye to the goodman of the house, The Master saith, Where is the guestchamber, where I shall eat the **passover** with my disciples?

16. SIN is put for sin offering.

Genesis 4:7 (emphasis added)
If thou doest well, shalt thou not be accepted? and if thou doest not well, **sin** lieth at the door. And unto thee *shall be* his desire, and thou shalt rule over him.

It was a sin offering lying at the door, not sin.

Hosea 4:8 (emphasis added)
They eat up the **sin** of my people, and they set their heart on their iniquity.

People can't literally eat sin; this is a *metonymy* where the word "sin" is put for the sin offering, meaning an animal that was sacrificed. People ate the sin offering, meaning the animal or animals that were sacrificed.

2 Corinthians 5:21 (emphasis added)
For he hath made him *to be* **sin** for us, who knew no sin; that we might be made the righteousness of God in him.

How important to recognize the *metonymy* in this verse where it reads that he, Jesus Christ, was made a sin offering for us in order that we might be made the righteousness of God in him.

17. FAITH put for the thing believed.

Acts 6:7 (emphasis added)
And the word of God increased; and the number of the disciples multiplied in Jerusalem greatly; and a great company of the priests were obedient to the **faith**.

What were the great company of priests obedient to? The thing to be believed, which was the gospel of God concerning the Lord Jesus Christ.

Ephesians 4:5 (emphasis added)
One Lord, one **faith**, one baptism,

We know that the word "faith" in this context cannot refer to a belief system because there are countless belief systems in the world. Rather, "faith" is used as a *metonymy* put for the thing which is to be believed; namely, the gospel of God concerning His Son Jesus Christ.

1 Timothy 4:1 (emphasis added)
Now the Spirit speaketh expressly, that in the latter times some shall depart from the **faith**, giving heed to seducing spirits, and doctrines of devils;

Those spoken of here departed from the "faith" meaning the thing believed, the right doctrine.

18. SPIRIT ("Holy Ghost" or "spirit" in these examples from the KJV) is put for the information that God communicates.[5]

Luke 1:67 (emphasis added)
And his father Zacharias was filled with the **Holy Ghost**, and prophesied, saying,

Before a person can prophesy for God, he or she needs information from God. And so this use of the word "spirit" (Greek *pneuma hagios*) is a *metonymy* for the information that God communicates.

Acts 4:8 (emphasis added)
Then Peter, filled with the **Holy Ghost**, said unto them, Ye rulers of the people, and elders of Israel,

We know from Acts 2 that Peter was filled with the gift of holy spirit on the day of Pentecost, so this reference does not refer to receiving the gift. In other words, this verse does not say that Peter received the gift of holy spirit a second time. Instead, the word "spirit" is a *metonymy* for the information that comes from God. The words that are recorded in that passage are the words that God gave to Peter, and then Peter spoke them to the elders of Israel and rulers of the people there gathered.

> **Acts 4:31** (emphasis added)
> And when they had prayed, the place was shaken where they were assembled together; and they were all filled with the **Holy Ghost**, and they spake the word of God with boldness.
> the things of God.

> **Luke 1:80** (emphasis added)
> And the child grew, and waxed strong in **spirit**, and was in the deserts till the day of his shewing unto Israel.

To grow strong in spirit is to grow strong in the things of God.

> **Acts 18:25** (emphasis added)
> This man was instructed in the way of the Lord; and being fervent in the **spirit**, he spake and taught diligently the things of the Lord, knowing only the baptism of John.

To be fervent in the spirit is to be fervent in the things of God.

> *Metonymy* is a noun or name put for a related noun or name.

Do all metonymies bring emphasis?

Like any other figure of speech, *metonymy* may bring emphasis or call our attention to a particular passage or word in Scriptures. But it is doubtful that every *metonymy* brings attention or adds emphasis to every passage in which it occurs. For example, in English when we refer to a computer mouse, we use *metonymy*, a figure that uses a noun (mouse) to refer to an associated noun (mouse-shaped computer device). This particular figure is so common now in our English vernacular that it can hardly be said to draw our attention or to add emphasis.

The same might be said of some common *metonymies* used in the lands and times of the Bible. For example, in the Bible the word "house" is a common *metonymy* for the members in a household, as seen in the following verse:

> **2 Samuel 3:1a** (emphasis added)
> Now there was long war between the **house** of Saul and the **house** of David:

These words are not literal: "house" is a *metonymy* for the members of their households. In this example, the word "house" is certainly a figure of speech, but does it bring emphasis or draw the reader's attention to the particular word in this particular verse? Not necessarily. It's just a common *metonymy* that occurs in the Hebrew language.

In this example, words are used in a non-literal manner, but they don't necessarily have any emphatic force. We should recognize, therefore, that there are some non-literal expressions or words in the Bible that are figurative but don't necessarily carry emphasis. For more information about how a figure may or may not bring emphatic force or arrest our attention, please see Appendix 3.

Chapter 19
Metalepsis

(double metonymy) 609

me-ta-LEP-sis

> *Metalepsis* is a double *metonymy*.

Liddell and Scott's lexicon gives thirteen different meanings for the word *metalepsis*, and some rhetoricians view this figure as either a figure of grammar or rhetoric (Lanham 99).[6] However, in this book, the figure *metalepsis* refers to a double *metonymy*. The Silva Rhetoricae defines *metalepsis* as "A metonymical substitution of one word for another which is itself figurative."

Metalepsis occurs when one word is used to signify two related things. In the following verse, the word "roof" is put for two things:

Genesis 19:8
Behold now, I have two daughters which have not known man; let me, I pray you, bring them out unto you, and do ye to them as *is* good in your eyes: only unto these men do nothing; for therefore came they under the shadow of my **roof**.

Here the word "roof" is put for the entire house and for the protection it provides.

In the New Testament, a commonly occurring *metalepsis* is in the phrase "cross of Christ" where the word "cross" is put for two related things. First, the cross is put for the death of Jesus Christ, it being the instrument of his crucifixion. And second, the cross is put for all that was accomplished for mankind by his dying on the cross. The following three verses contain the figure *metalepsis* where the word "cross" is a double *metonymy*, put both for Christ's death and also for all that was accomplished by his death.[7]

 ## FROM THE SCRIPTURES

1 Corinthians 1:17
For Christ sent me not to baptize, but to preach the gospel: not with wisdom of words, lest the **cross of Christ** should be made of none effect.

Galatians 6:12
As many as desire to make a fair shew in the flesh, they constrain you to be circumcised; only lest they should suffer persecution for the **cross of Christ**.

Philippians 3:18
(For many walk, of whom I have told you often, and now tell you even weeping, *that they are* the enemies of the **cross of Christ**:

Metalepsis also occurs in the phrase "blood of Christ" where the word "blood" is a double *metonymy*, used to signify both the shed blood (meaning death) and also all that was accomplished by his death.

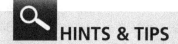 ## HINTS & TIPS

Not every occurrence of the word "blood" or "cross" is a *metalepsis*. The context would help to determine whether or not this figure, or another, might occur.

Ephesians 2:13
But now in Christ Jesus ye who sometimes were far off are made nigh by the **blood** of Christ.

Colossians 1:14
In whom we have redemption through his **blood**, *even* the forgiveness of sins:

1 John 1:7

But if we walk in the light, as he is in the light, we have fellowship one with another, and the **blood** of Jesus Christ his Son cleanseth us from all sin.

Metalepsis is a double *metonymy*.

Chapter 20
Synecdoche

(part for whole; whole for part) 613

sin-EK-duh-kee

> *Synecdoche* is an exchange of one idea for a related idea,
> often a part for the whole or a whole for the part.

Because the figure of speech *synecdoche* occurs when a part of something is
used to express the whole of something, it might be considered to be a type
of *metonymy*. But *synecdoche* is narrower than *metonymy*.[8] It isn't enough
for the words to be related; one must be part of the whole, or a whole
put for the part. When a captain commands "All hands on deck!" he uses
synecdoche where the hands are put for the sailors. When a car enthusiast
says to the owner of a Porsche, "I like your wheels," he uses *synecdoche*
where part of the car ("wheels") is put for the whole car.

FROM GENERAL CULTURE

Part for the Whole

- The rancher lost count of his herd because he had more than
  1000 **head** of cattle.

"Head" of cattle is put for the entire cow. A head is part of a cow.

- The young man asked Mr. Selfridge for his daughter's **hand**
  in marriage.

161

"Hand" is put for the person. A hand is part of a person.

• The latest census shows that there are 18,997 **souls** in that city.

"Souls" is put for people. A soul is part of a person.

Another example of part-for-the whole *synecdoche* occurs when a species is put for the genus most commonly when the word "man" is used as a *synecdoche* to signify both men and women. Consider the following verses:

> **Genesis 1:26-27**
> And God said, Let us make **man** in our image, after our likeness: and let them have dominion over the fish of the sea, and over the fowl of the air, and over the cattle, and over all the earth, and over every creeping thing that creepeth upon the earth.
> So God created **man** in his *own* image, in the image of God created he him; male and female created he them.

Here we see that God made man in His own image and then refers to "man" as "them" meaning "male and female." This is an example of a very common *synecdoche* where a part (species) is put for the whole (genus).[9] While the English word "man" often means a male person, in the Bible, the word translated "man" (*anthropos* in Greek) may also refer to a person or a human being, and not just a male. The context would help to determine if the word "man" (*anthropos*) is literal or figurative, meaning a *synecdoche* of a part (species) put for the whole (genus).

Figures of Speech Used in the Bible Explained and Illustrated arranges *synecdoche* in four main categories with 20 sub-categories. While one can certainly glean much understanding from this organization, in the interest of keeping things simple, I divide *synecdoche* into two main categories: 1) part-for-whole, and 2) whole-for-part. Students should note, however, that Bullinger's detailed classification amplifies and clarifies the relationship that exists between the word used in substitution for the word being substituted. The simple classification system I use does not provide that insight.

FROM THE SCRIPTURES

Part for the Whole

1. FLESH AND BLOOD is put for human beings.

   Matthew 16:17 (emphasis added)
   And Jesus answered and said unto him, Blessed art thou, Simon Barjona: for **flesh and blood** hath not revealed *it* unto thee, but my Father which is in heaven.

   Galatians 1:16 (emphasis added)
   To reveal his Son in me, that I might preach him among the heathen; immediately I conferred not with **flesh and blood**:

HINTS & TIPS

1. This figure usually occurs with nouns. Look for a part to represent a whole, or a whole to represent a part.
2. It isn't enough for the word used in substitution to be related to the word meant; it must be part of that word.
3. A noun like "belly" may be a *metonymy* in one instance but a *synecdoche* in the next.
4. A word like "flesh" may be used as *synecdoche* but carry different meanings. In each case, a careful consideration of the context will help to determine the figure's meaning.
5. Not all *synecdoches* bring emphatic force to a word or passage.

Ephesians 6:12 (emphasis added)
For we wrestle not against **flesh and blood**, but against principalities, against powers, against the rulers of the darkness of this world, against spiritual wickedness in high *places*.

2. FLESH is put for human beings, people.

   Psalm 145:21 (emphasis added)
   My mouth shall speak the praise of the Lord: and let all **flesh** bless his holy name for ever and ever.

   Romans 3:20a (emphasis added)
   Therefore by the deeds of the law, shall no **flesh** be justified in his sight.

3. FLESH is put for the old nature, or evil desires of the old nature.

Romans 8:3-9 (emphasis added)
For what the law could not do, in that it was weak through the **flesh**, God sending his own Son in the likeness of sinful **flesh**, and for sin, condemned sin in the **flesh**:
That the righteousness of the law might be fulfilled in us, who walk not after the **flesh**, but after the Spirit.
For they that are after the flesh do mind the things of the flesh; but they that are after the Spirit the things of the Spirit.
For to be carnally minded *is* death; but to be spiritually minded *is* life and peace.
Because the carnal mind *is* enmity against God: for it is not subject to the law of God, neither indeed can be.
So then they that are in the **flesh** cannot please God.
But ye are not in the **flesh**, but in the Spirit, if so be that the Spirit of God dwell in you. Now if any man have not the Spirit of Christ, he is none of his.

4. MAN is put for both sexes.[10]

Psalm 1:1 (emphasis added)
Blessed *is* the **man** that walketh not in the counsel of the ungodly, nor standeth in the way of sinners, nor sitteth in the seat of the scornful.

Psalm 112:1 (emphasis added)
Praise ye the LORD. Blessed *is* the **man** *that* feareth the LORD, *that* delighteth greatly in his commandments.

5. SOUL is put for the person, including one's self.

Genesis 12:5 (emphasis added)
And Abram took Sarai his wife, and Lot his brother's son, and all their substance that they had gathered, and the **souls** that they had gotten in Haran; and they went forth to go into the land of Canaan; and into the land of Canaan they came.

Romans 13:1 (emphasis added)
Let every **soul** be subject unto the higher powers. For there is no power but of God: the powers that be are ordained of God.

Psalm 17:13 (emphasis added)
Arise, O LORD, disappoint him, cast him down: deliver my **soul**
from the wicked, *which* is thy sword:

In this instance, the word "soul" is a *synecdoche* signifying the individual speaking. He is asking God to deliver himself from the wicked. Note how the NIV translates this figure:

Psalm 17:13 (NIV)
Rise up, LORD, confront them, bring them down; with your
sword rescue me from the wicked.

In this version, the figure of speech is a little clearer than in the KJV.

6. HEAD is put for the person.

2 Kings 2:3 (emphasis added)
And the sons of the prophets that were at Bethel came forth
to Elisha, and said unto him, Knowest thou that the Lord will
take away thy master from thy **head** to day? And he said, Yea,
I know *it*; hold ye your peace.

Psalm 7:16 (emphasis added)
His mischief shall return upon his own **head**, and his violent
dealing shall come down upon his own pate.

Proverbs 10:6 (emphasis added)
Blessings *are* upon the **head** of the just: but violence covereth
the mouth of the wicked.

7. FACE is put for the person, often meaning one's presence.

Acts 20:25 (emphasis added)
And now, behold, I know that ye all, among whom I have gone
preaching the kingdom of God, shall see my **face** no more.

Psalm 69:17 (emphasis added)
And hide not thy **face** from thy servant; for I am in trouble: hear
me speedily.

Genesis 35:7 (emphasis added)
And he built there an altar, and called the place Elbethel: because there God appeared unto him, when he fled from the **face** of his brother.

8. BELLY put for the person, often meaning one's appetites.

Romans 16:18 (emphasis added)
For they that are such serve not our Lord Jesus Christ, but their own **belly**; and by good words and fair speeches deceive the hearts of the simple.

Note how the NIV translates this figure:

Romans 16:18 (NIV) (emphasis added)
For such people are not serving our Lord Christ, but **their own appetites**. By smooth talk and flattery they deceive the minds of naive people.

This version gives one possible meaning of the figure rather than a word-for-word translation.

Philippians 3:19 (emphasis added)
Whose end is destruction, whose God *is their* **belly**, and *whose* glory *is* in their shame, who mind earthly things.)

Note how the NASB translates this figure:

Philippians 3:19 (NASB) (emphasis added)
Whose end is destruction, whose god is **their appetite**, and whose glory is in their shame, who set their minds on earthly things.

This English translation gives one possible meaning of the figure rather than a word-for-word translation.

9. FEET is put for the person or persons, often in respect to haste.

Proverbs 1:16 (emphasis added)
For their **feet** run to evil, and make haste to shed blood.

Proverbs 6:18 (emphasis added)
An heart that deviseth wicked imaginations, **feet** that be swift in running to mischief,

Romans 10:15 (emphasis added)
And how shall they preach, except they be sent? as it is written, How beautiful are the **feet** of them that preach the gospel of peace, and bring glad tidings of good things!

10. SPIRIT is put for the new nature.

Romans 7:6 (emphasis added)
But now we are delivered from the law, that being dead wherein we were held; that we should serve in newness of **spirit**, and not *in* the oldness of the letter.

Romans 8:4 (emphasis added)
That the righteousness of the law might be fulfilled in us, who walk not after the flesh, but after the **Spirit**.

Galatians 5:5 (emphasis added)
For we through the **Spirit** wait for the hope of righteousness by faith

Philippians 3:3 (emphasis added)
For we are the circumcision, which worship God in the **spirit**, and rejoice in Christ Jesus, and have no confidence in the flesh.

> *Synecdoche* is an exchange of one idea for a related idea, often a part for the whole or a whole for the part.

 # FROM THE SCRIPTURES

Whole for the Part

1. WORLD, EARTH is put for parts of it.

Isaiah 13:11 (emphasis added)
And I will punish the **world** for *their* evil, and the wicked for their iniquity; and I will cause the arrogancy of the proud to cease, and will lay low the haughtiness of the terrible.

From the context we see that this prophecy is against the Babylonians, so the word "world" is a *synecdoche* where the "world" is put for parts of it (Babylon).

Luke 2:1 (emphasis added)
And it came to pass in those days, that there went out a decree from Caesar Augustus, that all the **world** should be taxed.

Caesar Augustus would have ordered a census for the Roman Empire, not for the entire inhabited world. This is a *synecdoche* where the whole ("world") is put for part of it (the Roman Empire).[11]

2. EAST is put for land or countries east of Jerusalem.

Ezekiel 25:4 (emphasis added)
Behold, therefore I will deliver thee to the men of the **east** for a possession, and they shall set their palaces in thee, and make their dwellings in thee: they shall eat thy fruit, and they shall drink thy milk.

Matthew 2:1 (emphasis added)
Now when Jesus was born in Bethlehem of Judaea in the days of Herod the king, behold, there came wise men from the **east** to Jerusalem,

3. SOUTH is put for the land or countries south of Jerusalem.

Joshua 10:40 (emphasis added)
So Joshua smote all the country of the hills, and of the **south**, and of the vale, and of the springs, and all their kings: he left none remaining, but utterly destroyed all that breathed, as the LORD God of Israel commanded.

Jeremiah 13:19 (emphasis added)
The cities of the **south** shall be shut up, and none shall open *them*: Judah shall be carried away captive all of it, it shall be wholly carried away captive.

4. NORTH is put for the land or countries north of Jerusalem.

Jeremiah 6:1 (emphasis added)
O ye children of Benjamin, gather yourselves to flee out of the midst of Jerusalem, and blow the trumpet in Tekoa, and set up a sign of fire in Bethhaccerem: for evil appeareth out of the **north**, and great destruction.

Jeremiah 50:3 (emphasis added)
For out of the **north** there cometh up a nation against her, which shall make her land desolate, and none shall dwell therein: they shall remove, they shall depart, both man and beast.

> *Synecdoche* is an exchange of one idea for a related idea, often a part for the whole or a whole for the part.

Notes

1. While most scholars agree that *metonymy* exists only with nouns, some say that this figure might also occur with other parts of speech like verbs (re: *Figures of Speech Used in the Bible Explained and Illustrated* pgs.552-557).

2. Students should be aware that according to some rhetoricians, *metalepsis* also carries a broader meaning than provided here and is used to describe "any metaphorical usage resulting from a series or succession of figurative substitutions" (*OED*).

3. There is often confusion between *metonymy* and metaphor and between *metonymy* and *synecdoche*. Discrepancies regarding figures of comparison and transference abound with little consensus amongst and between scholars.

4. For a comprehensive discussion of the various types of relationships that might exist in a *metonymy*, see *Figures of Speech Used in the Bible Explained and Illustrated* (pgs. 538-609).

5. This is a partial list of the ways in which the word "spirit" might be used in the Bible as a *metonymy*. For more examples see Appendix 2.1 of Christopher C. Geer's *Walking in God's Power®: A Biblical Studies Series Intermediate Class Student Study Guide*.

6. Sister Miriam Joseph defines *metalepsis* as a figure that "attributes a present effect to a remote cause" (158).

7. Examples of *metalepsis* from general culture proved to be difficult to locate, which is why this chapter omits such examples.

8. Bullinger lists 20 different types of *synecdoche* while Vilant Macbeth, Leith, and others consider *synecdoche* to be a subset of *metonymy*.

9. Species is a subordinate group to a genus.

10. Because this *synecdoche* is so common in the Scriptures, it is worth considering if and when such a figure of speech brings emphasis to a verse or passage. It's also worth noting that in the KJV, the Greek word *anthropos* is frequently translated "man" when it may mean "a person" or "a human being" and not just males.

11. According to *Gill's Exposition of the Entire Bible*, this census reached only the Roman Empire, which because of its size, was, as Ptolemy Evergetes calls his kingdom, "the world." Gill also points out that the Syriac version renders verse eleven, "that all the people of his empire might be enrolled," and that the Persic version translates this verse, "that they should enrol [sic] all the subjects of his kingdom."

SECTION 6
FIGURES OF COMPARISON

FIGURES OF COMPARISON

Figures of comparison are some of the most common types of figurative expressions used in language and some of the most difficult to understand. Figures like simile, metaphor, and parable are viewed from various perspectives, and so definitions are wide ranging and often conflicting. In addition, whole books have been devoted to metaphor and parable, which makes a short discussion of these figures extremely challenging. The definitions in this section are offered with this background in mind. Readers are kindly referred to the endnotes in this section, which contain secondary source information for corroboration and further study.

While there are numerous figures of comparison, Section 6 covers five of the most common figures of comparison used in the Bible: simile, metaphor, *hypocatastasis*, parable, and allegory.[1] When it comes to identifying and understanding these figures, the danger lies in drawing parallels to things that are not meant to be in a comparative relationship. Writing about metaphor in general, Benjamin Keach observes, "there must be great care and accuracy used to find out the reason of the similitude, and the scope or intention of the comparison, lest there may be an aberration from the proper coherence of the text, or the analogy of faith" (37). In other words, we need to read the context very carefully when considering figures of comparison used in the Bible and not get carried away and begin to ascribe parallel meanings beyond what is stated or implied in the Scriptures. As we will see, with many figures of comparison, the context elaborates on or illuminates the point or points of comparison intended in the figure.

Not only is reading the context important when considering figures of comparison, it is also necessary to understand the terms used in the comparison in light of biblical culture. Perhaps no figure of speech is more reliant on an understanding of biblical culture than a figure of comparison. For example, consider the comparison made in the following verse:

Psalm 23:1-6
The Lord *is* my shepherd; I shall not want.
He maketh me to lie down in green pastures: he leadeth me beside the still waters.
He restoreth my soul: he leadeth me in the paths of righteousness for his name's sake.

Yea, though I walk through the valley of the shadow of death, I will fear no evil: for thou *art* with me; thy rod and thy staff they comfort me.
Thou preparest a table before me in the presence of mine enemies: thou anointest my head with oil; my cup runneth over. Surely goodness and mercy shall follow me all the days of my life: and I will dwell in the house of the Lord for ever.

Here the Psalmist compares God to a shepherd. The details of this comparison may be lost, however, if we don't understand something about shepherding during Biblical times.

In the lands and times of the Bible, during certain times of the year shepherds would spend weeks away from their village with their flock so that they could graze on green pastures. Shepherds protected, guided, and watched over these docile animals. And because they are timid, sheep will not always drink from turbulent waters, so being led to still waters connotes a shepherd's care and a freedom from anxiety for the animals. A shepherd would bind up the wounds of his flocks and would lead the animals through narrow, at times precarious passages. Sheep need constant protection, and shepherds used clubs ("rod" of verse 4) to ward off predators. They used a staff, a long stick sometimes with a crooked end, to direct and corral their flock. Because sheep were constantly pestered by flies and gnats, a shepherd would use an oily ointment to treat the heads of these animals to relieve them from these annoying pests. W. Phillip Keller, a shepherd who cared for sheep in the Near East, writes that the anointing the head with oil spoken of in verse five refers to this practice. All the details spoken of in this Psalm indicate a caring, loving, and provident shepherd.[2] If we don't know about the cultural background of the Biblical shepherd, then we miss the depth and beauty of this comparison.

And so when considering figures of comparison in the Bible, it is important to carefully consider the context and to endeavor to understand the terms used in the comparison in light of biblical culture and customs.

Chapter 21
Simile

(comparison by resemblance) 726

SIM-i-lee

> Simile is a comparison based on resemblance usually keyed by "like" or "as."

The word "simile" comes from the Latin word *similis* meaning like or similar, and this figure expresses how two things are like or similar to each other.[3] Simile is a figure of comparison that explicitly states a similarity between things in other respects unalike. Generally, there is only one point of comparison in a simile. For example, when we say, "Getting the two parties to agree on an issue is like herding cats," we use a simile.

- "like herding cats"

The act of getting two parties to agree is compared to the act of herding cats, which, as any cat owner will attest, is virtually impossible. (Trying to corral animals that are both extremely agile and extremely recalcitrant is maddening business.) Using this simile emphasizes the near-impossibility of the task. Note that the simile is not meant to convey a comparison on multiple levels as if to suggest that the two groups are furry, whiskered creatures that like to eat mice, and so forth. There is one point of comparison.

FROM GENERAL CULTURE

- "Researching a topic online is like drinking from a fire hydrant."

Because water is released from a fire hydrant at a furious rate, this simile draws a comparison between the volume of information available online. Stated literally, we could write, "The Internet provides more information that one can possibly assimilate." But stated figuratively, we emphasize how overwhelmed one might feel by the volume of information the Internet provides. Note how we aren't meant to draw a comparison between research and water in regards to it being wet, or it being a liquid, or it being made from hydrogen and oxygen, and so forth. There is one point of comparison.

Humorists like to use unexpected similes to draw attention to something or to provide comic substance. English humorist P.G. Wodehouse is famous for his witty, unexpected similes:

- "He paused and swallowed convulsively, like a Pekingese taking a pill."
(P.G. Wodehouse, *The Code of the Woosters*, 1938)
- "Pauline . . . remained in Chuffy's arms gurgling like a leaky radiator."
(P.G. Wodehouse, *Thank You, Jeeves*, 1934)
- "Old Bassett had been listening to these courtesies with a dazed expression on the map—gulping a bit from time to time, like a fish that has been hauled out of a pond on a bent pin and isn't at all sure it is equal to the pressure of events." (P.G. Wodehouse, *The Code of the Woosters*, 1938)

Song lyrics also use lots of comparisons, like simile:

Wide, **wide as the ocean, high as the Heaven above**;
Deep, **deep as the deepest sea** is my Savior's love.
I, though so unworthy, still am a child of His care;
For His Word teaches me that His love reaches me everywhere.
(Charles A. Miles, "Wide, Wide as the Ocean")

In this song, the Savior's love is described using three similes where the songwriter compares the wideness of the ocean, the highness of the heavens, and the deepness of the sea to the Savior's love. What a beautiful way to express the depth of the Savior's love.

FROM THE SCRIPTURES

Example 1
Proverbs 16:24 (emphasis added)
Pleasant words *are **as an honeycomb***, sweet to the soul, and health to the bones.

Today, as in antiquity, honeycomb is known for its sweetness and healing properties. In this verse, "pleasant words" are compared to a honeycomb, and then an elaboration of the comparison provided. Pleasant words are like honey in regards to sweetness and healing properties. Honeycomb

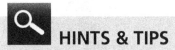

HINTS & TIPS

1. Look for one point of comparison.
2. Look for key words "like" and "as."
3. Consider the context for clues about the comparison.

is also very sticky, but we aren't meant to make that comparison as well. Note how the specifics of the comparison are provided in the immediate context.

Example 2
Genesis 26:4 (emphasis added)
And I will make thy seed to multiply **as the stars of heaven**, and will give unto thy seed all these countries; and in thy seed shall all the nations of the earth be blessed;

Speaking to Abraham, God here promises Abraham that his seed (*metonymy* for offspring) would multiply as the stars of heaven, meaning innumerable. We aren't meant to think that the figure supplies other points of comparison: Abraham's offspring are not like the stars in heaven in that they are made of gaseous substances or are suspended in space thousands of miles from Earth. The simile provides one point of comparison.

Note that not all similes using the same word convey the same comparison. In the following verse, we see a simile using the word "star" but with a different meaning.

Example 3
Philippians 2:15 (ISV) (emphasis added)
So that you may be blameless and innocent, God's children

without any faults among a crooked and perverse generation, among whom you shine like **stars** in the world

Note how in this verse, sons of God are compared to stars not in regards to their number as we saw in Genesis 26:4 but in regards to their ability to shine, meaning to cast light.

Example 4
1 Thessalonians 5:1-2 (emphasis added)
But of the times and the seasons, brethren, ye have no need that I write unto you.
For yourselves know perfectly that the day of the Lord so cometh **as a thief in the night**.

A thief doesn't announce his arrival, and so the time of his coming is completely unknowable. In the same way, no one knows the day or time of the day of the Lord. The comparison underscores the unpredictability of this time period.

Example 5
Luke 22:44 (emphasis added)
And being in an agony he prayed more earnestly: and his sweat was **as it were great drops of blood** falling down to the ground.

Sometimes the simile in this verse is overlooked. His sweat was "as it were" (*hosei* in Greek meaning "like" or "as") great drops of blood. A comparison is made between his sweat and great drops of blood, perhaps as a way to emphasize the profound intensity of that moment. Note how the ESV translates this verse:

Luke 22:44 (ESV) (emphasis added)
And being in an agony he prayed more earnestly; and his sweat became **like** great drops of blood falling down to the ground.

In this Bible version, the simile is properly supplied, making the figure a bit more obvious than in the KJV.

Example 6
Psalm 1:1-4
Blessed *is* the man that walketh not in the counsel of the ungodly, nor standeth in the way of sinners, nor sitteth in the seat of the scornful.
But his delight *is* in the law of the LORD; and in his law doth he meditate day and night.
And he shall be **like a tree planted by the rivers of water**, that bringeth forth his fruit in his season; his leaf also shall not wither; and whatsoever he doeth shall prosper.
The ungodly *are* not so: but *are* **like the chaff** which the wind driveth away.

Verse 3 and verse 4 contain similes. In verse 3, the godly man (described in verse 1 and 2) is compared to a tree planted by a river, which is an ideal place for a tree to be planted. Such a tree would be regularly watered and therefore would bear fruit in season, in accordance with God's creative design. In contrast, in verse 4 the ungodly man is compared to chaff, which is the unused and unusable part of grain. During winnowing, this light chaff is blown away by the wind while the heavier kernel of grain falls to the ground. With this simile, the ungodly man is compared to something worthless that blows away in the wind while the godly man is compared to something that will flourish.

> Simile is a comparison based on resemblance ususally keyed by "like" or "as."

Chapter 22
Metaphor

(comparison using two nouns) 735

MET-a-phor

> Metaphor is a comparison where one thing is declared to be another thing.

From Aristotle to George Lakoff, scholars have written about metaphor, each offering his own definition and theory about metaphor's significance and meaning. Each year literary scholars, cognitive linguists, anthropologists, poets, and others publish articles and books on metaphor and comment on its significance in society. Few figures are more misunderstood than metaphor, and few engender more controversy in the academic community. In addition, classifications of metaphor differ widely amongst disciplines. Because *Go Figure!* is an introduction to figures of speech, this chapter on metaphor provides a basic definition of the figure and offers easy-to-understand examples. Readers are kindly asked to be aware that this figure has been the topic of many book-length discussions and that this chapter does not purport to be a comprehensive or authoritative treatment of this important figure of speech.

While the word "metaphor" is often used imprecisely in today's vernacular, rhetorically metaphor is a comparison where one thing is directly stated to be another thing, often by the use of a linking verb also called a substantive verb.[4] Simply put, a metaphor is a way of seeing something in terms of something else (Enos 440). A simple equation may help to illustrate this definition:

Noun IS Noun

If we say, "The child is like a lamb," we use a simile where the word "like" suggests that the child resembles a lamb in some way. However, a metaphor is a more direct type of comparison. If we say, "The child is a lamb," we use a metaphor.

Child IS Lamb

Some linguists refer to these words as *"phoros"* and "principal subject." In the example quoted above, the word "child" would be the *phoros* and the word "lamb" would be the principal subject.

Generally speaking, a metaphor is considered to be a stronger comparison than a simile. In *Strange Figures: The Figurative Language of the Bible*, James Neil writes: "It is in its nature a figure full of rugged power. Its very brevity and abruptness lend it force and sublimity" (20). In a similar vein, Bullinger writes that a simile "gently states" a comparison while metaphor "boldly and warmly declares one thing IS the other" (735). So we can expect that a metaphor is typically a stronger figure of comparison than a simile.

What is the function of a metaphor? That is a difficult question to answer, but many believe that metaphor allows us to see things in fresh ways. Aristotle wrote: "Now strange words simply puzzle us; ordinary words convey only what we know already; it is from metaphor that we can best get hold of something fresh. . . the metaphors must not be far-fetched, or they will be difficult to grasp, nor obvious, or they will have no effect. The words, too, ought to set the scene before our eyes" (qtd in Joseph 145). This new way of seeing things is particularly interesting when we consider the extensive use of metaphor in the Gospels.

Similarly, linguists suggest that metaphor may direct our attention to something that would have been overlooked if stated literally: "Each metaphor orients us differently, motivates different questions, leads to different insights," Enos writes (440). Like most figures of speech, metaphor may arrest our attention because it expresses thought in a non-literal manner. Here are some other functions of metaphor as they occur in language and general literature:

- Direct and deflect our attention
- Create perspectives
- Shape attitudes
- Motivate actions
- Lead to insights, attitudes, and actions
- Help us to see things in a new light

FROM GENERAL CULTURE

Many aphorisms rely on metaphor where one thing is equated to another thing. "Life is a bowl of cherries" uses a metaphor with a linking verb. Considered to be a positive aphorism, this saying means that life, like, cherries, is sweet. Or consider the use of metaphor in this sentence: "Toronto's Eaton Centre is a beehive of activity on Boxing Day." In this example, the busyness of a shopping mall is compared to the busyness of a beehive.

Metaphor is a common figure found in song lyrics:

> She is a flower, You are the rain
> She gets more beautiful with every passing day
> She is my flower and You are the sun
> She gets more beautiful because of how You love
> How You love.
> (tobyMac, "Made to Love")

The woman in the song is compared to a flower that grows more beautiful everyday while God is compared to the sun and rain that nourishes the flower and is essential to its growth. (tobyMac, a Christian songwriter, purposefully capitalizes the pronoun "You" in order that we may understand that God is the implied antecedent of the pronoun.)

Metaphor can be difficult to understand if the comparison is not spelled out. Because of the potential for ambiguity, writers often supply an explanation or elaboration after the metaphoric statement. For example Peggy Noonan writes, "Humor is the shock absorber of life; it helps us take the blows." (*What I Saw at the Revolution*, 1990). In this case, the writer clarifies the comparison. Humor is like a shock absorber in that it helps to absorb shocks or unpleasant experiences. We aren't meant to think that humor is like a shock absorber in that it costs $89.95 to replace on your car. Or consider the following sentence: "Time is a dressmaker." In what way is time like a dressmaker? Because the comparison between time and a dressmaker might not be clear, the writer adds a brief elaboration: "Time is a dressmaker specializing in alterations." (Faith Baldwin, *Face Toward the Spring*, 1956). It is helpful to keep this in mind as we read and consider metaphors in the Bible.

Frequently, when metaphor is used in Scripture, some sort of elaboration follows; therefore, considering the context becomes paramount to understanding this figure of speech. Note this example:

> **Isaiah 40:6-8** (emphasis added)
> The voice said, Cry.
> And he said, What shall I cry?
> **All flesh *is* grass**,
> and all the goodliness thereof *is* as the flower of the field:
> the grass withereth, the flower fadeth:
> because the spirit of the LORD bloweth upon it:
> surely the **people *is* grass**.
> The grass withereth, the flower fadeth:
> but the word of our God shall stand for ever.

There are two metaphors in this passage: "all flesh is grass" and "the people is grass." In the first, the word "flesh" is a *synecdoche* for people, so these two metaphors are saying the same thing albeit in slightly different words: people are grass. But in what way are people like grass? The context sheds light on the comparison. Grass withers and flowers fade—this is the comparison made to people. People are like grass not in that they are green and pliant but in that they wither away, like grass. In other words, their temporal existence is relatively short.

It's also important to note the cultural meaning of the *phoros* and principal subject used in this metaphor. In other words, we should consider the nature of grass in Bible times and not think anachronistically about our own notions of modern grass treated with chemical fertilizers. James Neil describes the peculiar nature of grass found throughout the Bible lands:

> The 'grass' of the Bible is . . . the chief charm of Palestine, their variety, beauty, and abundance forming a sight never to be forgotten. Yet they only last like this in their fullness for some two brief months. About the first of May, the *shirocco*, the burning

east or south-east wind of the Bible, begins to blow, coming up from Arabia's thousand miles of sand desert, . . .and with a heat like the blast of a furnace. Sometimes . . . in a single day, it cuts down and destroys all the rare and delicate beauty of this wealth of wild growth. What more striking or affecting picture could be drawn of man's frailty and mortality; and how natural is the prophet's strong emotion, as he records the thought, evinced by the use of a *Metaphor!* (21).

When reading Isaiah 40:6-8, it's therefore helpful to know something about the nature of grass grown during Bible times. The context helps us to see the point of comparison between man and grass while knowledge of biblical culture helps us to understand the specific cultural details involved in this comparison.

 FROM THE SCRIPTURES

Example 1
Psalm 84:11a (emphasis added)
For the **LORD God *is* a sun and shield:**
the LORD will give grace and glory:

In verse eleven, we find the metaphor: "The Lord God is a sun and shield." (Because Hebrew has no verb "to be," the verb is often supplied in italic print in the Old Testament, as it is in verse eleven.) What comparison is meant here? We know that the sun can both destroy and give life. But in the context, we see that this comparison is meant to imply something good. God is compared to a sun, which provides essential warmth to the earth and essential life to living things. And God is compared to a shield, which protects. This is in harmony with the line that follows: the Lord will give grace and glory.

Example 2
Jeremiah 50:6 (emphasis added)
My **people hath been lost sheep**: their shepherds have caused them to go astray,   they have turned them away *on* the mountains: they have gone from mountain to hill, they have forgotten their resting place.Here the prophet Jeremiah compares God's people to lost sheep. The context provides the point of comparison.

Example 3
John 15:1-5 (emphasis added)
I am the true vine, and my Father is the husbandman.
Every branch in me that beareth not fruit he taketh away: and every *branch* that beareth fruit, he purgeth it, that it may bring forth more fruit.
Now ye are clean through the word which I have spoken unto you. Abide in me, and I in you. As the branch cannot bear fruit of itself, except it abide in the vine; no more can ye, except ye abide in me.
I am the vine, ye *are* the branches: He that abideth in me, and I in him, the same bringeth forth much fruit: for without me ye can do nothing.

There are many metaphors in the Gospel of John like the one in verse one where Jesus declares, "I am the true vine," and in verse five, where he again declares "I am the vine." This is a metaphor. The point of comparison is explained in the context: Just as a branch can't bear fruit by itself unless it abides in the vine, so too can't Jesus's disciples bear fruit unless they abide in him. (Note that there are other metaphors in this passage: "my father is the husbandman" and "ye are the branches.")

Example 4
1 Corinthians 10:4 (emphasis added)
And did all drink the same spiritual drink: for they drank of that spiritual Rock that followed them: and that **Rock was Christ**.

Here Christ is compared to "that Rock," making this a metaphor.

Metaphor is a comparison where one thing is declared to be another thing.

186

Chapter 23
Hypocatastasis

(implied comparison) 735

hi-po-ca-ta-STAY-sis

> *Hypocatastasis* is an implied comparison.

Both metaphor and *hypocatastasis* are comparisons, but *hypocatastasis* is implied while metaphor is stated. *Hypocatastasis* also does not use a linking verb and does not follow the *phoros* = principal subject formula. Because there is often a misunderstanding between these two figures, perhaps it would help to consider them side-by-side:

Metaphor: The lawyer is a shark! (stated comparison)

Hypocatastasis: The shark won his tenth case this year! (implied comparison)

Some rhetoricians assert that the comparison in *hypocatastasis* is more forceful than the comparison in either metaphor or simile.[5]

FROM GENERAL CULTURE

Many nicknames are implied comparisons.

- The King (Elvis Presley)

Despite what you hear at Graceland, Elvis Presley wasn't a monarch, so this is *hypocatastasis*. At the height of his career in the 1950s, Elvis Presley was called "the king" because of the way in which he dominated the record charts. For similar reasons, Michael Jackson was known as "the King of Pop" because, like Presley, Jackson had preeminence in the popular music industry in his heyday.

- The Iron Lady (Margaret Thatcher)

England's Prime Minister from 1979-1990, Margaret Thatcher was known as "the iron lady." Despite what her critics might say, Thatcher wasn't literally made out of iron. The implied comparison in this figure is that Thatcher had a firm leadership style and uncompromising political views.

Slang and vernacular speech are filled with examples of *hypocatastasis*. When we refer to a friend or an enemy as "dog," or call a woman a "doll," or a sloppy eater a "pig" or a health practitioner a "quack," we use *hypocatastasis*. The following are common examples from colloquial speech:

- Couch potato (person is compared to an inert object that sits on a couch)
- Backstabber (person who speaks ill of you when you aren't present)
- Dough (money)
- Guts (fortitude, courage)
- Hottie (someone who is physically attractive)
- Jam (predicament)

Consult an online dictionary of slang, and you will find an almost endless list of this type of implied comparison, often referred to as a metaphor.

 FROM THE SCRIPTURES

Example 1
John 2:19 (emphasis added)
Jesus answered and said unto them, destroy this **temple**, and in three days, I will raise it up.

Here Jesus Christ refers to his body as "this temple," an implied comparison. He doesn't use *simile* ("my body is like the temple"), or a *metaphor* with a linking verb ("my body is the temple") but *hypocatastasis*.

Example 2
Matthew 12:34a (emphasis added)
O generation of **vipers**, how can ye, being evil, speak good things?

Addressing the Pharisees mentioned in verse 24, Jesus Christ compares them to vipers, which are dangerous and poisonous snakes.

Example 3
Matthew 16:6 (emphasis added)
Then Jesus said unto them, Take heed and beware of the **leaven** of the Pharisees and of the Sadducees.

The doctrine of the Pharisees and the Sadducees is implied here, and it is compared to leaven, a rising agent used in baking. In the context, Jesus Christ's disciples thought he was talking literally about bread; they did not understand that he was speaking figuratively and that there was an implied comparison between leaven and doctrine. Rather than use *simile* ("their doctrine is like leaven") or metaphor with a linking verb ("their doctrine is leaven"), Jesus Christ uses *hypocatastasis* to emphasize how the doctrine of the Pharisees and Sadducees, like leaven in dough, spreads pervasively and is powerful in its effect.

Example 4
Luke 13:32 (emphasis added)
And he said unto them, Go ye, and tell that **fox**, Behold, I cast out devils, and I do cures to day and to morrow, and the third *day* I shall be perfected.

Speaking in response to certain Pharisees, Jesus Christ here calls Herod "that fox" not because Herod had bushy red hair but because of Herod's craftiness.

Example 5
Philippians 3:2 (emphasis added)
Beware of **dogs**, beware of evil workers, beware of the concision.

In this verse, the Apostle Paul is not warning the Philippians about canines. The word "dogs" is a *hypocatastasis* meaning people. Dogs were despised scavengers in the lands and times of the Bible, not cosseted house pets, so this is not a complimentary comparison. Note a similar use of *hypocatastasis* in the following verse:

> **Psalm 22:16** (emphasis added)
> For **dogs** have compassed me: the assembly of the wicked have inclosed me: they pierced my hands and my feet.

Again, the word "dog" in this verse in not literal; David was not surrounded by a pack of wild canines. This is a strong figure of comparison, likening David's enemies to a pack of dogs, which are animals that work in packs and attack their prey by encircling them. Note how the New Living Translation translates this verse:

> **Psalm 22:16 (NLT)** (emphasis added)
> My enemies surround me **like a pack of dogs;** an evil gang closes in on me. They have pierced my hands and feet.

The NLT here changes the figure to a simile thereby lessening the impact of the comparison.

Hypocatastasis is an implied comparison.

Chapter 24
Parabola

(parable) 751

pa-RA-bo-la

> Parable is an extended comparison in story form usually with one main point of comparison.

Let's consider what the Scriptures say about parables:

John 10:1-6 (emphasis added)
Verily, verily, I say unto you, He that entereth not by the door into the sheepfold, but climbeth up some other way, the same is a thief and a robber.
But he that entereth in by the door is the shepherd of the sheep.
To him the porter openeth; and the sheep hear his voice: and he calleth his own sheep by name, and leadeth them out.
And when he putteth forth his own sheep, he goeth before them, and the sheep follow him: for they know his voice.
And a stranger will they not follow, but will flee from him: for they know not the voice of strangers.
This **parable** spake Jesus unto them: but they understood not what things they were which he spake unto them.

In verse six we read that Jesus spoke a parable to them (the Pharisees) but that they did not understand what he said. This is a common response to many of the parables Jesus Christ taught: his audience did not understand him. Indeed, parable is one of the most difficult figures of speech to understand in the Scriptures.

The following record gives some insight into the purpose of the parables spoken by Jesus Christ:

Matthew 13:1-3a

The same day went Jesus out of the house, and sat by the sea side.
And great multitudes were gathered together unto him, so that he went into a ship, and sat; and the whole multitude stood on the shore.
And he spake many things unto them in parables, saying

Jesus Christ spoke many things in parables unto the "great multitude" that was gathered. Then follows one of those parables:

Matthew 13:3-9

And he spake many things unto them in parables, saying, Behold, a sower went forth to sow;
And when he sowed, some *seeds* fell by the way side, and the fowls came and devoured them up:
Some fell upon stony places, where they had not much earth: and forthwith they sprung up, because they had no deepness of earth:
And when the sun was up, they were scorched; and because they had no root, they withered away.
And some fell among thorns; and the thorns sprung up, and choked them:
But other fell into good ground, and brought forth fruit, some an hundredfold, some sixtyfold, some thirtyfold.
Who hath ears to hear, let him hear.

Next, the disciples (not the multitude) asked him why he spoke to the multitude in parables. Jesus Christ's response is worth careful consideration:

Matthew 13:9-17

Who hath ears to hear, let him hear.

And the disciples came, and said unto him, Why speakest thou unto them in parables? He answered and said unto them, Because it is given unto you to know the mysteries of the kingdom of heaven, but to them it is not given.

For whosoever hath, to him shall be given, and he shall have more abundance: but whosoever hath not, from him shall be taken away even that he hath.

Therefore speak I to them in parables: because they seeing see not; and hearing they hear not, neither do they understand.

And in them is fulfilled the prophecy of Esaias, which saith, By hearing ye shall hear, and shall not understand; and seeing ye shall see, and shall not perceive:

For this people's heart is waxed gross, and *their* ears are dull of hearing, and *their* eyes they have closed; lest at any time they should see with their eyes, and hear with *their* ears, and should understand with *their* heart, and should be converted, and I should heal them.

But blessed *are* your eyes, for they see: and your ears, for they hear.

For verily I say unto you, That many prophets and righteous *men* have desired to see *those things* which ye see, and have not seen *them*; and to hear *those things* which ye hear, and have not heard *them*.

In other words, Jesus spoke to the multitude in parables because they did not see, nor hear, nor understand. Their ears were dull of hearing, and they had closed their eyes. These are all figurative ways of saying that certain things were hidden from the multitude. The truths Jesus Christ spoke in parables were secret from some and were therefore difficult to understand. Note how the meaning of the parable is then given to his *disciples* who were willing to hear.

Matthew 13:18-23

Hear ye therefore the parable of the sower.

When any one heareth the word of the kingdom, and understandeth *it* not, then cometh the wicked *one*, and catcheth away that which was sown in his heart. This is he which received seed by the way side.

But he that received the seed into stony places, the same is he that heareth the word, and anon with joy receiveth it;

> Yet hath he not root in himself, but dureth for a while: for when tribulation or persecution ariseth because of the word, by and by he is offended.
> He also that received seed among the thorns is he that heareth the word; and the care of this world, and the deceitfulness of riches, choke the word, and he becometh unfruitful.
> But he that received seed into the good ground is he that heareth the word, and understandeth *it*; which also beareth fruit, and bringeth forth, some an hundredfold, some sixty, some thirty.

So the meaning of parables might not be immediately apparent. Keeping this in mind, we approach the topic of biblical parables with caution and with an understanding that they can be some of the most difficult parts of Scripture to grasp.

Many books have been written about parables, those occurring in the Bible and those in general literature. As such, there are many different opinions about the definition of this figure of speech, sometimes also called a rhetorical device. However, despite the diversity of definitions, most agree that a parable is a story with an extended comparison, usually with one main point of comparison. Bullinger describes a parable as "a story with a hidden meaning, without pressing in every detail, the idea of a comparison" (751). And Bible scholar Roy B. Zuck writes that a parable typically is a "true-to-life story to illustrate or illuminate a truth" (194). While the Greek word *parabole* has several meanings, in this chapter, we will only consider the meaning of a parable that is an extended comparison in story form. A parable may have more than one point of comparison, but it is often an extension of the one main point in order to render the comparison more vivid. [6]

Today teachers, speechwriters, preachers, and others who engage in public discourse frequently use parables as a means of illustrating a truth or as a way to engage their audience. If you've ever heard a keynote speaker open with a story from his childhood, one that illustrates the main point of his speech, then you've heard a modern day parable. These illustrative stories spark interest in the audience while also encouraging the listener to think about the possible connection being made.

There are many ways one might approach the study of biblical parables. The following are some characteristics of parables that might help the reader identify and appreciate this figure of speech. The reader is kindly asked to remember that these are merely offered as helpful guidelines and are not intended to serve as the only way, or even as a comprehensive way, to approach this field of study. Please note that while these characteristics are common to many parables, they are not present in all biblical parables.

1. Everyday elements

In the Bible, parables rely on verisimilitude, meaning having the appearance of being true or real, and not on fanciful or imaginary details.[7] Jesus frequently taught using parables, and these illustrations spoke of familiar occurrences like banquets, weddings, and harvests; they relied on familiar objects like birds, trees, seeds, and soil; and his parables were peopled with common folk like fishermen, children, slaves and masters. Note the everyday elements in the following parable.

> **Luke 15:3-7**
> And he spake this parable unto them, saying,
> What man of you, having an hundred sheep, if he lose one of them, doth not leave the ninety and nine in the wilderness, and go after that which is lost, until he find *it*?
> And when he hath found *it*, he layeth it on his shoulders, rejoicing.
> And when he cometh home, he calleth together *his* friends and neighbours, saying unto them, Rejoice with me; for I have found my sheep which was lost.
> I say unto you, that likewise joy shall be in heaven over one sinner that repenteth, more than over ninety and nine just persons, which need no repentance.

In this example, everyday elements include details about a shepherd and his sheep, along with someone rejoicing over something valuable that has been found.

2. Explanation in the context

A second point to keep in mind is that many parables explain the hidden meaning right in the story itself or in the near context. In the parable of the sower, for instance, (re: Matt. 13:3-8, Mark 4:3-8, Luke 8:5-8) the meaning of the parable is provided right in the context.[8]

Mark 4:1-8

And he began again to teach by the sea side: and there was gathered unto him a great multitude, so that he entered into a ship, and sat in the sea; and the whole multitude was by the sea on the land.

And he taught them many things by parables, and said unto them in his doctrine,

Hearken; Behold, there went out a sower to sow:

And it came to pass, as he sowed, some fell by the way side, and the fowls of the air came and devoured it up.

And some fell on stony ground, where it had not much earth; and immediately it sprang up, because it had no depth of earth:

But when the sun was up, it was scorched; and because it had no root, it withered away.

And some fell among thorns, and the thorns grew up, and choked it, and it yielded no fruit.

And other fell on good ground, and did yield fruit that sprang up and increased; and brought forth, some thirty, and some sixty, and some an hundred.

When his disciples asked him what this parable meant, Jesus Christ supplied them with this detailed answer.

Mark 4:14-20

The sower soweth the word.

And these are they by the way side, where the word is sown; but when they have heard, Satan cometh immediately, and taketh away the word that was sown in their hearts.

And these are they likewise which are sown on stony ground; who, when they have heard the word, immediately receive it with gladness;

And have no root in themselves, and so endure but for a time: afterward, when affliction or persecution ariseth for the word's sake, immediately they are offended.

And these are they which are sown among thorns; such as hear the word,

And the cares of this world, and the deceitfulness of riches, and the lusts of other things entering in, choke the word, and it becometh unfruitful.

And these are they which are sown on good ground; such as hear the word, and receive *it*, and bring forth fruit, some thirtyfold, some sixty, and some an hundred.

3. Purpose Statement

A third point to keep in mind is that many parables are introduced with a "purpose statement" where a parable is given in response to a specific situation or to address a specific point. Keeping these purpose statements in mind may help us to understand the meaning of the parable. Note the purpose statement in the following example:

> **Luke 18:9-14** (emphasis added)
> **And he spake this parable unto certain which trusted in themselves that they were righteous, and despised others:**
> Two men went up into the temple to pray; the one a Pharisee, and the other a publican.
> The Pharisee stood and prayed thus with himself, God, I thank thee, that I am not as other men *are*, extortioners, unjust, adulterers, or even as this publican.
> I fast twice in the week, I give tithes of all that I possess.
> And the publican, standing afar off, would not lift up so much as *his* eyes unto heaven, but smote upon his breast, saying, God be merciful to me a sinner.
> I tell you, this man went down to his house justified *rather* than the other: for every one that exalteth himself shall be abased; and he that humbleth himself shall be exalted.

Verse nine declares that Jesus spoke this parable unto certain people who "trusted in themselves that they were righteous, and despised others." This parable is given in response to this specific situation and to these specific individuals. Keeping the purpose statement in mind helps us to understand the comparison being made and not to attach all sorts of analogous meanings to the parable that might not be intended.

Note the purpose statement at the opening of this parable:

> **Luke 18:1-8** (emphasis added)
> And he spake a parable unto them *to this end*, **that men ought always to pray, and not to faint**;
> Saying, There was in a city a judge, which feared not God, neither regarded man:

And there was a widow in that city; and she came unto him, saying, Avenge me of mine adversary.

And he would not for a while: but afterward he said within himself, Though I fear not God, nor regard man;

Yet because this widow troubleth me, I will avenge her, lest by her continual coming she weary me.

And the Lord said, Hear what the unjust judge saith.

And shall not God avenge his own elect, which cry day and night unto him, though he bear long with them?

I tell you that he will avenge them speedily. Nevertheless when the Son of man cometh, shall he find faith on the earth?

According to verse one, this parable was given to teach the truth that men ought always to pray and not to faint, meaning to give up. (It is NOT intended to draw a comparison between the unjust judge of verse two and God.) Of course, not all parables have purpose statements. But if they do, they often occur at the beginning or at the end of a parable.

4. Rhetorical Questions

Rhetorical questions are frequently used in parables, and keeping these questions in mind might help us to remember the hidden meaning or main point of the parable. For example, note how Jesus Christ uses several rhetorical questions in this parable:

Luke 15:1-10 (emphasis added)
Then drew near unto him all the publicans and sinners for to hear him.

And the Pharisees and scribes murmured, saying, This man receiveth sinners, and eateth with them.

And he spake this parable unto them, saying,

What man of you, having an hundred sheep, if he lose one of them, doth not leave the ninety and nine in the wilderness, and go after that which is lost, until he find it?
And when he hath found *it*, he layeth *it* on his shoulders, rejoicing.

And when he cometh home, he calleth together *his* friends and neighbours, saying unto them, Rejoice with me; for I have found my sheep which was lost.

I say unto you, that likewise joy shall be in heaven over one sinner that repenteth, more than over ninety and nine just persons, which need no repentance.

Either what woman having ten pieces of silver, if she lose one piece, doth not light a candle, and sweep the house, and seek diligently till she find *it*?

And when she hath found *it*, she calleth *her* friends and *her* neighbours together, saying, Rejoice with me; for I have found the piece which I had lost.

Likewise, I say unto you, there is joy in the presence of the angels of God over on sinner that repenteth.

In this example, the two rhetorical questions are similar in function. Both help the listener to stop and to consider the value of something that is lost and the effort expended in finding that valuable something. Therefore, when reading this parable, it is helpful to keep the specific rhetorical questions in mind.[9]

5. End stress

Roy B. Zuck notes that many parables conclude with an "end stress in which the last element of a parable is the most important" (202). Often, this end stress is keyed by concluding words like "so likewise," "therefore," and "so" as in the following example:

Matthew 18:23-35 (emphasis added)
Therefore is the kingdom of heaven likened unto a certain king, which would take account of his servants.

And when he had begun to reckon, one was brought unto him, which owed him ten thousand talents.

But forasmuch as he had not to pay, his lord commanded him to be sold, and his wife, and children, and all that he had, and payment to be made.

The servant therefore fell down, and worshipped him, saying, Lord, have patience with me, and I will pay thee all.

Then the lord of that servant was moved with compassion, and loosed him, and forgave him the debt.

But the same servant went out, and found one of his fellowservants, which owed him an hundred pence: and he laid hands on him, and took *him* by the throat, saying, Pay me that thou owest.

And his fellowservant fell down at his feet, and besought him, saying, Have patience with me, and I will pay thee all.

And he would not: but went and cast him into prison, till he should pay the debt.

So when his fellowservants saw what was done, they were very sorry, and came and told unto their lord all that was done.

Then his lord, after that he had called him, said unto him, O thou wicked servant, I forgave thee all that debt, because thou desiredst me:

Shouldest not thou also have had compassion on thy fellowservant, even as I had pity on thee?

And his lord was wroth, and delivered him to the tormentors, till he should pay all that was due unto him.

So likewise shall my heavenly Father do also unto you, if ye from your hearts forgive not every one his brother their trespasses.

Note how the end stress here is keyed by the words "so likewise," and the meaning of the parable is spelled out. (Other examples of parables with end stress include Matthew 25:1-13, Luke 12:16-21, Luke 17:7-10). Look for concluding words like "therefore," "and so," and "likewise" used in parables, as these usually key the end stress or final point to be made in the parable.

FROM THE SCRIPTURES

In the Bible, parables are often introduced with the phrase, "and he spoke a parable unto them" or something along those lines. But some parables, like this one in 2 Samuel 12, are not identified:

Example 1
2 Samuel 12:1-10

And the Lord sent Nathan unto David. And he came unto him, and said unto him, There were two men in one city; the one rich, and the other poor.

The rich *man* had exceeding many flocks and herds:

But the poor *man* had nothing, save one little ewe lamb, which he had bought and nourished up: and it grew up together with him, and with his children; it did eat of his own meat, and drank of his own cup, and lay in his bosom, and was unto him as a daughter.

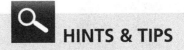

HINTS & TIPS

1. Look for everyday elements.
2. Look for explanation in the context.
3. Look for "purpose statement."
4. Look for rhetorical questions.
5. Look for "end stress."

And there came a traveller unto the rich man, and he spared to take of his own flock and of his own herd, to dress for the wayfaring man that was come unto him; but took the poor man's lamb, and dressed it for the man that was come to him.

And David's anger was greatly kindled against the man; and he said to Nathan, As the Lord liveth, the man that hath done this *thing* shall surely die:

And he shall restore the lamb fourfold, because he did this thing, and because he had no pity.

And Nathan said to David, Thou *art* the man. Thus saith the Lord God of Israel, I anointed thee king over Israel, and I delivered thee out of the hand of Saul;

And I gave thee thy master's house, and thy master's wives into thy bosom, and gave thee the house of Israel and of Judah; and if *that had been* too little, I would moreover have given unto thee such and such things.

Wherefore hast thou despised the commandment of the Lord, to do evil in his sight? thou hast killed Uriah the Hittite with the sword, and hast taken his wife *to be* thy wife, and hast slain him with the sword of the children of Ammon.

Now therefore the sword shall never depart from thine house; because thou hast despised me, and hast taken the wife of Uriah the Hittite to be thy wife.

In this record, the prophet Nathan confronts King David by speaking a parable.

Example 2
Luke 17:5-10

And the apostles said unto the Lord, Increase our faith.

And the Lord said, If ye had faith as a grain of mustard seed, ye might say unto this sycamine tree, Be thou plucked up by the root, and be thou planted in the sea; and it should obey you.

But which of you, having a servant plowing or feeding cattle, will say unto him by and by, when he is come from the field, Go and sit down to meat?

And will not rather say unto him, Make ready wherewith I may sup, and gird thyself, and serve me, till I have eaten and drunken; and afterward thou shalt eat and drink? Doth he thank that servant because he did the things that were commanded him? I trow not.

So likewise ye, when ye shall have done all those things where are commanded you, say, We are unprofitable servants: we have done that which was our duty to do.

Some parables are long and detailed while others are quite short, like this one. Note how this parable opens with rhetorical questions and concludes with an end stress, keyed by the words "so likewise ye."

Example 3
Matthew 25:1-13

Then shall the kingdom of heaven be likened unto ten virgins, which took their lamps, and went forth to meet the bridegroom.

And five of them were wise, and five *were* foolish.

They that *were* foolish took their lamps, and took no oil with them:

But the wise took oil in their vessels with their lamps.

While the bridegroom tarried, they all slumbered and slept.

And at midnight there was a cry made, Behold, the bridegroom cometh; go ye out to meet him.

Then all those virgins arose, and trimmed their lamps.

And the foolish said unto the wise, Give us of your oil; for our lamps are gone out.

But the wise answered, saying, *Not so*; lest there be not enough for us and you: but go ye rather to them that sell, and buy for yourselves.

And while they went to buy, the bridegroom came; and they that were ready went in with him to the marriage: and the door was shut.

Afterward came also the other virgins, saying, Lord, Lord, open to us.

But he answered and said, Verily I say unto you, I know you not. Watch therefore, for ye know neither the day nor the hour wherein the Son of man cometh.

Note the "end stress" in verse 13, keyed by the word "therefore."

Parable is an extended comparison in story form usually with one main point of comparison.

Chapter 25

Allegory

(allegory) 748

AL-le-gor-y

> Allegory is an extended comparison in story form with several points of comparison.

Like parable, allegory is an extended comparison with a hidden meaning; but allegory may or may not contain true-to-life details, and allegory has several or numerous analogous parts. As Zuck puts it, "a parable usually has one major point of comparison, whereas an allegory has several points of comparison" (221). Allegory is made up of a sustained comparison that may continue through whole sentences or through entire passages. Allegories may even be book length. In English literature, Edmund Spenser's *Faerie Queene* (1590) and John Bunyan's *Pilgrim's Progress* (1678) are book-length allegories. In modern times, the novels *Animal Farm* (1945) and *The Lord of the Flies* (1954) are all literary allegories where numerous analogies are sustained throughout the length of the work.

FROM GENERAL CULTURE

Example 1

Allegory can be quite simple and short:

> All the world's a stage, And all the men and women merely players; They have their exits and their entrances, And one man

in his time plays many parts, His acts being seven ages. (*As You Like It,* II, vii)

"All the world's a stage" is a metaphor, comparing the world to a stage. Then the comparison is continued where men and women are compared to actors who take their exits and entrances off and on stage. The comparison continues as one man is compared to an actor who has many roles in a play, and his lifespan is compared to a seven-act play. Even though this is a short passage, it is still an allegory, technically speaking.

Example 2

Consider how a garden comparison is continued throughout this passage from *Othello*:

> Our bodies are our gardens, to the which our wills are gardeners. So that if we will plant nettles or sow lettuce, set hyssop and weed up thyme, supply it with one gender of herbs or distract it with many—either to have it sterile with idleness, or manured with industry—why, the power and corrigible authority of this lies in our wills. (*Oth.*, I.3.322)

Note how the metaphor of a garden is sustained throughout this passage and that many terms (though not all) have a double significance. Our bodies are equated with gardens; our wills, with gardeners. And then actions (idleness or industry) are compared to sowing in sterile soil or in well-fertilized soil. But the plants mentioned—nettles, lettuce, hyssop, thyme—do not have a stated secondary meaning. We aren't meant to let our imagination run wild and say that the nettles represent bad thoughts, the lettuce, a weak will and so forth. So while allegory often has several points of comparison, not every detail has a secondary meaning.

It's important to note that even in longer allegories, not every character or object has a correlative, symbolic meaning. For instance, in the allegorical short story "Young Goodman Brown" (1835) by Nathanael Hawthorne, several of the main characters and several key objects have an allegorical significance. Literary critics have suggested that the character "Faith" represents religious faith while the character called "The Old Man" symbolizes the devil. However, that doesn't mean that every character in the story has this type of double, symbolic meaning. In addition, there are several key objects in the story with allegorical significance. Faith's pink hair ribbons are thought to symbolize innocence while the Old Man's walking staff (carved into the shape of a serpent) is thought to symbolize evil. However, that doesn't mean that every physical object in the story has a double meaning.

Because an allegory is an extended comparison with several points of comparison, it will necessarily have several items that carry a double meaning. However, that doesn't mean that every item in an allegory has to have a correlative meaning. This is important to keep in mind as we consider allegory in the Scriptures.

 # FROM THE SCRIPTURES

The following are some guidelines to consider when studying allegory in the Bible.

 ## HINTS & TIPS

1. Look for an extended comparison.
2. Look for an explanation of the points of comparison in the passage.
3. Avoid ascribing meaning to details in the allegory that are not explained.
4. Look for the main truth in the allegory.

Example 1
Psalm 23:1-6

The LORD *is* my shepherd; I shall not want.
He maketh me to lie down in green pastures: he leadeth me beside the still waters.
He restoreth my soul: he leadeth me in the paths of righteousness for his name's sake.
Yea, though I walk through the valley of the shadow of death, I will fear no evil: for thou *art* with me; thy rod and thy staff they comfort me.
Thou preparest a table before me in the presence of mine enemies: thou anointest my head with oil; my cup runneth over.
Surely goodness and mercy shall follow me all the days of my life: and I will dwell in the house of the LORD for ever.

Psalm 23 is an allegory beginning with a metaphor. Note how the opening metaphor, "The Lord is my shepherd" is then extended throughout the passage. The points of comparison are delineated in verses two to five, and the main truth is summed up in verse six, "Surely goodness and mercy shall follow me all the days of my life: and I will dwell in the house of the Lord forever."

Example 2
Judges 9:7-15
And when they told *it* to Jotham, he went and stood in the top of mount Gerizim, and lifted up his voice, and cried, and said unto them, Hearken unto me, ye men of Shechem, that God may hearken unto you.
The trees went forth *on a time* to anoint a king over them; and they said unto the olive tree, Reign thou over us.
But the olive tree said unto them, Should I leave my fatness, wherewith by me they honour God and man, and go to be promoted over the trees?
And the trees said to the fig tree, Come thou, *and* reign over us.
But the fig tree said unto them, Should I forsake my sweetness, and my good fruit, and go to be promoted over the trees?
Then said the trees unto the vine, Come thou, *and* reign over us.
And the vine said unto them, Should I leave my wine, which cheereth God and man, and go to be promoted over the trees?
Then said all the trees unto the bramble, Come thou, *and* reign over us.
And the bramble said unto the trees, If in truth ye anoint me king over you, *then* come *and* put your trust in my shadow: and if not, let fire come out of the bramble, and devour the cedars of Lebanon.

Even though some versions of the King James Bible label this as "Jotham's parable of the trees," this passage is more accurately an allegory with the numerous points of comparison explained in verses 16-20. (Note also the use of personification in this passage where trees, vines, and brambles are portrayed as having the human ability of speech.)

Example 3
Galatians 4:21-31
Tell me, ye that desire to be under the law, do ye not hear the law?

For it is written, that Abraham had two sons, the one by a bondmaid, the other by a freewoman.

But he *who* was of the bondwoman was born after the flesh; but he of the freewoman was by promise.

Which things are an allegory: for these are the two covenants; the one from the mount Sinai, which gendereth to bondage, which is Agar.

For this Agar is mount Sinai in Arabia, and answereth to Jerusalem which now is, and is in bondage with her children.

But Jerusalem which is above is free, which is the mother of us all.

For it is written, Rejoice, *thou* barren that bearest not; break forth and cry, thou that travailest not: for the desolate hath many more children than she which hath an husband.

Now we, brethren, as Isaac was, are the children of promise.

But as then he *that* was *born* after the flesh persecuted him that was born after the Spirit, even so it is now.

Nevertheless what saith the scripture? Cast out the bondwoman and her son: for the son of the bondwoman shall not be heir with the son of the freewoman.

So then, brethren, we are not children of the bondwoman, but of the free.

In this passage, Hagar and Sarah are metaphors for the two covenants. The verses that follow extend this metaphor, delineating the details of the comparison; finally, the allegory concludes with the main point: "we are not children of the bondwoman, but of the free." Note how verse 24 states, "which things are an allegory."

Example 4
Ephesians 6:10-17
Finally, my brethren, be strong in the Lord, and in the power of his might.

Put on the whole armour of God, that ye may be able to stand against the wiles of the devil.

For we wrestle not against flesh and blood, but against principalities, against powers, against the rulers of the darkness of this world, against spiritual wickedness in high *places*.

Wherefore take unto you the whole armour of God, that ye

may be able to withstand in the evil day, and having done all, to stand.
Stand therefore, having your loins girt about with truth, and having on the breastplate of righteousness;
And your feet shod with the preparation of the gospel of peace;
Above all, taking the shield of faith, wherewith ye shall be able to quench all the fiery darts of the wicked. And take the helmet of salvation, and the sword of the Spirit, which is the word of God:

In this passage, believers are admonished to be strong in the lord and in the power of his might. They are told to put on the "whole armour of God," which is a metaphor. Verses 13 to 17 then extend this metaphor, making this passage an allegory. Following are the items enumerated in the allegory:

- The loins are girt with truth[10]
- The breastplate is righteousness
- The feet are covered with the gospel of peace
- The shield is faith
- The helmet is salvation
- The sword of the spirit is the Word of God

Note that while prayer is certainly part of being strong in the lord and in the power of his might, it is not part of the armor allegory found in verses 13-17. Note also how the main purpose of the allegory might be found in verse 11, "that ye may be able to stand against the wiles of the devil" and in verse thirteen, "that ye may be able to withstand in the evil day, and having done all, to stand."

Allegory is an extended comparison in story form with several points of comparison.

Notes

1. While endeavoring to define parable and allegory, I have avoided the definition that states parable is an extended simile and that allegory is an extended metaphor because this formula does not apply in every instance. For example, the Scriptures call John 10:1-10 a parable, and yet this passage is an extended metaphor. Plus, such a narrow definition might hinder rather than help a student seeking to identify these figures of comparison.

2. Many sources such as a Bible dictionary, Bible encyclopedia, or a book on biblical manners and customs will provide information about shepherds and shepherding in biblical times. For a particularly enlightening description of shepherding see *A Shepherd Looks at Psalm 23* by W. Phillip Keller.

3. In addition to "like" and "as," the following words might also be used in similes: "but as," "so," "just as," "similar, similar to," "as it were," and so forth.

4. I am aware that metaphor may exist without a substantive verb, but this chapter only handles metaphors with a linking verb mainly because they are easier to identify than metaphors without linking verbs and because some metaphors without linking verbs are thought to be a different figure of speech, *hypocatastasis*.

5. Students wishing to study this figure may run into difficulty because the name *hypocatastasis* is obsolete, and most scholars now call this type of comparison a metaphor. Very few rhetoricians or linguists use this term today aside from those who cite or reference Bullinger. However, online sources have begun to bring this term back into use, and its name may yet come back into circulation. Because this figure is used extensively in the Scriptures, and because the distinction between it and metaphor are worth noting, I have retained its classical name in this book. It is also interesting that *hypocatastasis* is one of two figures of speech used most often by Jesus Christ (the other being *erotesis*.)

6. The Greek word *parabole* can also refer to a short saying, sometimes also called a similitude: (re: Mark 7:16-17, Luke 14:7-8, Luke 5:34, etc.) The word is also used to refer to a proverb (re: Luke 4:23). See Zuck page 195 for more examples. Parables also occur in the Old Testament. For more information, see Zuck pages 196-197.

7. A notable exception to this would be Luke 16:19-31, the parable of Lazarus in Abraham's bosom. For more about this parable, see Victor Paul Wierwille's *Are the Dead Alive Now?* (pg. 71-76).

8. For a detailed discussion of this parable, see Christopher C. Geer's "Profitable Word-Pictures," *Open My Eyes That I Might See*, pgs. 119-127.

9. Not every question used in a parable is rhetorical. In the parable spoken to Simon in Luke 7:42-43, Jesus asks Simon a non-rhetorical question that is asked to elicit an answer. Simon therefore answers him.

10. Many translations of verse fourteen offer "the belt of truth" instead of "loins girth with truth." A Roman soldier would have tied his midsection ("loins") with a belt. What's more, in the lands and times of the Bible, free-flowing clothing would be cinched at the waist whenever a person was about to work or undertake other activities. Charles Welch writes, "To an Eastern whose garments were loose and flowing, the girding of the loins was the initial act of preparedness for service" (520).

SECTION 7
RHETORICAL QUESTIONS

RHETORICAL QUESTIONS

Questions are an integral part of communication. Normally, we ask a question because we want an answer. If I ask, "What time is Kristin's wedding shower?" or "Does Chad's Coffee Shop serve sandwiches?" I want to get an answer. Questions like this are found in the Scriptures and are not figures of speech.

John 9:1-3
And as *Jesus* passed by, he saw a man which was blind from *his* birth.
And his disciples asked him, saying, Master, who did sin, this man, or his parents, that he was born blind?
Jesus answered, Neither hath this man sinned, nor his parents: but that the works of God should be made manifest in him.

From the context we see that Jesus Christ's disciples asked him this question because they wanted an answer. Jesus answered them.

A question becomes figurative when it is asked not to obtain an answer but to bring about a certain emphasis or effect. This is a *rhetorical question*, an interrogative construction that implies but doesn't expect an answer. Many scholars use the name *erotesis* (or *erotema*) to signify the rhetorical question.[1] Here's an example of a rhetorical question in the Bible:

Genesis 18:25
That be far from thee to do after this manner, to slay the righteous with the wicked: and that the righteous should be as the wicked, that be far from thee: Shall not the Judge of all the earth do right?

"Shall not the Judge of all the earth do right?" is a rhetorical question, asked without expecting an answer. This could have been written in a declarative form: The Judge [God] of all the earth shall absolutely do right." But when expressed in a question, a certain effect is achieved; it causes the listener to stop and to supply the answer in his mind while also bringing emphasis to the implied answer. In Genesis 18:25 the implied answer is—YES!

Questions are used for different reasons, but fundamentally a question causes the reader or listener to stop and to think. Teachers use questions in the classroom as a way to encourage student engagement. Advertisers use questions for similar reasons:

- "Got milk?"
- "What can Brown do for you?"
- "Have you driven a Ford lately?"
- "What would you do for a Klondike bar?"

Whether we realize it or not, these rhetorical questions help us stop and think about the question and about the answer. Rhetorical questions are used to accomplish any number of things:

- to rebuke
- to admonish
- to avoid
- to express strong emotion
- to arrest attention
- to cause the listener to pause, wonder, or consider deeply
- to raise doubt

Consider the first question used in the Scriptures:

Genesis 3:1
Now the serpent was more subtil than any beast of the field, which the LORD God had made. And he said unto the woman, Yea, hath God said, Ye shall not eat of every tree of the garden?

This question was asked by the serpent (*hypocatastasis* for Satan) to instill doubt in Eve. He asked this question so that she would stop and think about his words.

Rhetorical questions are also used to express deep emotion like alarm, wonder, fear, and astonishment. When a repairman hands us an outrageously expensive estimate and we respond, "Are you kidding me?" we aren't expecting an answer. We are expressing strong emotion, like anger or surprise. "How in the world is Michael going to get that couch up the stairs by himself?" and "Is the President of the United States really coming over to give Abby his autograph?" are examples of rhetorical questions used to express strong emotion.

The study of questions in the Bible is vast. According to Bullinger there are 3298 questions in the Scriptures: 2274 in the Old Testament and 1024 in the New Testament. Some are questions asked by God to man, some are asked by man of God, and others are questions a person asks himself. Because this is an enormous field of study, a comprehensive discussion of all the different kinds of questions in the Bible remains outside the scope of this book. However, for those wishing to study this field in more depth, Bullinger offers nineteen classifications of questions, and the specificity of these categories can be helpful to students interested in this topic.[2]

Go Figure! covers four types of rhetorical questions that occur in the Scriptures:

1. *Erotesis* in negative affirmation
2. *Erotesis* in negative negation
3. *Erotesis* in affirmative negation
4. *Erotesis* in strong emotion

1. In negative affirmation

In English, interrogative pronouns (who/whom, that/which, what, where, when, why, how) signify that a question is being asked. In Greek, when the adverb *ou* or one of its cognate forms introduce a question, it indicates an implied affirmative answer. Note the following example:

1 Corinthians 3:16
Know ye not *(ou)* that ye are the temple of God, and *that* the Spirit of God dwelleth in you?

In this example, the question in Greek is introduced by the negative adverb *ou*, which anticipates an answer in the affirmative. When asked, "Don't you know that you are the temple of God and that the Spirit of God dwells in you?" The emphatic answer would be "Yes, we do!" This type of question implies an emphatic, affirmative answer.

2. In negative negation

When the Greek negative adverb *me* introduces a question, a negative answer is expected as in the following series of questions:

1 Corinthians 1:13
Is Christ divided? *(me)* was Paul crucified for you? Or *(me)* were ye baptized in the name of Paul?

The second and third questions are introduced in the Greek by the negative adverb *me*, which anticipates an answer in the negative. In other words, when asked, "Was Paul crucified for you? Or were you baptized in the name of Paul?" the emphatic answer would be, "No, he wasn't!" and "No, we weren't!"

3. In affirmative negation

A third type of question may be asked in a positive manner that prompts a negative response. These types of questions are not introduced with a specific adverb, but the context often signifies that a question in affirmative negation occurs.

Genesis 18:14

Is any thing too hard for the LORD? At the time appointed I will return unto thee, according to the time of life, and Sarah shall have a son.

Spoken by an angel to Abraham, this question is asked in an affirmative manner that implies a strong negative response.

4. In strong emotion

A fourth type of rhetorical question occurs when the speaker or writer uses an interrogative construction to express strong emotion. For example, when God told Abraham that he would have a son by his wife, Sarah, who was well passed childbearing years, Abraham responded with these questions:

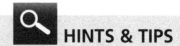

HINTS & TIPS

1. Not every question that occurs in the Scriptures is translated as a question in the King James Version.
2. To determine if a question is rhetorical, it is necessary to read the context.
3. Check a research tool like an interlinear to determine if a specific Greek adverb is used to introduce the question. This may help to determine the implied emphatic answer.

Genesis 17:17

Then Abraham fell upon his face, and laughed, and said in his heart, Shall a *child* be born unto him that is an hundred years old? And shall Sarah, that is ninety years old, bear?

Abraham did not ask these questions in doubt; rather, he asked them as a way to express his strong emotion, which would naturally have include joy and perhaps astonishment.

Chapter 26

Erotesis

(in negative affirmation)

air-o-TEE-sis

> Rhetorical question introduced by a negative adverb
> anticipating an affirmative answer.

The English language does not have negative adverbs that cue a particular response, but the Greek language does. When the Greek negative adverb *ou* introduces a question, an affirmative answer is expected. Something similar in English might be, "You don't want to win $1million, do you?" Though stated in the negative ("you don't want"), the implied answer is in the affirmative, and a very emphatic affirmative at that.

 FROM THE SCRIPTURES

Example 1
Acts 9:21
But all that heard *him* were amazed, and said; Is not *(ou)* this he that destroyed them which called on this name in Jerusalem, and came hither for that intent, that he might bring them bound unto the chief priests?

In the Greek, the adverb *ou* introduces this question, so the implied or anticipated answer would be in the affirmative.

Example 2
Acts 21:38

Art not *(ou)* thou that Egyptian, which before these days madest an uproar, and leddest out into the wilderness four thousand men that were murderers?

In the Greek, the adverb *ou* introduces this question, so the implied or anticipated answer would be in the affirmative.

Example 3
1 Thessalonians 2:19

For what *is* our hope, or joy, or crown of rejoicing? *Are* not *(ou)* even you in the presence of our Lord Jesus Christ at his coming?

In the Greek, the adverb *ou* introduces this question, so the implied or anticipated answer would be in the affirmative.

Example 4
2 Thessalonians 2:5

Remember ye not *(ou)*, that, when I was yet with you, I told you these things?

In the Greek, the adverb *ou* is used to introduce this question, so the implied or anticipated answer would be in the affirmative.

Example 5

In the Scriptures, questions sometimes occur in a series or group and might be evaluated both individually and as part of a larger context. For example, the ninth chapter of 1 Corinthians contains 20 questions. Let's consider some of these questions individually.

1 Corinthians 9:1

Am I not *(ou)* an apostle? am I not *(ou)* free? have I not *(ou)* seen Jesus Christ our Lord? are not *(ou)* ye my work in the Lord?

The questions in verse one are introduced with the negative adverb *ou*, so the anticipated answer is in the emphatic affirmative.

1 Corinthians 9:8
Say I these things as a man? or saith not *(ou)* the law the same also?

The second question in this verse is introduced with the negative adverb *ou*, so the anticipated answer is in the emphatic affirmative.

1 Corinthians 9:13
Do ye not *(ou)* know that they which minister about holy things live *of the things* of the temple? and they which wait at the altar are partakers with the altar?

1 Corinthians 9:24
Know ye not *(ou)* that they which run in a race run all, but one receiveth the prize? So run, that ye may obtain.

The questions in verses 13 and 24 are both introduced with the negative adverb *ou*, so the anticipated answer is in the emphatic affirmative.

After looking at the individual questions, we next consider the context. Verse three reads, "Mine answer to them that do examine me is this." The word for "answer" is the Greek word *apologia*, which is a legal term meaning a defense given in the face of an accusation. In this chapter Paul is responding to accusations about his authority as an apostle and about his freedom in Christ. It's interesting to note how often Paul uses questions as a means of responding to these unjust accusations.

> Rhetorical question introduced by a negative adverb anticipating an affirmative answer.

Chapter 27
Erotesis

(in negative negation)

air-o-TEE-sis

> Rhetorical question introduced with a negative adverb
> anticipating a negative answer.

The English language does not have negative adverbs that cue a particular response, but the Greek language does. When the Greek negative adverb *me* introduces a question, a negative answer is expected. Something similar in English might be, "You don't want to get your tooth extracted without anesthesia do you?" The implied answer is, NO! and a very emphatic "no" at that. In Greek, the negative adverb cues the specific response.

FROM THE SCRIPTURES

Example 1
Romans 3:5
But if our unrighteousness commend the righteousness of God, what shall we say? *Is (me)* God unrighteous who taketh vengeance? (I speak as a man)

In the Greek, the adverb *me* is used to introduce the second question in this verse, so the implied or anticipated answer would be in the negative.

Example 2
1 Corinthians 10:22

Do we provoke the Lord to jealousy? are we *(me)* stronger than he?

The KJV does not include the negative adverb, but in the Greek *me* is used to introduce the second question in this verse, so the implied or anticipated answer would be in the negative. Note how the NASB translates this verse:

1 Corinthians 10:22 (NASB)

Or do we provoke the Lord to jealousy? We are not stronger than He, are we?

In this Bible version, the translators include the negative adverb "not," which is in the Greek texts.

Example 3
1 Corinthians 12:29

Are (me) all apostles? are *(me)* all prophets? are *(me)* all teachers? *are (me)* all workers of miracles?

The KJV omits the negative adverb, but in the Greek, *me* introduces all four of these short questions. Note how the ISV renders this verse:

1 Corinthians 12:29 (ISV)

Not *(me)* all are apostles, are they? Not *(me)* all are prophets, are they? Not *(me)* all are teachers, are they? Not *(me)* all perform miracles, do they?

In this Bible version, the translators include the negative adverb "not," which is in the Greek texts. The repetition of this negative adverb certainly draws attention to the implied negative answer.

> Rhetorical question introduced with a negative adverb anticipating a negative answer.

Chapter 28
Erotesis

(in affirmative negation)

air-o-TEE-sis

> Rhetorical question introduced in an affirmative manner anticipating a negative answer.

The Psalms are filled with rhetorical questions. Here are a few examples of those asked in an affirmative manner anticipating a negative response.

Psalm 11:3
If the foundations be destroyed, what can the righteous do?

Psalm 30:9
What profit is *there* in my blood, when I go down to the pit? Shall the dust praise thee? shall it declare thy truth?

Psalm 71:19
Thy righteousness also, O God, *is* very high, who hast done great things: O God, who is like unto thee!

Psalm 118:6
The LORD *is* on my side; I will not fear: what can man do unto me?

 # FROM THE SCRIPTURES

The following verses in Romans 10 include four rhetorical questions asked in affirmative negation:

Example 1
Romans 10:14-15

How then shall they call on him in whom they have not believed? and how shall they believe in him of whom they have not heard? and how shall they hear without a preacher?
And how shall they preach, except they be sent? as it is written, How beautiful are the feet of them that preach the gospel of peace, and bring glad tidings of good things!

If we keep the figure of speech in mind, here's how these verses might read:

Romans 10:14-15 (emphasis added)

How then shall they call on him in whom they have not believed? [**THEY CAN'T!**] and how shall they believe in him of whom they have not heard? [**THEY CAN'T!**]
and how shall they hear without a preacher? [**THEY CAN'T!**]
And how shall they preach, except they be sent? [**THEY CAN'T!**]
as it is written, How beautiful are the feet of them that preach the gospel of peace, and bring glad tidings of good things!

This figure draws our attention to the truth that one cannot believe until one hears and that one cannot hear until one preaches and that one cannot preach until one is sent. In drawing our attention to the implied negative answer, the *erotesis* reminds us of the importance of proclaiming the gospel of God concerning His Son Jesus Christ so that others might hear and believe and be saved.

This type of *erotesis* also occurs three times in Romans 8:

Example 2
Romans 8:33-35

Who shall lay any thing to the charge of God's elect? *It is* God that justifieth.

Who *is* he that condemneth? *It is* Christ that died, yea rather, that is risen again, who is even at the right hand of God, who also maketh intercession for us.
Who shall separate us from the love of Christ? *shall* tribulation, or distress, or persecution, or famine, or nakedness, or peril, or sword?
In these three verses, three questions are asked in the affirmative with an anticipated negative response. With the figure in mind, here's how the verses might read:

Romans 8:33-35 (emphasis added)
Who shall lay any thing to the charge of God's elect? [**NO ONE!**]
It is God that justifieth.
Who *is* he that condemneth? [**NO ONE!**] *It is* Christ that died, yea rather, that is risen again, who is even at the right hand of God, who also maketh intercession for us.
Who shall separate us from the love of Christ? [**NO ONE!**] *shall* tribulation, or distress, or persecution, or famine, or nakedness, or peril, or sword?

The repetition of this type of question used in quick succession draws attention to the emphatic answer supplied by the reader.

Example 3
Hebrews 1:5a
For unto which of the angels said he at any time, Thou art my Son, this day have I begotten thee?

The rhetorical question in this verse suggests a response in strong negation: NONE of the angels were referred to by God as His only begotten Son.

Rhetorical question introduced in an affirmative manner anticipating a negative answer.

Chapter 29
Erotesis

(in strong emotion)

air-o-TEE-sis

> Rhetorical question asked in strong emotion.

When a person unexpectedly receives a spectacular gift, her first response might be something like, "Are you kidding me?" The person isn't expecting an answer but is using a rhetorical question to express strong emotion. Whether in poetry or in speeches, on greeting cards or in advertising slogans, rhetorical questions are a common way to express strong emotion.

FROM GENERAL CULTURE

Example 1

"Your father was a ballplayer," she said. "He could have played in college, you know? You should have said something about that."

Frank laughed. What kind of person offered constructive criticism at a funeral? What kind of literate mourner had the nerve to deconstruct a eulogy?

(Sherman Alexie, "What Ever Happened to Frank Snake Church?")

This dialogue takes place after the narrator, Frank, has just given his father's eulogy. The use of questions underscores his strong emotion—indignation.

Example 2

That man over there says that women need to be helped into carriages, and lifted over ditches, and to have the best place everywhere. Nobody ever helps me into carriages, or over mud-puddles, or gives me any best place! And ain't I a woman? Look at me! Look at my arm! I have ploughed and planted, and gathered into barns, and no man could head me! And ain't I a woman? I could work as much and eat as much as a man - when I could get it - and bear the lash as well! And ain't I a woman? I have borne thirteen children, and seen most all sold off to slavery, and when I cried out with my mother's grief, none but Jesus heard me! And ain't I a woman? Must I argue the wrongfulness of slavery? Is that a question for republicans? Is it to be settled by the rules of logic and argumentation, as a matter beset with great difficulty, involving a doubtful application of the principle of justice, hard to understand? (Sojourner Truth, "Ain't I a Woman?")

This excerpt from a speech given by a former slave to an 1851 women's rights convention is punctuated with rhetorical questions, which convey moral indignation while drawing attention to the need for the women's rights movement to advocate for equality for women of all races.

Example 3

Hath not a Jew eyes?
Hath not a Jew hands, organs, dimensions, senses, affections, passions?
If you prick us, do we not bleed, if you tickle us, do we not laugh?
If you poison us, do we not die?
(Merchant of Venice 3.1.58-68)

In these well-known lines from Shakespeare, the character Shylock uses a series of questions to draw attention to the ethnic bias Jews at that time were subjected to. Depending on how an actor interprets these lines, these questions might be asked in a sorrowful way thereby expressing sadness or weariness, or they might be asked in an aggressive way thereby expressing anger. However the actor interprets these lines, the questions are used to express strong emotion.

FROM THE SCRIPTURES

Example 1
Genesis 4:9
Then the LORD said to Cain, "Where is Abel your brother?" And he said, "I do not know. Am I my brother's keeper?"

The first question, "where is Abel your brother?" is asked by God to elicit an answer. Cain answers with a lie," I do not know." Then, Cain uses a rhetorical question ("Am I my brother's keeper?") to demonstrate strong emotion, sarcasm.

Example 2
John 7:45-48
Then came the officers to the chief priests and Pharisees; and they said unto them, Why have ye not brought him? The officers answered, Never man spake like this man. Then answered them the Pharisees, Are ye also deceived? Have any of the rulers or of the Pharisees believed on him?

In this record, the chief priests and Pharisees were furious that the officers did not bring Jesus Christ to them and were incensed over the possibility that these officers might believe on Jesus Christ. The first question, "Why haven't you brought him?" is not a rhetorical question, and so is answered by the officers. But the questions that follow are rhetorical used here to express strong emotion—accusatory anger.

Example 3
Psalm 139:7-8
Whither shall I go from thy spirit?
or whither shall I flee from thy presence?
If I ascend up into heaven, thou *art* there:
if I make my bed in hell, behold, thou *art there.*

The Psalms are filled with questions used to convey strong emotion like awe or amazement, typically at the greatness and fidelity of God. Here the psalmist uses questions to express his amazement or astonishment over the truth that no matter where he goes, God is still with him. It is a beautiful expression of deep emotion.

Example 4
Psalm 13: 1-6

How long wilt thou forget me, O LORD? for ever? how long wilt thou hide thy face from me?

How long shall I take counsel in my soul, *having* sorrow in my heart daily? how long shall mine enemy be exalted over me?

Consider *and* hear me, O Lord my God: lighten mine eyes, lest I sleep *the sleep of* death;

Lest mine enemy say, I have prevailed against him; *and* those that trouble me rejoice when I am moved.

But I have trusted in thy mercy; my heart shall rejoice in thy salvation.

I will sing unto the Lord, because he hath dealt bountifully with me.

The Psalms sometime express the anguish or despair we humans all feel at one time or another. In the first two verses of Psalm 13, the psalmist asks a series of rhetorical questions that express the anguish he felt at the time. By the time he reaches verse five, however, the psalmist has resolved his strong emotion and declares that he will trust in God's mercy, rejoice in God's salvation, and sing unto the Lord.

The Book of Job contains 329 questions, more than any other book in the Bible. Is it any wonder given the extreme gamut of emotions Job experiences that the rhetorical question is so often used in this book?

Example 5
Job 10: 1-10

My soul is weary of my life; I will leave my complaint upon myself; I will speak in the bitterness of my soul.

I will say unto God, Do not condemn me; shew me wherefore thou contendest with me.

Is it good unto thee that thou shouldest oppress, that thou shouldest despise the work of thine hands, and shine upon the counsel of the wicked?

Hast thou eyes of flesh? or seest thou as man seeth?

Are thy days as the days of man? *are* thy years as man's days,

That thou enquirest after mine iniquity, and searchest after my sin?

Thou knowest that I am not wicked; and *there is* none that can deliver out of thine hand.

Thine hands have made me and fashioned me together round
about; yet thou dost destroy me.
Remember, I beseech thee, that thou hast made me as the clay;
and wilt thou bring me into dust again?
Hast thou not poured me out as milk, and curdled me
like cheese?

It's clear from the context that Job is speaking out of deep emotion: he says
that he is weary of his life and that his soul is bitter. (The NASB translates
verses 1-3 a little more forcefully, "I loathe my own life; I will give full vent
to my complaint; I will speak in the bitterness of my soul.") How fitting that
the rhetorical question is used to convey such deep emotions.

Example 6
Luke 1: 41-45
And it came to pass, that, when Elisabeth heard the salutation
of Mary, the babe leaped in her womb; and Elisabeth was filled
with the Holy Ghost:
And she spake out with a loud voice, and said, Blessed *art* thou
among women, and blessed *is* the fruit of thy womb.
And whence *is* this to me, that the mother of my Lord should
come to me?
For, lo, as soon as the voice of thy salutation sounded in mine
ears, the babe leaped in my womb for joy.
And blessed *is* she that believed: for there shall be a performance
of those things which were told her from the Lord.

In this passage, a rhetorical question is asked to express the extreme joy
Elisabeth must have felt in knowing that her cousin, Mary, was pregnant with
the long anticipated Messiah.

Rhetorical question asked in strong emotion.

Notes

1. There is some debate amongst rhetoricians whether or not a question is a figure of speech or if it is a device used in persuasion. I consider questions to be figures of speech when they are asked not for information or for an answer but for a certain effect or to imply a specific emphatic answer. However, students might wish to note that not all scholars consider rhetorical questions true figures of speech.

2. See *Figures of Speech Used in the Bible Explained and Illustrated*, (pgs. 943-957).

SECTION 8
IDIOMS AND OTHER FAMILIAR FIGURES

IDIOMS AND OTHER FAMILIAR FIGURES

According to some sources, there are 20 essential American idioms people needs to know in order to sound like a native speaker:

1. (To) Hit the books
2. (To) Hit the sack
3. (To) Twist someone's arm
4. Up in the air
5. (To) Stab someone in the back
6. (To) Lose your touch
7. (To) Sit tight
8. (To) Pitch in
9. (To) Go cold turkey
10. (To) Face the music
11. (To be) On the ball
12. (To) Ring a bell
13. Rule of thumb
14. (To be) Under the weather
15. (To) Blow off steam
16. (To) Look like a million dollars/bucks
17. (To) Cut to the chase
18. (To) Find your feet
19. (To) Get over something
20. (To) Keep your chin up

An idiom is an expression that is not literal but has a culture-specific meaning attached to it. For instance, if we take the individual words "quit cold turkey" at their literal face value, they have no meaning. But most Americans know what this expression means: to give up totally and suddenly an addictive habit or substance. Idioms are unique to groups, languages, and cultures and are an intricate part of the fabric of language. There are many idioms in the Bible that are derived from the land and culture and languages of the time period. Individual words and whole phrases can be used idiomatically. Here are some idioms that occur frequently in the Bible:

- Children of men
- Breaking bread
- Answered and said
- And it came to pass

- Lifting up the face
- Stiff necked

When studying the Scriptures, knowledge of idioms helps us to understand what we're reading. *Go Figure!* covers 19 biblical idioms, with numerous examples provided for further study.

Like idiom, irony is a figure of speech that when not recognized can end in confusion or misunderstanding. I'm sure we've all be on the receiving end of an email or text that was meant ironically, but we took it literally and problems ensued. That's why we often use emoticons when texting or in emails: they convey tone of voice in a visual form. In print, irony can be difficult to detect. If I write: "I just love those new purple, pink, and green chintz curtains," it's difficult to determine if I am being ironic or literal. (Ironic—I'm more a beige-and-white-stripe kind of girl.) In print, irony is usually cued by the context. Chapter 31 gives numerous examples of rhetorical irony and discusses the difference between irony and sarcasm.

Finally, Section 8 closes with the figure *oxymoron*. The word "*oxymoron*" comes from the Greek *oxus* meaning sharp or acute, and *moros* meaning dull or foolish. So an *oxymoron* is a wise saying that seems foolish. *Oxymoron* can also be understood as any paradoxical words appearing close together. In American English vernacular, *oxymoron* is often quite funny, probably because paradox is central to comedy. Here are a few examples of English *oxymoron*s:

- Awfully good
- Crash landing
- Deafening silence
- Good grief!
- Old news

Chapter 30
Idioma

(idioms)

i-di-O-ma

Idioms are non-literal, culture-specific expressions.

Idioms are non-literal expressions that are unique or peculiar to a specific language or group. Here are some commonly used American idioms:

- My bad!
- A chip on your shoulder
- Rub someone the wrong way
- Jump the gun
- Once in a blue moon
- Out of the blue
- Piece of cake
- Costs an arm and a leg
- Hit the books
- Let the cat out of the bag
- When pigs fly
- Pig out

When a non-native speaker interprets idiomatic expressions literally, he misses the intended meaning. Read the following sentence literally: "I told him to take the chip off his shoulder, and that if he hit the books, the test would be a piece of cake." A literal reader might ask, why does he have a potato chip on his shoulder? Why would he strike his calculus textbook? And how can a test be made out of a dessert? It's essential to understand the intended meaning behind idioms and not to read the words literally.

Idioms are unique to each language. Roy Zuck gives the following interesting example of how idioms are culture-specific:

> In English, 'he has a hard heart,' means 'he is indifferent to the needs of others.' But the same expression, . . . in the Shipibo language of Peru means, 'he is brave.' Shipibo does have an idiom, which means a person is indifferent. It is, 'His ears have no holes.' English has the idiom 'a horse of a different color,' but in Spanish, the corresponding idiom is translated 'flour from a different bag.' (165)

In other words, idiomatic expressions vary from culture to culture. So while an idiom may mean one thing in one culture, the same idiom may mean something else in another.

Idioms may even be unique to a specific area or geographic region. How many Americans understand the meaning of these common British idioms?[1]

- Any road
- Bob's your uncle!
- Cheeky
- Donkey's Years
- The Full Monty
- Gob-smacked
- Jack the lad
- To Have A Butcher's
- Lose The Plot
- Made Redundant
- Mind the queue!
- Off One's Trolley
- Shambolic
- Spend A Penny
- Throw A Spanner In The Works
- Tickety-Boo

As we can see, idioms may be unique to a specific language or group and may even vary amongst people speaking the same language.

The question remains: Are idioms really figures of speech? Some scholars consider idioms to be part of figurative language while some do not. Because idioms are stated in a non-literal way, I consider them to be figurative and have therefore included them in this book. In addition, because knowledge of biblical idioms can greatly enhance a reader's understanding of the Bible, I have included a chapter on idioms in *Go Figure!*

It should be further noted that there is some debate about whether or not an idiom in the Bible brings emphasis to a passage. Many believe that even though idioms are figurative, they do not necessarily bring emphasis to a passage as other figures might because these expressions were common to native speakers and were an integral part of the Bible languages at the time.[2] However, it would be foolhardy to say that idioms never carry emphatic force in the Bible. As always, a consideration of the context will help to make that determination.

While unfamiliar idioms like "shake the dust off your feet" might arrest our attention today, to people of the Bible lands, such an expression might not necessarily or categorically arrest the attention. For example, when Americans refer to a frankfurter as a "hot dog," this expression does not raise any eyebrows because it is such a familiar idiom. To a non-native speaker, however, such an expression would certainly grab the attention. In this chapter, biblical idioms are listed in the hopes that readers might better understand some of these expressions as they are used in the Scriptures. Whether or not these expressions bring a divine emphasis may require further study and consideration.

 # FROM THE SCRIPTURES

When it comes to the Bible, there are hundreds of Hebrew and Greek idioms that have been translated into English. Furthermore, many scholars agree that although the New Testament is written in Greek, many of its idioms are Hebraic or Semitic in nature.[3] Michael D. Marlowe explains it thus:

> Although the language of the New Testament is fundamentally the *koine* or "common" Greek of the period in which it was written, the New Testament authors wrote in a Hebraic or Semitic style, which is not entirely idiomatic Greek. This stylistic

character may be seen in several areas, including the grammar, syntax, semantics, and rhetorical features of the text. Particular examples of this style are called linguistic Hebraisms, or, more broadly, Semitisms (a term which covers Aramaic influences as well as Hebrew).

Marlowe's point is that the Greek New Testament contains many Hebrew idioms even though it is written in Greek. E. W. Bullinger writes something similar: "While therefore, the *words* are Greek, the *thoughts* and *idioms* are Hebrew . . . the New Testament abounds with *Hebraisms*: i.e., expressions conveying Hebrew usages and thoughts in Greek words" (819).

Another point to consider is that a word or phrase may be idiomatic in one place but literal in another. Verbs such as "to eat" and "to drink" can have both a literal and an idiomatic meaning. Consider how the verb "to eat" is used in the following verse:

> **1 Kings 19:6** (emphasis added)
> And he looked, and, behold, *there was* a cake baken on the coals, and a cruse of water at his head. And he did **eat** and drink, and laid him down again.

In this verse, the verb "did eat" is literal, for the prophet ate the cake (and drank the water) mentioned. But note how this same verb might be used idiomatically:

> **Jeremiah 15:16** (emphasis added)
> Thy words were found, and I **did eat** them; and thy word was unto me the joy and rejoicing of mine heart: for I am called by thy name, O LORD God of hosts.

HINTS & TIPS

1. In order to determine if a word or phrase is used idiomatically or literally, it is important to read the context.

2. An idiom in one verse might not be an idiom in another.

3. An idiom may overlap with other figures of speech or with biblical customs and manners.

Clearly, the prophet Jeremiah did not literally eat the pieces of a scroll. Here the verb "ate" is used idiomatically to mean that he mentally digested or assimilated the words written on the scroll. This idiomatic meaning of the word "eat" is common in Greek and Hebrew where the idea of assimilation is suggested.

 # FROM THE SCRIPTURES

Example 1
Romans 16:4 (emphasis added)
Who have for my life **laid down their own necks**: unto whom not only I give thanks, but also all the churches of the Gentiles.

The expression "laid down their necks" means to risk their lives. We have similar idioms in English: "I risked my neck" or "I stuck out my neck" for you.

Example 2
Acts 23:3 (emphasis added)
Then said Paul unto him, God shall smite thee, *thou* **whited wall**: for sittest thou to judge me after the law, and commandest me to be smitten contrary to the law?

A "whited wall" is an idiom meaning a hypocrite. In the lands and times of the Bible, whitewash was used to cover up defects. (See also Matthew 23:27)

Example 3
Acts 1:21 (emphasis added)
Wherefore of these men which have companied with us all the time *that* the Lord Jesus **went in and out among us,**

The expression "to go in and out" is an idiom meaning to conduct one's daily life. (See also Acts 9:28).

Example 4
1 Samuel 25:27 (emphasis added)
And now this **blessing** which thine handmaid hath brought unto my lord, let it even be given unto the young men that follow my lord.

The word "blessing" might be an idiom meaning a material and tangible gift. Here the "blessing" or gift included 200 loaves, two bottles of wine, five sheep, five measures of parched corn, 100 clusters of raisins, and 200 cakes of figs. (See also Genesis 33:11, 2 Corinthians 9:5.)

Example 5
Ephesians 6:5 (emphasis added)
Servants, be obedient to them that are *your* masters according to the flesh, with **fear and trembling**, in singleness of your heart, as unto Christ;

"Fear and trembling" is an idiom meaning reverence and respect. (See also 2 Corinthians 7:15, Philippians 2:12)

Bullinger offers eleven categories of idioms, with a few examples under each. While much might be gleaned from using Bullinger's classification of idioms, in *Go Figure!* common biblical idioms are given with some examples. (In many cases, even if you weren't familiar with the idiom, you would probably be able to get the meaning by simply reading the context.)

1. to eat or drink: an idiom meaning to receive, to assimilate

> John 6:51
> John 6:53
> 1 Corinthians 12:13

2. to hear: an idiom meaning to understand, to perceive the sense of something (not just to hear sounds or words)

> Luke 8:15
> John 8:43,47
> Galatians 4:21

3. riches: an idiom meaning abundance (not just monetary wealth)

> Romans 2:4
> Ephesians 1:7
> Colossians 1:27
> Colossians 2:2

4. walk: an idiom meaning one's habit, conduct, or manner of life

> 2 Corinthians 5:7
> 1 Peter 4:3

2 Peter 2:10, 3:3
Jude:16, 18

5. edge of the sword: an idiom meaning in battle, warfare

Judges 1:8
Joshua 8:24
Luke 21:24

6. "son of" + quality: an idiom meaning belonging, pertaining, or devoted to that quality

Luke 10:6
Ephesians 5:6 ("children" in KJV)
1 Thessalonians 5:5 ("children" in KJV)

7. breaking of bread: an idiom meaning to eat, or to eat a meal

Luke 24:35
Acts 2:42
Acts 2:46

8. to open the mouth: an idiom meaning to speak (often at length)

Job 3:1
Job 33:2
Psalm 78:2
Proverbs 31:26

9. sons of God: an idiom sometimes meaning angels who believed God (not the rebellious angels)

Job 38:7
Daniel 3:25

10. give the hand: an idiom meaning to join in an alliance, to be in league with

Lamentations 5:6
Jeremiah 50:15
Ezekiel 17:18

11. to strike hands: an idiom meaning to make a promise

>Job 17:3
>Proverbs 22:26

12. by hands: an idiom meaning agency, or the means by which something occurs or takes place

>Acts 2:23
>Acts 5:12
>Acts 11:30, 14:3, 19:11

13. stiff-necked: an idiom meaning to be stubborn or obstinate

>Exodus 32:9, 33:5
>2 Chronicles 30:8
>Acts 7:51

14. spirit: an idiom sometimes used as meaning the life of man, its issues and characteristics[4]

>Acts 7:59
>Acts 19:21
>Acts 20:22

15. sand of (or by) the sea: an idiom to connote a vast number

>Genesis 41:49
>Isaiah 10:22
>Jeremiah 15:8

16. dust of the earth: an idiom to connote a vast number

>Genesis 13:16
>Genesis 28:14
>2 Chronicles 1:9

17. to gird up the loins: an idiom meaning to make or to get ready

        2 Kings 4:29
        Job 38:3
        1 Peter 1:13

18. answered and said: an idiom meaning to speak

        Genesis 18:27
        Job 40:1
        John 5:19

This phrase occurs nearly 200 times in the Bible and might be considered to be both a *pleonasm* (re: Chapter 10) and an idiom. Or it may be considered a pleonastic idiom.

19. gnashing of teeth: an idiom meaning anger, fury

        Psalm 35:16
        Matthew 13:50
        Acts 7:54

Idioms are non-literal, culture-specific expressions.

Chapter 31
Eironeia

(verbal irony) (807)

i-roe-NEE-uh

> Irony is to say one thing but to mean another, usually
> the opposite of what is said.

Verbal irony is a familiar figure of speech: it is to say one thing and to mean another, usually the opposite of what is meant.[5] When someone remarks that a three-hour wait at the doctor's office, "took no time at all," they are being ironic. To say, "I haven't seen you in ages" to someone we see daily or "Your room looks fantastic!" to a child with a disheveled bedroom is to use verbal irony. Irony has been described as a kind of "winking at each other" where we understand that what is said is the opposite of what is actually meant. Irony may be used for many purposes, but typically it is a rhetorical device used to drive home a point.

Today irony intersects with parody, satire, sarcasm, coincidence, and hypocrisy. Irony also comes in many forms such as situational irony, dramatic irony, Socratic irony, cosmic irony, postmodern irony, visual irony, and, even ironic punctuation![6] So it can be difficult to appreciate and identify verbal irony as a specific figure of speech. Because sarcasm and irony are often confused in contemporary culture, a brief discussion of the difference between these two figures is worth considering.

Sarcasm vs. Irony

Bullinger considers sarcasm as a specific type of irony that is used to taunt or to ridicule.

The *OED* defines sarcasm as, "a sharp, bitter, or cutting expression or remark; a bitter gibe or taunt." Indeed, the word "sarcasm" comes from the Greek *sarkosmos* meaning to tear the flesh, gnash the teeth, to speak bitterly. So sarcasm might be understood as a type of irony that has a specific purpose— to chide, deflate, scorn, ridicule, or mock. It has a cutting edge to it.

Many modern sources, however, make no distinction between sarcasm and irony. The Silva Rhetorica offers this definition of irony: "Speaking in such a way as to imply the contrary of what one says, often for the purpose of derision, mockery, or jest." Basically, this definition suggests that the intent of irony is often to deride, mock, or jest. But that isn't always the case. Sarcasm is a specific type of irony that serves a specific purpose. Another way to look at it is that while all sarcasm is ironic, not all irony is sarcastic. The difference between these two figures is worth keeping in mind, especially when we consider verbal irony used in the Scriptures.

Indeed, there are occurrences of sarcasm in the Bible where irony is used and the context indicates that the intent is to taunt, ridicule, or mock. Consider the following passage:

> **Nehemiah 4:1-3** (emphasis added)
> But it came to pass, that when Sanballat heard that we builded the wall, he was wroth, and took great indignation, and mocked the Jews. And he spake before his brethren and the army of Samaria, and said, **What do these feeble Jews? will they fortify themselves? will they sacrifice? will they make an end in a day? will they revive the stones out of the heaps of the rubbish which are burned**? Now Tobiah the Ammonite was by him, and he said, **Even that which they build, if a fox go up, he shall even break down their stone wall.**

Here, Sanballat and Tobiah use sarcasm to mock the Judeans who were rebuilding the wall at Jerusalem. The Judeans were not feeble, for God helped them. They did fortify themselves with God's help, they did offer sacrifices, and the walls were strong enough to withstand being broken down by the mere weight of a fox. In this record, the rhetorical question and *hyperbole* are also used, but the words are sarcastic, meant to mock the Judeans who were rebuilding the wall at Jerusalem.

Sarcasm is used in Elijah's response to the prophets of Baal:

1 Kings 18:27
And it came to pass at noon, that Elijah mocked them, and said, Cry aloud; for he *is* a god; either he is talking, or he is pursuing, *or* he is in a journey, or peradventure he sleepeth, and must be waked!

These words are not literal: idols do not talk, pursue, take journeys, or sleep. These words are spoken in order to taunt the worshippers of Baal.

Michal, Saul's daughter, uses sarcasm when she says to David: "How glorious was the King of Israel today!" (2 Sam 6:20). And Job's response to his three antagonists, "Surely you are the people, and wisdom will die with you" (Job 12:2) is heavy with sarcasm.

Irony in Antiquity

When considering verbal irony in the Scriptures, it is helpful to view irony in light of its characteristics and functions in antiquity, rather than in modernity. In his book *The Irony of Galatians*, Mark Nanos provides a comprehensive definition of irony as it was understood and used in antiquity, pointing out that irony was a "highly developed rhetorical and situational form" (34) in Paul's day and that it existed in many forms of writing, particularly in epistolary form. Audiences and orators alike were well acquainted with this familiar form. Nanos then offers the following insight regarding verbal irony's purpose in antiquity:

> Irony creates and exposes a tension between appearance (what is assumed to be the case) and reality, . . . [and that] following the employment of such irony, that this will be the view shared by the addressees and audience . . . . Thus, even in the early usage, we gain a view of the ability of irony to expose the error of appearances, to undermine and thereby correct perceptions through pretense. (35)

Nanos's point is that irony may help an audience distinguish between appearance and reality and to help correct its ways of thinking. This ironic framework would be understood by audience and addressee alike. Note how Nanos does not mention derision or mockery. Irony, Nanos continues, played "an overall positively valued role" in antiquity (37). It is therefore probably a good idea for us not to bring negative connotations of sarcasm into our understanding of irony as it is used in the Scriptures.

FROM GENERAL CULTURE

Example 1
The more New Yorkers like something, the more disgusted they are. "The kitchen was all Sub-Zero: I want to kill myself. The building has a playroom that makes you want to break your own jaw with a golf club." I can't take it. (Tinay Fey, *Bossypants*)

Giving examples of how New Yorkers express joy by feigning disgust, Fey depicts the irony embedded in this type of language. The speaker doesn't literally want to kill herself or break her own jaw with a golf club; she is speaking ironically saying one thing but meaning just the opposite.

Example 2
". . . pleasant and relaxed as a coiled rattlesnake." (*Breakfast of Champions*)

A rattlesnake coils up before it strikes. Few things in nature contain as much pent up energy and venom as a coiled rattlesnake. So to describe this animal as "pleasant and relaxed" is to use irony, for just the opposite is meant: it is dangerous and volatile.

Example 3
Why, I think it's more of a waltz, really. Isn't it? We might just listen to the music a second. Shall we? Oh, yes, it's a waltz. Mind? Why, I'm simply thrilled. I'd love to waltz with you.

I'd love to waltz with you. I'd love to waltz with you. I'd love to have my tonsils out, I'd love to be in a midnight fire at sea. Well, it's too late now. We're getting under way. Oh. Oh, dear. Oh, dear, dear, dear. Oh, this is even worse than I thought it would be. I suppose that's the one dependable law of life—everything is always worse than you thought it was going to be. Oh, if I had any real grasp of what this dance would be like, I'd have held out for sitting it out. Well, it will probably amount to the same thing in the end. (Dorothy Parker, "The Waltz")

In the short sketch the narrator repeatedly says one thing to her dance partner (given in italic print) when she means just the opposite (given in regular print). The woman says she would love to waltz when in reality she would rather "have her tonsils out." When her partner steps on her feet, she declares, "No, of course it didn't hurt. Why it didn't a bit. Honestly" when in reality she calls it a "shin splint." She declares, "Oh, they're going to play another encore. Oh goody!" when she has no desire to keep dancing. The story continues after this manner where the narrator says one thing to her dance partner but means exactly the opposite. The incongruity between what is said and what is meant supplies the humor in the story.

 FROM THE SCRIPTURES

Example 1
Ezekiel 20:39 (emphasis added)
As for you, O house of Israel, thus saith the Lord GOD; Go ye, **serve ye every one his idols**, and hereafter *also*, if ye will not hearken unto me: but pollute ye my holy name no more with your gifts, and with your idols.

It is impossible that God would command His people to serve idols, so these words are ironic where what is said "go ye, serve ye every one his idols" is the opposite of what is meant

Example 2
Judges 10:9-14 (emphasis added)
Moreover the children of Ammon passed over Jordan to fight also against Judah, and against Benjamin, and against the house of Ephraim; so that Israel was sore distressed. And the children of Israel cried unto the LORD, saying, We have sinned against thee, both because we have forsaken our God, and also served Baalim. And the LORD said unto the children of Israel, *Did* not

I deliver you from the Egyptians, and from the Amorites, from the children of Ammon, and from the Philistines? The Zidonians also, and the Amalekites, and the Maonites, did oppress you; and ye cried to me, and I delivered you out of their hand. Yet ye have forsaken me, and served other gods: wherefore I will deliver you no more. **Go and cry unto the gods which ye have chosen; let them deliver you in the time of your tribulation.**

In verse fourteen, the words are ironic, for God certainly does not wish His people to cry unto false gods, nor does He suggest that these false gods will deliver them in a time of tribulation. The words are an example of divine irony.

Example 3
2 Corinthians 11:5 (emphasis added)
For I suppose I was not a whit behind the **very chiefest apostles**.

The words "very chiefest apostles" in Greek are *huperlian apostolon*, which might be translated "super-apostles." This phrase is meant ironically, for it refers to the false apostles and deceitful workers mentioned in 2 Corinthian 11:13. Note how some translations or versions identify the irony in 2 Corinthians 11:5 by using quotation marks around the phrase "super apostle."

2 Corinthians 11:5 (NIV)
I do not think I am in the least inferior to those "super-apostles."

2 Corinthians 11:5 (NLT)
But I don't consider myself inferior in any way to these "super apostles" who teach such things.

2 Corinthians 11:5 (Holman CSB)
Now I consider myself in no way inferior to the "super-apostles."

2 Corinthians 11:5 (ISV)
I do not think I'm inferior in any way to those "super-apostles."

2 Corinthians 11:5 (NET)
For I consider myself not at all inferior to those "super-apostles."

These five versions use quotation marks around the phrase "super apostle": this is an example of ironic punctuation where quotation marks are used to signify that the words are meant ironically. Rendered thus, the irony becomes more apparent than in the KJV.

Example 4
1 Corinthians 4:8-10 (emphasis added)
Now ye are full, now ye are rich, ye have reigned as kings without us: and I would to God ye did reign, that we also might reign with you.
For I think that God hath set forth us the apostles last, as it were appointed to death: for we are made a spectacle unto the world, and to angels, and to men.
We *are* **fools for Christ's sake, but ye** *are* **wise in Christ; we** *are* **weak, but ye** *are* **strong; ye** *are* **honourable, but we** *are* **despised.**

In this example, the words in bolded print are meant ironically.

Example 5
1 Corinthians 6:1-5a (emphasis added)
Dare any of you, having a matter against another, go to law before the unjust, and not before the saints? Do ye not know that the saints shall judge the world? and if the world shall be judged by you, are ye unworthy to judge the smallest matters? Know ye not that we shall judge angels? how much more things that pertain to this life? If then ye have judgments of things pertaining to this life, **set them to judge who are least esteemed in the church**. I speak to your shame.

In this passage, the Apostle Paul, by revelation addresses the problem with believers taking other believers to court to be judged by unbelievers. He then ironically advises, "set them to judge who are least esteemed in the church," made clear by the added phrase: "I speak to your shame." (Something similar in our vernacular might be: "Set the least esteemed to judge—Not!")

Some English translations and versions render this verse as a question.

1 Corinthians 6:4 (NIV)
Therefore, if you have disputes about such matters, do you ask for a ruling from those whose way of life is scorned in the church?

1 Corinthians 6:4 (NLT)

If you have legal disputes about such matters, why go to outside judges who are not respected by the church?

1 Corinthians 6:4 (ESV)

So if you have such cases, why do you lay them before those who have no standing in the church?

1 Corinthians 6:4 (NASB)

So if you have law courts dealing with matters of this life, do you appoint them as judges who are of no account in the church?

Translating this verse as a question rather than as an ironic statement loses the emphatic force.

Example 6

Galatians 1:6 (emphasis added)
I **marvel** that ye are so soon removed from him that called you into the grace of Christ unto another gospel:

The word "marvel" might also be translated as "shocked" or "astonished" and is likely meant ironically. In other words, Paul was not at all shocked that the Galatians were removed unto "another gospel." According to Mark Nanos, this type of ironic address was common in Greek epistolary writing.

> Irony is to say one thing but to mean another, usually the opposite of what is said.

Chapter 32

Oxymoron

(wise-folly) 816

ox-E-mo-ron

> Oxymoron is a wise saying that appears foolish, or two
> contradictory words juxtaposed for effect.

When two contradictory words are placed in conjunction for a special effect, this is the figure of speech, *oxymoron*. The word comes from the Greek *oxus*, meaning sharp or acute, and *moros*, meaning dull or foolish. Bullinger offers a broader definition when he writes that an *oxymoron* is "a wise saying that seems foolish" (816). Both definitions will be considered in this chapter.[8]

FROM GENERAL CULTURE

Today, *oxymoron* is often understood in a generalized way, meaning any contradictory phrase or paradoxical saying, as in the following:

Example 1
- Deafening silence
- True fiction
- Working vacation
- Seriously funny
- Plastic silverware
- Genuine imitation
- Cruel kindness
- Blessed misfortunes

Example 2 (emphasis added)
...Yet from those flames
No light, but rather **darkness visible**
Served only to discover sights of woe.
                    —Milton, *Paradise Lost* 1.62-64

In this example, Milton suggests that flames "radiate a positive, palpable darkness which extinguishes light" (Edgeworth 97). The idea of flames emitting darkness is paradoxical.

Example 3
Richard Lanham offers these examples of *oxymoron* and notes how they convey some humor:

- Act natural
- Pretty ugly
- Academic administration
- Jumbo shrimp
- Fast asleep

 # FROM THE SCRIPTURES

Example 1
Matthew 16:25 (emphasis added)
For whosoever will **save** his life shall **lose** it: and whosoever will **lose** his life for my sake shall **find** it.

How can one save something and lose it, or lose something and find it? This is an *oxymoron*, a wise saying that seems foolish.

Example 2
Acts 2:24 (emphasis added)
Whom God hath raised up, having loosed the **pains of death**: because it was not possible that he should be holden of it.

The phrase "pains of death" might also be translated "birth pangs of death." This is an *oxymoron* where contradictory terms (birth pains/death) are placed in conjunction.

Example 3
Philippians 3:19 (emphasis added)
Whose end *is* destruction, whose God is *their* belly, and *whose* **glory** *is* in their **shame**, who mind earthly things.)

Here opposing words "glory" and "shame" are juxtaposed, making this an *oxymoron*.

Example 4
2 Corinthians 12:10 (emphasis added)
Therefore I take pleasure in infirmities, in reproaches, in necessities, in persecutions, in distresses for Christ's sake: for when I am **weak**, then am I **strong**.

How can a person be strong when he is weak? This is an *oxymoron*, drawing attention to the truth that when Paul was weak in his own strength, he was strong in the power of Christ, which is mentioned in verse nine.

Example 5
1 Timothy 5:5-6 (emphasis added)
Now she that is a widow indeed, and desolate, trusteth in God, and continueth in supplications and prayers night and day. But she that liveth in pleasure is **dead** while she **liveth**.

Note how this figure of speech in verse six draws attention to the widow who lives in pleasure, which is set in contrast to the widow in verse five who trusts in God and continues in supplications and prayers. The ISV more forcefully translates this figure:

1 Timothy 5:5-6 (ISV)
A woman who has no other family members to care for her and who is left all alone has placed her hope in God and devotes herself to petitions and prayers night and day. But the self-indulgent widow is just as good as dead.

> Oxymoron is a wise saying that appears foolish, or two contradictory words juxtaposed for effect.

Notes

1. This list of British idioms is kindly supplied by Oonagh Buchanan who lives in London and verifies that these idioms are still in use today. Here is the meaning of the idioms:

- Any road = anyway or any how
- Bob's your uncle! = 'there you are'! or 'and that's it!'
- Cheeky = rude or disrespectful but in a clever way
- Donkey's Years = 'for ages' as in 'I haven't see you for ages' or 'a long time'
- The Full Monty = the whole package
- Gobsmacked = very shocked or surprised
- Jack the lad = a cool dude!
- To Have A Butcher's = to have a look/peep
- Lose The Plot = to have no idea what one is doing
- Made Redundant = let go from a job
- Mind the queue! = get in line
- Off One's Trolley = mad, crazy
- Shambolic = very badly managed
- Spend A Penny = go to the loo/bathroom
- Throw A Spanner In The Works = screw things up, or add a complication to a situation
- Tickety-Boo = everything is great!

2. Linguists often refer to idioms as "dead metaphors" because the native speaker no longer thinks about the original or literal sense of the words but only the idiomatic sense (Zuck 166).

3. Bullinger, Mounce, Marlowe, etc

4. The definition of this idiom is from *A Journey Through the Acts and Epistles, Vol. 1* (p. 52, etc.).

5. As with many figures of speech, the definition of irony is difficult to pin down. Greek rhetoricians speak of irony as a "glib and underhand way to take someone in" (qtd. in Cuddin 458) while Roman rhetoricians, particularly Cicero and Quintilian, define irony as a rhetorical figure where the meaning was contrary to the words used. By the nineteenth-century, irony is no longer considered to be a figure of speech but a way of seeing things, a mode or a style of writing. As Cuddon so aptly puts it, "no definition will serve to cover every aspect of its nature" (460). Still, the idea that irony is a type of incongruity or discrepancy between words and their meaning prevails.

6. For a thoroughgoing and enjoyable discussion of the many forms of irony, see Jon Winokur's *The Big Book of Irony*, which of course is pocketsize.

7. In classical rhetoric, irony may be divided into more specific forms such as *antiphrasis* (irony of one word), *paralepsis* (drawing attention to something while pretending to pass over it), *epitrope* (ironic permission), or *permutatio* (irony spanning phrases, clauses, sentences or longer passages).

8. There is some discrepancy about the definition of this figure. Some consider oxymoron to be a type of "compressed" paradox while others view paradox as a different figure of speech, a statement that appears to be self-contradictory but nonetheless contains valuable truth.

APPENDIX 1

"BEAUTIFUL FEET: A LOOK AT SEVEN FIGURES OF SPEECH IN ROMANS 10:8-15"

The topic of eternal life is perhaps one of the most important, if not the most important topic for a person to consider in his or her lifetime. When it comes to eternal life—how to receive it, who might receive it, and what it means—there are many ideas, opinions, and traditions that circulate in Christian circles. And yet the Bible is very clear about the subject of eternal life.

John 3:16-17
For God so loved the world, that he gave his only begotten Son, that whosoever believeth in him should not perish, but have everlasting life.
For God sent not his Son into the world to condemn the world; but that the world through him might be saved.

In these verses, it is clear that in order to receive eternal or everlasting life, one must believe in God's "only begotten Son," Jesus Christ. This promise is made to "whosoever" meaning anyone. These verses also tell us what God's motivation was in sending His Son into the world: because God loved the world and in order that the world might be saved, and not condemned.

In 1 Timothy, we read more about God's desire for humanity regarding salvation.

1 Timothy 2:3-5
For this is good and acceptable in the sight of God our Saviour;
Who will have all men to be saved, and to come unto the knowledge of the truth.
For *there* is one God, and one mediator between God and men, the man Christ Jesus;

From these verses we see that it is God's will that all men (*anthropos* in the Greek meaning people or humankind) be saved and to come to knowledge of the truth. We also see that there is one mediator between God and men, the man Christ Jesus. It is God's will that all people be saved, irrespective of their nationality, gender, social class, or any other outward markers that separate or distinguish one group from another. These verses also tell us that the mediator between God and men is Christ Jesus. These verses do not suggest that there are many mediators to choose from.

It is to this important topic—salvation—that we turn our attention. How does salvation come about? What needs to take place before a person might be saved, or have eternal life? In the book of Romans, there is a passage that helps to answer these questions.

Romans 10:8-15

But what saith it? The word is nigh thee, *even* in thy mouth, and in thy heart: that is, the word of faith, which we preach;

That if thou shalt confess with thy mouth the Lord Jesus, and shalt believe in thine heart that God hath raised him from the dead, thou shalt be saved.

For with the heart man believeth unto righteousness; and with the mouth confession is made unto salvation.

For the scripture saith, Whosoever believeth on him shall not be ashamed.

For there is no difference between the Jew and the Greek: for the same Lord over all is rich unto all that call upon him.

For whosoever shall call upon the name of the Lord shall be saved.

How then shall they call on him in whom they have not believed? and how shall they believe in him of whom they have not heard? and how shall they hear without a preacher?

And how shall they preach, except they be sent? as it is written, How beautiful are the feet of them that preach the gospel of peace, and bring glad tidings of good things!

In this passage from Romans 10, the Apostle Paul by revelation tells us about salvation: how salvation comes about, to whom salvation is available, what needs to take place if one is to be saved. From this passage we see that in order to be saved, it is necessary to fulfill only two requirements: confess with the mouth the Lord Jesus and believe in the heart that God raised him from the dead. Once those two requirements are fulfilled, a person is born again, or saved, and that person is the recipient of eternal life.

In this key passage, there are a number of figures of speech that call our attention to significant details regarding salvation. The figures are *repetitio*, *metonymy*, *gnome*, *litotes*, *erotesis*, *synecdoche*, and *anadiplosis*. These are not all of the figures of speech one might find in this passage, but they are some key figures worth considering in light of the all-important subject of salvation. In studying figures of speech used in the Bible, it is helpful to keep two questions in mind: what is the unique characteristic of the figure, and how might that figure bring emphasis to the passage or verse?

figures of speech

Figures of speech are rhetorical devices used in written and oral communication often for the purpose of bringing emphasis or calling attention to what is communicated because they express something in a non-literal or unusual or ungrammatical way. For example a beleaguered student might say, "I have a ton of homework tonight." This is a non-literal expression, for the student doesn't literally have 2000 pounds of calculus and French homework. But because she is overwhelmed with work, she uses the figure of speech *hyperbole* (or exaggeration) to express the depth of her feeling. Figures like *hyperbole* are often referred to as "figures of thought" because they express thoughts in a non-literal manner.

Another way language becomes figurative is when it departs from normal rules of grammar or syntax. For instance, the figure *polysyndeton* repeats conjunctions more than ordinary usage would require, as in this example from Tim O'Brien's *The Things They Carried*: "As a medic, Rat Kiley carried a canvas satchel filled with morphine and plasma and malaria tablets and surgical tape and comic books and all the things a medic must carry. . ." Ordinarily, a conjunction comes between the last two items in a series, not between each item as it is in this example from O'Brien. Grammatical figures of repetition like *polysyndeton* often bring emphasis to writing. As we consider figurative language in the Bible, it is helpful to remember that these expressions are either figures of thought or figures of grammar. The characteristic of the individual figure helps to determine how it may bring emphasis in a passage.

repetitio

Repetitio is the repetition of the same word or words irregularly in the same passage.

The first figure to consider in Romans 10:8-15 is *repetitio*, which is the repetition of the same word or words irregularly in the same passage.

Romans 10:8-10 (emphasis added)
But what saith it? The word is nigh thee, *even* in thy **mouth**,
and in thy **heart**: that is, the word of faith, which we preach;
That if thou shalt confess with thy **mouth** the Lord Jesus, and
shalt believe in thine **heart** that God hath raised him from the
dead, thou shalt be saved.
For with the **heart** man believeth unto righteousness; and with
the **mouth** confession is made unto salvation.

In these three verses the word "heart" and "mouth" are repeated three
times in close proximity. Because there is no distinguishable pattern to their
repetition, their use might be considered to be the figure *repetitio*. Why would
these words merit our attention? In the context, both the heart and the mouth
are central to what it means to be saved. According to this passage, there are
only two criteria for salvation: to confess with the mouth (the Lord Jesus) and
to believe in the heart (that God has raised him from the dead) expressed in
verses nine and ten. The repetition of these key words draws attention to the
truth that to be saved involves the heart and the mouth as opposed to good
works, ethical behavior, reciting the "sinner's prayer," and so forth.

metonymy

Metonymy is a noun or name put for a related noun or name.

There is another figure of speech in these verses, *metonymy,* a figure of
exchange where one noun is put for another related noun. *Metonymy* occurs
in verse ten where the heart is put for the innermost part of the being.
According to verses 8-10, believing takes place in the heart. This cannot
mean the literal, blood pumping, four-chambered organ lying deep within
the chest cavity. The word "heart" is used figuratively, meant to indicate the
depth of a person's mind or being.

American English vernacular uses *metonymy* with the word "heart" routinely.
If we want someone to put forth concerted effort, we say, "Put your heart
into it." If we think a person has a kind disposition, we might describe her
as having a "good heart." When we say, "I love you with all my heart," we
mean that we love someone with all our being. In these examples, we don't
literally mean the physical, blood-pumping organ. We mean something else

like effort or disposition or the whole being. This is the figure *metonymy* where the word "heart" means something other than the literal organ.

> **Romans 10:8-10** (emphasis added)
> But what saith it? The word is nigh thee, *even* in thy mouth, and in thy **heart**: that is, the word of faith, which we preach;
> That if thou shalt confess with thy mouth the Lord Jesus, and shalt believe in thine **heart** that God hath raised him from the dead, thou shalt be saved.
> For with the **heart** man believeth unto righteousness; and with the mouth confession is made unto salvation.

In the Scriptures, the word "heart" is often used figuratively. Like our own expressions, it can mean different things, which is determined by the context. Here in the context of Romans 10, the word "heart" in verses 8-10 refers to the depth of the mind, or the depth of a person's being. Just as the physical heart lies deep within the chest cavity, so does believing lie deep within one's being or one's mind. This figure again emphasizes the heart and the believing that is to take place in the heart regarding the resurrection if one desires to be saved.

Some Christians today think that in order to be saved one must "let Jesus" into their heart. Some Christians today think that in order to be saved one must pray "the sinner's prayer" or to confess one's sins. Note that in Romans 10:8-15 the heart is mentioned in these verses, but there is no mention of inviting anyone or anything into the heart. Note that in Romans 10:8-15 the mouth and confession is mentioned, but there is no mention of confessing one's sins or saying a confessional prayer. However, the Scriptures do empathically say that in order to be saved, one must believe in the heart, or in the depth of one's being. What are we to believe in order to be saved? That God has raised Jesus from the dead. The Scriptures also declare that we are to confess with our mouth. What are we to confess in order to be saved? The Lord Jesus. There are two simple requirements if one wishes to be saved: confess with the mouth and believe in the heart. With two figures of speech, *repetitio* and *metonymy,* God makes these two criteria emphatic.

litotes

Litotes is understatement using the negative to express the positive in a high degree.

The figure of speech *litotes* is a type of understatement that uses the negative to express the positive in a high degree. For instance, when we want to say something is easy to understand we say, "It isn't rocket science." Rocket science, of course, is notoriously complex and difficult to grasp. This is *litotes* where the negative ("not rocket science") is used to express the positive ("it's simple") in a high degree. We see this figure in the following verse:

> **Psalm 51:17** (emphasis added)
> The sacrifices of God *are* a broken spirit: a broken and a contrite heart, O God, thou **wilt not despise**.

Litotes occurs in the expression "wilt not despise." Rather than write that God will accept a broken and contrite heart, the psalmist, by revelation, uses a figure of speech, which uses the negative to express the positive in a high degree. Here, *litotes* emphasizes God's acceptance of a broken and contrite heart. The same figure is used in the following verse from Acts:

> **Acts 12:18** (emphasis added)
> Now as soon as it was day, there was **no small stir** among the soldiers, what was become of Peter.

In this verse, "no small stir" is a *litotes* used to emphasize the big commotion amongst the soldiers.

Note how other English versions translates this verse:

> **Acts 12:18 (ISV)**
> When morning came, there was a great commotion among the soldiers as to what had become of Peter.

> **Acts 12:18 (Aramaic Bible Plain English)**
> When it was morning, there was a great uproar among the Soldiers about Shimeon: "What happened to him?"

In these versions, the meaning of the figure is given rather than a word-for-word rendering.

This same figure occurs in Romans 10:11.

> **Romans 10:11** (emphasis added)
> For the scripture saith, Whosoever believeth on him **shall not be ashamed**.

Litotes occurs in the expression "shall not be ashamed." The Greek word translated "be ashamed" is *kataischyna*, which might be understood as to make ashamed, to disgrace, or to dishonor. Rather than express this in the positive—whoever believes in him shall be highly satisfied—the Apostle Paul, by revelation, writes it in the negative, "will not be ashamed." The figure draws emphasis to the truth that whoever believes on Jesus Christ will be highly satisfied or highly fulfilled.

erotesis

> *Erotesis* in affirmative negation: A rhetorical question asked in a positive manner that prompts a negative response.

Did you know that there are more than 3000 questions in the Bible with at least a thousand occurring in the New Testament alone? According to E. W. Bullinger, the figure of speech *erotesis* (rhetorical question) is one of the two most common figures used by Jesus Christ. What is the function of rhetorical questions in the Scriptures? Are we supposed to focus on the question or on the answer? Do they all serve the same purpose? And what exactly is a rhetorical question?

Questions are common literary devices that can be used for various effects. Bullinger lists 19 classifications of *erotesis* used in the Bible each with its own characteristic and effect. Some questions are used to cause the reader to wonder, to consider, or to search out the answer to the question posed. A question becomes figurative when it is asked not to obtain an answer but to bring about a certain emphasis or effect. Many scholars use the term *erotesis* to signify the rhetorical question. Rhetorical questions are not used to elicit information but to draw attention. They might also be used to affirm or to deny something strongly. Consider the rhetorical questions used in this passage from the gospel of Matthew:

Matthew 7:9-11
Or what man is there of you, whom if his son ask bread, will he give him a stone?
Or if he ask a fish, will he give him a serpent?
If ye then, being evil, know how to give good gifts unto your children, how much more shall your Father which is in heaven give good things to them that ask him?

These rhetorical questions are not meant to elicit a response but are used as a way of drawing attention to the subject matter; namely, that God gives good and not evil gifts. Jesus Christ could have stated this in declarative sentences: "A man won't give his son a stone if he asks for bread. A man won't give his son a fish if he asks for a serpent." Instead, he uses the interrogative form to help the listeners to stop and to think about the subject matter—God's goodness.

Human writers may use questions haphazardly or with imprecision, but when questions occur in the Scriptures, they occur for a divine purpose. The context and the nature of the question will help to determine its emphasis. Let's consider the series of questions occurring in Romans 10:14-15.

Romans 10:14-15

How then shall they call on him in whom they have not believed?
and how shall they believe in him of whom they have not heard?
and how shall they hear without a preacher?
And how shall they preach, except they be sent? as it is written,
How beautiful are the feet of them that preach the gospel of
peace, and bring glad tidings of good things!

There are four questions in these two verses. The type of question in verses 14-15 is *erotesis* in affirmative negation, meaning that the question is asked in a positive way and that a negative answer is supplied in the mind of the reader. This is considered to be a very emphatic way of communicating a negative response. We see this type of *erotesis* in Romans 8:33-35.

Romans 8:33-35

Who shall lay any thing to the charge of God's elect? *It is* God
that justifieth.
Who *is* he that condemneth? *It is* Christ that died, yea rather,
that is risen again, who is even at the right hand of God, who
also maketh intercession for us.
Who shall separate us from the love of Christ? *shall* tribulation, or
distress, or persecution, or famine, or nakedness, or peril, or sword?

In these verses, three questions are asked in the affirmative, which the mind answers emphatically in the negative. With the *erotesis* in mind, here's how the verses might read:

Romans 8:33-35 (emphasis added)

Who shall lay any thing to the charge of God's elect? [NO ONE!] *It is* God that justifieth.

Who *is* he that condemneth? [NO ONE!]*It is* Christ that died, yea rather, that is risen again, who is even at the right hand of God, who also maketh intercession for us.

Who shall separate us from the love of Christ? [NO ONE!] *shall* tribulation, or distress, or persecution, or famine, or nakedness, or peril, or sword?

This type of question underscores the negative implied response.

Now let's return to Romans 10:14-15. Keeping in mind the figure *erotesis* in affirmative negation, here's how the four questions might read:

1. How then shall they call on him in whom they have not believed? [THEY CAN'T!]
2. How shall they believe in him of whom they have not heard? [THEY CAN'T!]
3. How shall they hear without a preacher? [THEY CAN'T!]
4. How shall they preach, except they be sent? [THEY CAN'T!]

This figure draws our attention to the truth that one cannot believe until one hears and that one cannot hear until one preaches and that one cannot preach until one is sent. In other words, if no one preaches the gospel, then no one hears the gospel. And if no one hears the gospel, no one can believe the gospel, and then no one might be saved. In drawing our attention to the implied negative answer, this figure of speech reminds us of the importance of proclaiming the gospel of God concerning His Son Jesus Christ so that others might hear and believe and be saved. We may think about how nice it would be for others to be saved. We might even pray for others to be saved. But the truth is that if someone does not proclaim the gospel of God concerning His Son, Jesus Christ, others might not have the opportunity to hear, to believe, and to be saved.

gnome

Gnome is a partial, modified, or complete quotation.

In literature, when an author chooses to quote from or allude to another work, he does so typically as a claim to cultural authority. Speechwriters strategically use quotes as a way to add heft to their own words or to connect to a particular past tradition. Writers commonly quote from other writers in part or in whole as a way to add dimension or authority to their own works.

The New Testament is filled with partial, modified, or complete quotations from the Old Testament; in many cases this constitutes the figure of speech *gnome*. Often (but not always) these quotes are cued by the phrase, "as it is written." *Gnome*s come in many varieties including partial quotes, indirect quotes, direct quotes, and modified quotes. Let's consider the *gnome* that occurs in Romans 10:15.

> **Romans 10:15** (emphasis added)
> And how shall they preach, except they be sent? as it is written,
> **How beautiful are the feet of them that preach the gospel of peace, and bring glad tidings of good things!**

This is a partial quote from the following verse:

> **Isaiah 52:7** (emphasis added)
> **How beautiful** upon the mountains **are the feet of him that bringeth good tidings**, that publisheth **peace**; that **bringeth good tidings of good**, that publisheth salvation; that saith unto Zion, Thy God reigneth!

Looking at these verses in close proximity, we can see that Romans 10:15 is not a direct quote, taken word-for-word, but that it is similar in wording to the Old Testament verse. It is worth considering which words are quoted in Romans and how those words might relate to the immediate context.

In the Septuagint, the phrase "bringeth good tidings" in Isaiah 52:7 is used twice and is translated from one word *euaggelizo*. We see similar wording in Romans 10:15 where the phrases "preach the gospel" and "bring glad tidings" are also translated from the same singular Greek word, *euaggelizo*. In Isaiah the person mentioned brings good tidings of peace and of good. In Romans, the person mentioned also brings good tidings of peace and of good (*ta agatha*). What is emphasized in this *gnome* are the words repeated from Isaiah: the preaching of the gospel and that the gospel is a gospel of peace and of good.

What a blessing it is to remember that the gospel of God is good news, not bad news. In 2 Corinthians 4:4 and 1 Timothy 1:11, this good news is referred to as the "glorious" gospel, meaning praiseworthy, excellent, or magnificent. And what a blessing it is to remember that the gospel of God is news of peace with God, not strife or hostility. This peace is further articulated in the book of Ephesians.

Ephesians 2:14
For he is our peace, who hath made both one, and hath broken down the middle wall of partition *between us*;

According to this verse, Jesus Christ is our peace, meaning that because of his accomplishments, there is no more hostility between Judean and Gentile (those who believe on him). Further, because of the accomplishments of Jesus Christ, there is no more hostility between God and man. Far more than meaning that the gospel of peace brings us a tranquil state of mind, the gospel of peace signifies all that Christ accomplished for us in regards to removing enmity with God. The *gnome* makes emphatic these truths about the gospel of God.

synecdoche

Synecdoche is an exchange of one idea for a related idea often a part for the whole or a whole for the part.

Embedded in this quotation in Romans 10:15 is a curious expression, "beautiful feet." The word "beautiful" in this verse is the Greek word *horaios*. Before we consider the figurative meaning of the word "feet," we might first investigate the meaning of *horaios*, translated "beautiful" in KJV. According to Richard C. Trench, this word has several meanings, one of which is to give the sense of something being timely in the way that a flower that reaches its peak exhibits the most beauty. Other sources give the meaning of *horaios* as timely, seasonable, or opportune. Given the context of this word, "timely" would be a better translation of *horaios* than beautiful. How timely are the feet of those who preach the gospel. Why? Because this is the glorious gospel of God concerning His Son Jesus Christ, the gospel of salvation, and one might certainly consider it to be timely. Note how the New English Translation gives the following for Romans 10:15:

Romans 10:15 (NET)
And how are they to preach unless they are sent? As it is written, "How timely is the arrival of those who proclaim the good news."

This translation gives the word "timely" for *horaios*. Keeping in mind that the word *horaios* in this verse means timely, seasonable, or opportune, we next need to consider why the word "feet" is used to describe those who proclaim the gospel of peace. A common figure of speech used in the Bible is *synecdoche* where a body part is used to represent the whole person. Here in Romans 10:15, the part (feet) is put for the whole (person). But why would feet be used to represent a person proclaiming the gospel, rather than the mouth or the hands? What is significant about the feet? If we look at other verses that use *synecdoche* of the feet, we might glean some understanding of this curious expression.

Proverbs 1:16 (emphasis added)
For their **feet run to evil** and make haste to shed blood.

In the context, the plural pronoun "their" in verse 16 refers to "sinners" in verse 10. These sinners are described in verses 10-14 as seeking to murder innocent people without a cause so that they can plunder their goods. They are also described in verse 16 as having feet that run to evil and make haste to shed blood, meaning to murder. It isn't their feet that commit these actions; it is the men themselves. In this verse, the figure of speech *synecdoche*, where a body part (feet) is put for the whole man, emphasizes the action these men commit—stealing from the innocent and murdering without a cause. But because the feet are described as running, as opposed to walking, this also indicates haste.

Another occurrence of *synecdoche* of feet occurs in the following verse:

Proverbs 6:18 (emphasis added)
An heart that deviseth wicked imaginations, **feet that be swift** in running to mischief.

In verses 16-19, the Scriptures list seven things that are an abomination to the Lord, one of them being "feet that be swift in running to mischief." This is the figure of speech *synecdoche*, where the feet are put for the person or people. Why the feet? Again, to underscore the action these men take and also how quickly these people run to evil. In this verse, their feet are described as "running" and being "swift," which indicates speed of action. It's as if to say that these men do not hesitate, they do not stop to consider, they are not held in check by a healthy conscience. We might say they run headlong to do evil or to inflict injury. There is a callousness implied, as if these men have absolutely zero hesitation in committing evil.

In Isaiah, we read another verse where *synecdoche* of feet is used.

> **Isaiah 59:4-8** (emphasis added)
> None calleth for justice, nor *any* pleadeth for truth: they trust in vanity, and speak lies; they conceive mischief, and bring forth iniquity.
> They hatch cockatrice' eggs, and weave the spider's web: he that eateth of their eggs dieth, and that which is crushed breaketh out into a viper.
> Their webs shall not become garments, neither shall they cover themselves with their works: their works *are* works of iniquity, and the act of violence *is* in their hands.
> Their **feet run to evil**, and they make haste to shed innocent blood: their thoughts are thoughts of iniquity; wasting and destruction *are* in their paths.
> The way of peace they know not; and *there is* no judgment in their goings: they have made them crooked paths: whosoever goeth therein shall not know peace.

The people referred to here are similar to the sinners described in Proverbs 1: their feet run to evil and they make haste to shed innocent blood. The figure of speech *synecdoche*, where the feet are put for the people, draws attention to the actions of these people and to the speed with which these individuals commit evil. Rather than say, "their feet walk to evil," the Scriptures declare that these men RUN to evil, connoting haste.

A fourth occurrence of *synecdoche* of feet is found in the book of Romans:

> **Romans 3:10-18** (emphasis added)
> As it is written, There is none righteous, no, not one:
> There is none that understandeth, there is none that seeketh after God.

They are all gone out of the way, they are together become
unprofitable; there is none that doeth good, no, not one.
Their throat *is* an open sepulchre; with their tongues they have
used deceit; the poison of asps *is* under their lips:
Whose mouth *is* full of cursing and bitterness:
Their **feet *are* swift to shed blood**:
Destruction and misery *are* in their ways:
And the way of peace have they not known:
There is no fear of God before their eyes.

In Romans 3:14, feet are used as a *synecdoche* to indicate the whole person.
Verse 15 quotes specifically from Isaiah 59:7-9. As we previously read, Isaiah
59 declares that "their feet run to evil and they make haste to shed blood."
However, in Romans only a part of the verse is quoted: "their feet are swift to
shed blood." Here again, we see *synecdoche* of feet in the context of haste
to commit evil, specifically, to murder.

In these four examples, we have seen that the word "feet" is used as a
synecdoche for the entire person, and we have seen that this *synecdoche*
of feet often occurs in the context of swiftness, haste, and running. The
question remains, what bearing might this have on the usage of *synecdoche*
of feet in Romans 10:15?

Because the context of Romans 10:15 is salvation and proclaiming the gospel
of God concerning His Son Jesus Christ, the *synecdoche* is used to convey the
need for action as well as the urgency of the message, especially since the
word "beautiful" might be better understood as meaning "timely." Just as
sinners run to commit evil, so too might believers demonstrate a readiness to
proclaim the gospel of God. In other words, in order for the gospel of God
to be heard and to be believed, someone must first act as a messenger and
deliver the gospel of God, rather than merely think about proclaiming the
gospel. The emphasis is on action—delivering the message—rather than, say,
merely intellectualizing the gospel. And the *synecdoche* calls attention to the
urgency of the times, especially since eternal life is at stake.

There are two other records worth considering in light of understanding why
feet are used in the context of preaching the gospel.

> **Nahum 1:15** (emphasis added)
> Behold upon the mountains the **feet of him that bringeth**

good tidings, that publisheth peace! O Judah, keep thy solemn feasts, perform thy vows: for the wicked shall no more pass through thee; he is utterly cut off.

In the lands and times of the Bible, news was carried from town to town and from village to village via messengers, usually someone who could run very quickly. And so when a messenger bearing good news was spotted coming into town, it would be a cause of celebration. The word "feet" here in Nahum 1:15 is a *synecdoche* for the messenger who is coming into town with good news. In effect, the townspeople would say, "Look! A messenger is coming over the mountain with good news!" This would be a cause of celebration and excitement.

In Ephesians 6:15, feet are again used in the context of the preaching the gospel.

Ephesian 6:10-17 (emphasis added)
Finally, my brethren, be strong in the Lord, and in the power of his might.
Put on the whole armour of God, that ye may be able to stand against the wiles of the devil.
For we wrestle not against flesh and blood, but against principalities, against powers, against the rulers of the darkness of this world, against spiritual wickedness in high *places*.
Wherefore take unto you the whole armour of God, that ye may be able to withstand in the evil day, and having done all, to stand.
Stand therefore, having your loins girt about with truth, and having on the breastplate of righteousness;
And your **feet shod with the preparation of the gospel of peace**;
Above all, taking the shield of faith, wherewith ye shall be able to quench all the fiery darts of the wicked.
And take the helmet of salvation, and the sword of the Spirit, which is the word of God:

In verse 15, the feet are described as being shod, meaning bound with the preparation, meaning readiness of the gospel of peace. This is not literal: God does not want us to cover our feet with pages from the Bible. Rather, the word "feet" is used figuratively as a *synecdoche* to indicate the entire believer who displays a readiness to preach the gospel of peace. The word "feet" is used here as a way to connote both the urgency of the message and the joyful readiness of the messenger.

In these examples, the word "feet" is used as a *synecdoche* where a body part is put for the whole person and where the feet are connected to haste, to swiftness, and to running thereby connoting a sense of haste, or a sense of urgency. In Nahum, *synecdoche* of feet is put for a messenger who brings good news of peace. Understandably, such a messenger is eagerly and joyfully received. In Romans 10:15 the figure *synecdoche* occurs to emphasize both the need for a messenger in regards to salvation and the need for urgency in delivering the good news.

anadiplosis

> *Anadiplosis* is the *repetition* of the same word or words at the end of one sentence, phrase, or clause and at the beginning of the next.

Anadiplosis is a figure of repetition where the same word repeats at the end of one sentence (phrase or clause) and at the beginning of the next. Because the figure repeats one thought at the end of a sentence and at the beginning of the next, it often reflects a logical progression of thought. Like most figures of repetition, *anadiplosis* also highlights the repeated words. Consider the following occurrences of *anadiplosis* in the Scriptures:

Roman 8:17 (emphasis added)
And if children, then **heirs**; **heirs** of God, and joint-heirs with Christ; if so be that we suffer with *him*, that we may be also glorified together.

The repetition of the word "heirs" at the end of the first phrase and at the start of the next makes this the figure *anadiplosis*.

Sometimes in the Scriptures, we see a repeated *anadiplosis*, as in the following example:

Luke 12:58 (emphasis added)
When thou goest with thine adversary to the magistrate, *as thou art* in the way, give diligence that thou mayest be delivered

from him; lest he hale thee to the **judge**, and the **judge** deliver thee to the **officer**, and the **officer** cast thee into prison.

This repeated *anadiplosis* (judge-judge, officer-officer) shows a logical progression. First one is brought before a judge; then the judge hands one over to the officer; and, finally, the officer casts one into prison. (Note that the conjunction "and" does not affect this figure of speech.)

In Romans 10:14-15, we find a repeated *anadiplosis*:

> **Romans 10:14-15** (emphasis added)
> How then shall they call on him in whom they have not **believed**? and how shall they **believe** in him of whom they have not **heard**? and how shall they **hear** without a **preacher**? And how shall they **preach**, except they be sent? as it is written, How beautiful are the feet of them that preach the gospel of peace, and bring glad tidings of good things!

Note how three words are repeated at or near the end of one sentence and at the beginning of the next: believed-believe; heard-hear; preach-preach. (In verses 14 and 15, the words "how then" interrupt the repetition but do not affect the figure.) Taking the figure of speech into account, here's how these repeated words might appear if arranged in a logical progression:

            Preacher
            Preach
                        Heard
                        Hear
                                    Believed
                                    Believe

This *andadiplosis* draws attention to the progression of events or line of action leading to salvation: the sent ones preach the gospel of God concerning His Son Jesus Christ. Then once the gospel of God is preached, one can hear the message. Then once one hears the message, one can choose to believe the gospel. And then once one believes the gospel, he or she may call upon the name of the Lord and be saved. Hurrah! This complex figure of speech draws attention to the words that are repeated (preach, hear, believe) as well as to the logical progression of thought or line of action leading to salvation.

conclusion

Romans 10:8-15 is a pivotal section in the Scriptures, for it shows the way of salvation. In this section, there are several key figures of speech that might be considered. Two figures, *repetitio* (the repetition of the same word or words irregularly in the same passage) and *metonymy* (one noun or name put for a related noun or name) emphasize the words "heart" and "mouth" reminding us of the two requirements needed for salvation: confess Jesus as Lord and believe that God raised him from the dead. The figure *litotes* (understatement using the negative to express the positive to a high degree) emphasizes the fulfillment and joy one finds in believing the gospel of God concerning His Son Jesus Christ. Several rhetorical questions (*erotesis*) draw our attention to the truth that salvation does not come about without someone first proclaiming the gospel of God. In drawing our attention to the implied negative answer, this figure of speech reminds us of the importance of proclaiming the gospel of God so that others might hear and believe and be saved. Quotations (*gnome*) from the Old Testament stress that the gospel is good news and that it is a gospel of peace. *Synecdoche* (part for the whole) draws our attention to the need for a messenger in God's plan of salvation as well as the urgency of the message. The repeated *anadiplosis* (repetition of the same word or words at the end of one sentence, phrase, or clause and at the beginning of the next) emphasizes the line of action leading to salvation. While one might find other figures of speech in Romans 10:8-15, these seven figures undoubtedly shed light on a section of the Scriptures that deals with the all-important subject of salvation.

How marvelous of God to make the way of salvation plain and clear and to make the promise of eternal life freely available to all. May we remember that God wants ALL people to be saved and to come to the knowledge of the truth. May we, like the Apostle Paul, be eager to proclaim the gospel of God concerning His Son Jesus Christ.

Romans 1:15-16
So, as much as in me is, I am ready to preach the gospel to you that are at Rome also.
For I am not ashamed of the gospel of Christ: for it is the power of God unto salvation to every one that believeth; to the Jew first, and also to the Greek.

APPENDIX 2

SELECT PRINT AND DIGITAL RESOURCES FOR FURTHER RESEARCH

The following is a brief annotated bibliography of some helpful resources on rhetoric and figurative language.

BOOKS

Bullinger, E. W. *Figures of Speech Used in the Bible Explained and Illustrated.* Grand Rapids: Baker Books, 1968.

> The definitive work on the topic, recognized by scholars from around the world and quoted by researchers past and present, this book is the single most important work on the topic. Indispensible, exhaustive, and erudite, the book can be nonetheless be difficult to use because of Roman numerals, complex categorizations, and Greek, Hebrew, and Latin phrases given without translation. Digital version (available through Logos Software) replaces Roman numbering with Arabic and is searchable.

Enos, Theresa. *The Encyclopedia of Rhetoric and Composition.* London: Routledge, 1996.

> A comprehensive reference book focusing on rhetoric, not figurative language. However, numerous individual figures are comprehensively defined as well as other rhetorical terms.

Espy, Willard R. *The Garden of Eloquence: A Rhetorical Bestiary.* New York: Harper & Row, 1983.

> A short encyclopedia of figures conceived as a bestiary, which is a type of book popular in medieval times written about real and imaginary animals. Bizarre illustrations aside, the definitions and examples are helpful, and Espy's lighthearted approach is delightful.

Joseph, Sister Miriam. *Shakespeare's Use of the Arts of Language.* Philadelphia: Paul Dry Books, 2005.

> Widely respected, scholarly, and elegantly written book on rhetorical strategies in the works of William Shakespeare.

Comprehensive examples and definitions of dozens of figures of speech. Particularly helpful in explaining how figurative language brings emphasis or conveys a particular effect. However, figures are listed alphabetically in the index under the heading "figures of speech and vices of language" making for time-consuming research. Some examples from the Bible are cited.

Lanham, Richard. *A Handlist of Rhetorical Terms*. Berkeley: U of California P, 1991.

Excellent, inexpensive book on figures of speech in general literature with some material on broader rhetorical concerns. Examples are mostly drawn from Renaissance literature, so terminology is not always consistent with classical sources. Rich bibliography and insightful, witty introduction.

Leith, Sam. *Words Like Loaded Pistols: Rhetoric from Aristotle to Obama*. New York: Basic Books, 2012.

This book would be a good starting point to learn about the history of rhetoric. This is not a book about figures of speech *per se* though there are a few examples interspersed throughout. Leith's genial, tongue-in-cheek writing style makes the history lesson palatable. Glossary of terms probably the most helpful. Especially good for those wanting to study models of classical rhetoric, which may have bearing on Scripture study.

Macbeth, John Walker Vilant. *The Might and Mirth of Literature*. New York: Harper, 1875.

Exhaustive in its scope, listing more than 220 figures in literature and examples from 600 authors, Vilant Macbeth's Victorian writing style takes getting used to and his examples from arcane poetry are difficult to understand. However, he does give examples from the Bible, although finding these in the print version is painstaking business. The digital version is recommended making searching much easier.

Neil, James. *Strange Figures: Or, the Figurative Language of the Bible*. London: Marshall, 1895.

A short, valuable work discussing ten figures of speech used in the Bible. A contemporary of Bullinger, Neil served as a minister in Palestine, writing several small volumes about the customs and culture of the Bible lands. Neil's familiarity with biblical culture and his understanding of how figures function in Scripture are inestimable. Highly readable and insightful. No digital copy to date, and print version seems difficult to find in the U.S.

Quinn, Arthur. *Figures of Speech: 60 Ways To Turn A Phrase.* Salt Lake City: Gibbs M. Smith, 1982.

Highly recommended, especially for beginners. This slim volume provides succinct definitions and accessible examples, a few from Scripture. Many of Quinn's definitions appear in the *Encyclopedia of Rhetoric and Composition*.

Winokur, Jon. *The Big Book of Irony.* New York: St. Martin's Press, 2007.

Concise book about the history of irony, types of irony, and definitions of irony, with many examples from general culture. This is not a scholarly treatment of the subject and offers no bibliography. But there is a fun test at the end to determine if you are ironic, and the book itself is very readable. (The hilarious cover is worth the price of the book.)

Zuck, Roy B. *Basic Bible Interpretation.* Wheaton, IL: Victor Books, 1991.

Chapter 7 offers a wonderful overview of figures of speech in clear, lucid writing with many examples from the Scriptures. Especially helpful is his explanation of the various ways figures function and his exercises at the end of each chapter. Canonical and topical indices are very helpful.

DIGITAL RESOURCES

http://www.americanrhetoric.com/index.htm

Website with valuable links to many resources both general and scholarly and with a focus on rhetoric. "Rhetorical in Sound" tab offers interesting auditory examples of many figures.

http://rhetoric.byu.edu/

The Silva Rhetorica is provided by Dr. Gideon Burton of Brigham Young University and provides extensive list of classical and renaissance rhetoric. Offers many useful links that would be of interest to both beginner and advanced student. Few examples from the Bible.

http://rhetfig.appspot.com/list

Wiki cataloguing an astonishing 1489 figures of speech providing name, source, earliest source, synonyms, etymology, type, linguistic domain, definitions, and copious examples. Affiliated with University of Waterloo, Canada. A spectacular online resource.

APPENDIX 3

APPENDIX 3

Q1: Do figures of speech in the Bible occur in English, or in Hebrew and Greek?

A1: Figures in the Bible occur in the Hebrew and the Greek.

Working in English is a good starting point when researching figures of speech used in the Bible because many figures are reflected in an English translation like the King James Version. However, because Hebrew and Greek are the original languages of the Bible, the figures occur in Hebrew and Greek. Therefore, it is necessary to verify a figure's existence in the biblical languages. An interlinear or other translation tool is necessary.

This is especially important when considering grammatical figures like figures of repetition because an English translation often does not retain these figures. Unlike the Semitic writing style, which is imbued with natural repetitions, English writing styles tend to frown on repetition. For example Isaiah 26:3 reads, "Thou wilt keep *him* in perfect peace *whose* mind *is* stayed *on thee*: because he trusteth in thee." In the Hebrew, the word "perfect" and "peace" are the same word (*shalom*) making this the figure *epizeuxis*. The KJV, however, does not reflect the figure, likely because the translators considered it to be a poor stylistic translation. So while English is a good starting point, when readers suspect figurative language, it is necessary to verify the wording in the biblical languages if one wishes to speak with any confidence in this field. In addition, it might be helpful to note that some English translations, particularly Young's Literal Translation (1862), are more apt to retain figures of speech than more literary English translations or versions.

In *Go Figure!* the wording of each biblical example has been verified in the original languages. Notes or alternative translations have been included where the KJV does not reflect the figure.

Q2: What is the origin of the names of figures?

A2: In the western literary tradition, the names of figures of speech originated from classical antiquity, meaning Greek and Roman culture and have come down to us from the Greek and Latin languages.

Some of these names have been transliterated into English. For instance, the name of the figure "metaphor" comes from the Greek word μεταφορά, transliterated *metaphora*. The Romans named this figure *translatio*. For the most part, the original Greek name of a figure (transliterated) is still in use today amongst rhetoricians. However, a few figures that are prevalent in English are more commonly known by their English name. The figure *prosopopeia* is referred to today by most general sources as personification, yet scholars also use the classical name.

It's important to remember that the names of figures, except those mentioned in Scripture like allegory and parable, are manmade and are therefore subject to discrepancies and inconsistencies. In addition, many figures have multiple names. For example, the figure of speech *prolepsis* has two other Greek names, *procatalepsis* and *apantesis*, and three Latin names, *occupatio*, *anteoccupatio*, and *praemonitio*. In English, we would call this rhetorical figure "anticipation." When studying this field, it's important to remember that a figure might have several different names and that differences in spelling also commonly occur. In addition, the classical names of some figures sometimes change over time as words and terms fall in and out of use. For instance, the figure *tapeinosis* (also spelled *tapinosis*) is today more commonly referred to as the figure *litotes*.

In *Go Figure!* I have endeavored to retain the classical nomenclature for continuity and because these names are, for the most part, still in use today. In a few cases, I have chosen the modern use of a name if the older name is now obsolete. Alternative names for a figure are frequently provided in the endnotes.

Q3: Do all figures in the Bible have a name?

A3: No.

Not all figures occurring in the Scriptures have specific names, meaning that their occurrence might not conform to a specific figure that has been named. For example, the word "name" occurs three times in Philippians 2:9-10, yet this repetition does not conform to a specific pattern of one of the grammatical figures and therefore might not be assigned a particular name. Yet the word occurs three times in close proximity for emphasis, as the context indicates. Similarly, the phrase "confidence in the flesh" occurs three times in close proximity in Philippians 3:3-4 and is meant to draw attention to that phrase, as the context suggests. Yet the nature and pattern of repetition does not neatly fit into one of the known figures of repetition. It is more important to recognize that the phrase is repeated in an unusual manner and therefore adds emphasis to the passage than it is to agree on a specific name of the figure of speech.

Identifying unnamed figures of speech is outside the scope of *Go Figure!*

Q4: Where do your definitions of figures come from?

A4: Numerous scholarly sources.

Rhetoricians, literary scholars, classicists, linguists of all stripes, and other scholars who study language are all interested in this field and approach this topic from different perspectives, bringing with them their own theoretical apparatuses and their own vocabularies and intellectual preferences. A literary scholar might consider an expression to be a metaphor while a linguist may consider that same expression to be a metonymy. Discrepancies over definitions of figures abound, even amongst those working in the same discipline. What's more, definitions of some figures change over time, and there is frequently no consensus amongst scholars about the precise definition of a particular figure.

Without a doubt, the definitive work in this field is E. W. Bullinger's *Figures of Speech Used in the Bible Explained and Illustrated*. This work has always been my starting point for naming and defining a figure of speech. Another helpful source, the 20-volume *Oxford English Dictionary* is an invaluable aid, as it traces the history of a word's meaning and provides variant spellings. Reference books on rhetoric and online resources have also been invaluable. (See bibliography) The definitions in *Go Figure!* are derived from numerous literary sources spanning several centuries and from other books written by rhetoricians, linguists, and classicists. Variant definitions are discussed in the endnotes.

Q5: Is context important when studying figures of speech?

A5: Context is King.

I use a metaphor to draw attention to the importance of considering the context when studying figures of speech in the Bible. When seeking to identify a figure of speech and when seeking to understand how the figure might bring emphasis to a verse or passage of Scripture, it is paramount to read and to carefully consider the context in which the figure occurs. This might necessitate reading the whole passage or chapter or perhaps reading the entire book to gain an understanding of the context. In other words, it isn't enough to identify a figure purely by a grammatical formula.

When seeking to identify a figure of speech it is helpful to ask: does this passage indicate that a particular thought might be emphasized by a figure? What is God's intent in this passage? Let's consider how the figure, *litotes*, is used in the following verse:

> **Acts 5:42** (emphasis added)
> And daily in the temple, and in every house, they **ceased not** to teach and preach Jesus Christ.

"Ceased not" is *litotes*, a figure of understatement using the negative to express the positive in a high degree. We aren't able to determine this from a consideration of grammar but we can from the context. In Acts 5 we read that the apostles had been put in prison and had been commanded by various religious leaders in Jerusalem <u>not</u> to speak in the name of Jesus Christ. The apostles were then rescued out of prison by an angel and were commanded by the angel to "go, stand, and speak in the temple to the people all the words of this life." They obeyed this command. The apostles were then brought before the Sanhedrin and the high priest and were sternly reminded that they were forbidden to teach in the name of Jesus Christ. Peter responded, "We ought to obey God rather than men" (verse 29). The apostles were then beaten and commanded again <u>not</u> to speak in the name of Jesus. They were released, but they kept right on teaching and preaching Jesus Christ. The *litotes* in verse 42 makes emphatic their persistence in speaking about Jesus Christ, despite the prohibitions and punishments of antagonistic and powerful men. The figure highlights their obedience to God rather than to men.

Note how a number of English Bibles render this verse:

> **Acts 5:42 (NASB)**
> And every day, in the temple and from house to house, they kept right on teaching and preaching Jesus as the Christ.

> **Acts 5:42 (ISV)**
> Every day in the Temple and from house to house they kept teaching and proclaiming that Jesus is the Messiah.

In these versions, the meaning of the figure of speech is given rather than a word-for-word translation.

Let's consider another figure of speech, irony, and how reading the context is key in identifying and appreciating this figure:

1 Corinthians 6:4b
set them to judge who are least esteemed in the church.

In the context, we see that this cannot be literal but in fact is the figure irony, where the opposite of what is said is meant. The next phrase reads, "I speak to your shame." And verse seven asks, "Is it so that there is not a wise man among you? No; not one that shall be able to judge between his brethren?" Irony is used in verse six to arrest the reader's attention. In fact, irony is used frequently in this epistle (re: 1 Corinthians 4:8-10, 6:4, 9:4, 11:19, and 12:31.) Understanding the context helps to determine if a word or words are figurative or literal, and understanding the context helps to determine if and how a figure brings emphasis.

In *Go Figure!* care has been taken to discuss the context of each Biblical example given, but space prohibits a lengthy discussion of the context of each example. The onus is on the reader to verify this by carefully considering the context for him or herself.

Q6: What is the function of figures of speech?

A6: The function of figures of speech may vary.

Here is a partial list of the ways in which a figure might function in writing:

- Add emphasis
- Intensify feeling
- Diminish impact
- Arrest attention
- Appeal to emotion
- Cite authority
- Add ornamentation
- Bolster an argument
- Add aesthetic flourish
- Add zest or impact
- Reflect vernacular speech

- Dramatize feeling
- Serve as a mnemonic device
- Achieve a desired auditory quality
- Achieve a desired cadence or rhythm
- Serve a social function within a group
- Add comic value

Bullinger writes that figures in the Bible are "always for the purpose of giving additional force, more life, intensified feeling, and greater emphasis" (vi). It's important to remember that in Bullinger's day, figurative language was considered to be a *weakened* form of expression. So to some degree, the statement made in his introduction to *Figures of Speech Used in the Bible Explained and Illustrated* is in response to the intellectual climate of his time. Note what Bullinger says about the times in which he was writing:

> Whereas to-day [*sic*] "Figurative language" is ignorantly spoken of as though it made less of the meaning, and deprived the words of their power and force. A passage from God's Word is quoted; and it is met with the cry, "Oh, that is figurative"— implying that its meaning is weakened, or that it has quite a different meaning, or that it has no meaning at all. But the very opposite is the case. For an unusual form (*figura*) is never used except to *add* force to the truth conveyed, emphasis to the statement of it, and depth to the meaning. (vi)

In other words, Bullinger brings new light to the field by arguing that figurative language in the Bible adds emphasis and force to language, not weakens it, as his contemporaries then assumed. However, while figures of speech may bring emphasis or call attention to the reader, figures of speech in the Bible may also serve other functions.

In *Go Figure!* care has been taken to point out how a figure functions in the specific context of the examples provided, but a lengthy discussion of these various functions is outside the scope of the book.

Q7: Do figures of speech mark out what is important in the Scriptures?

A7: No.

Certainly, identifying figures of speech might help us to recognize what might be emphasized in a particular passage, but we need to make a distinction here between emphasis and importance. (According to the *OED*, importance means to have added significance, greater weight, or more consequence.) Because all Scripture is God-breathed, or God-inspired, all of it is important. We dare not toss aside a certain verse just because it might not contain a figure of speech or to consider a passage less important than another simply because it is stated literally rather than figuratively. Rather than say that figures of speech might mark out what is *important* in God's Word, perhaps it is better to say that figures of speech may mark out truths that are to be emphasized in a particular way and in a particular passage. Figurative language, because it may be stated in an unusual or non-literal manner, often arrests our attention. Figurative language adds more zest or intensified feeling to a passage, and figurative language often brings emphasis. But to claim that figures of speech mark out what is important in the Scriptures is to suggest there is a hierarchy of truth in the Scriptures.

Q8: Do all figures of speech in the Bible bring emphasis in every occurrence?

A8: No.

It is questionable whether or not some idioms and metonymies bring attention or add emphasis to a passage. This holds true for any language. For example, in English when we refer to a computer mouse, we use *metonymy,* a figure that uses a noun (mouse) to refer to an associated noun (mouse-shaped computer device). This particular figure is so common now in our English vernacular that it can hardly be said to draw our attention or to add emphasis. Or, take the familiar idiom "hot dog." Most Americans whose first language is English will know what this phrase means and will not take the words literally. Because this idiom is so common, it could hardly be said to draw attention even though it is figurative. In other words, some idioms and metonymies are, indeed, figurative, but they don't necessarily add emphatic force.

The same might be said of some metonymies or idioms used in the lands and times of the Bible. For example, in the Scriptures the word "house" is a common metonymy for the members in a household, as in the following verse:

2 Samuel 3:1a
Now there was long war between the house of Saul and the house of David:

These words are not literal: David and Saul's literal houses did not war; the members of their households fought one another. In this example, the word "house" is a *metonymy,* but does it bring emphasis or draw the reader's attention in this particular verse? Not necessarily. It's just a common metonymy that occurs in the Hebrew language.

Similarly, the idiomatic phrase "answered and said" occurs more than 300 times in the Bible. In many cases, the person speaking isn't literally answering a question, as in the following verse:

Genesis 40:18
And Joseph answered and said, This is the interpretation thereof:
The three baskets *are* three days:

In the context, Joseph isn't answering a question, so this is not literal. Rather, this is simply a common Hebrew idiom meaning "he said" or "he addressed." The idiom doesn't necessarily bring emphasis to the passage. But it might. A careful consideration of context would help us to make that determination.

In these examples, words or phrases are used in a non-literal manner, so they are certainly figurative, but such expressions become a normal part of the language and don't necessarily have any emphatic force. Each occurrence should be considered in light of the context and in light of other considerations for Scripture study.

Finally, it should be noted that a figure might bring emphasis in different ways. For example, *anaphora* has several functions. Like most figures of repetition, *anaphora* may emphasize the word that is repeated (e.g. Matthew 5:3-11). But *anaphora* might also emphasize the parallel or antithetical relationship between the sentence, phrase, or clause that is linked by the repeated word (e.g. Jeremiah 5:17). Finally, *anaphora* might also be used as a rhetorical device to bring the reader along to an end point or climax. In this case, the emphasis in *anaphora* lies on the end matter (e.g. Romans 8:33-35). As always, a careful consideration of the context helps to determine where the emphasis might lie.

Q9: If I can't identify or name figures of speech, can I still understand the Bible?

A9: Yes!

While it may be helpful to identify a figure of speech in the Bible, and while that knowledge may uncover hidden depths of meaning, knowledge of figures of speech isn't essential to understanding or believing the basic truths of the Word of God. For example, consider the following verse:

John 3:16
For God so loved the world, that he gave his only begotten Son, that whosoever believeth in him should not perish, but have everlasting life.

In this verse the word "world" is a metonymy put for the people in the world. But can we understand and believe the meaning of this verse without knowing about the figure of speech? Yes. Can we benefit from this verse without knowing that the metonymy exists? Certainly. While figures of speech may enhance our understanding of and appreciation for the divinely inspired Scriptures, knowledge of this field is not essential to understanding or to believing basic truths in the Bible.

Q10: What is the significance of several figures of speech occurring in one verse?

A10: I don't know exactly, but they sure arrest my attention!

BIBLIOGRAPHY

BIBLIOGRAPHY
BOOKS

Adamson, Sylvia, Ed. et al. *Renaissance Figures of Speech*. Cambridge: Cambridge UP, 20011.

Abrams, M.H. and Geoffrey Harpham. *A Glossary of Literary Terms*. Stamford, CT: Cengage, 2012/

Barry, Dave. *Dave Barry's Greatest Hits*. New York: Random, 2010.

Bullinger, E. W. *Figures of Speech Used in the Bible Explained and Illustrated*. London, 1898. Reprint Tenth Edition, Grand Rapids, MI: Baker Books, 1984.

Caplan, Harry. *An English Translation of Ad Herennium* London: William Heinemann Ltd., 1964.

Corbett, Edward P.J., *Classical Rhetoric for the Modern Student*. Oxford University Press, New York, 1971.

Cuddon, J. A. Ed. *Dictionary of Literary Terms*. New York: Penguin, 199.

Cummins, Walter J. *A Journey Through the Acts and Epistles: The Authorized King James Version with Notes and a Working Translation*, Vols. 1 and 2. Franklin, OH: Scripture Consulting, 2006.

Cummins, Walter J. *Scripture Consulting: Select Series*. "A Basis for Scripture Study." Franklin, OH: Scripture Consulting, 2010.

Dancygier, Barbara and Eve Sweetser. *Figurative Language*. Cambridge: Cambridge UP, 2014.

Enos, Theresa. *The Encyclopedia of Rhetoric and Composition*. London: Routledge, 1996.

Espy, Willard R. *The Garden of Eloquence: A Rhetorical Bestiary*. New York: Harper & Row, 1983.

Ferrari, Gloria. *Figures of Speech: Men and Maidens in Ancient Greece*. Chicago: Chicago UP, 2002.

Geer, Christopher C. *Open My Eyes That I Might See*. Glasgow, Scotland: Word Promotions Ltd., 2009.

Geer, Christopher C. *Walking in God's Power.® A Biblical Studies Series Intermediate Class Student's Study Guide*. Glasgow, Scotland: Word Promotions Ltd., 1995-2000. Appendix 2.2.

Joseph, Sister Miriam. *Shakespeare's Use of the Arts of Language*. Philadelphia: Paul Dry Books, 2005.

Keach, Benjamin. *Tropologia: A Key to Open Scripture Metaphor in Four Books*. London: William Hill Collingridge, 1858.

Lanham, Richard. *A Handlist of Rhetorical Terms*. Berkeley: U of California P, 1991.

Leith, Sam. *Words Like Loaded Pistols: Rhetoric from Aristotle to Obama*. New York: Basic Books, 2012.

Linnington, R. T. *The Rhetorical Speaker: And Poetical Class Book*. London: J. Souter, 1833.

Macbeth, John Walker Vilant. *The Might and Mirth of Literature*. New York: Harper and Brothers, 1875.

Metzger, Bruce M. *The New Testament Its Background, Growth, and Content*. Nashville, Abigdon: 2003.

Moliken, Paul, Ed. *Rhetorical Devices: A Handbook and Activities For Student Writers*. Clayton, DE: Prestwick House, 2007.

Nanos, Paul. *The Irony of Galatians: Paul's Letter in First-Century Context*. Minneapolis: Fortress Press, 2002.

Neil, James. *Strange Figures: The Figurative Language of the Bible*. London: Stanley Martin and Company, 1929.

Pallister, William. Between Worlds: The Rhetorical Universe of Paradise Lost. Toronto: U of Toronto P, 2013.

Peacham, Henry. *The Garden of Eloquence* (1593). New York: Delmar Scholars' Facsimiles & Reprints, Inc. 1977.

Quinn, Arthur. *Figures of Speech: 60 Ways To Turn A Phrase*. Salt Lake City: Gibbs M. Smith, 1982.

Ryan, Susan Elizabeth and Robert Indiana. *Figures of Speech*. New Haven, CT: Yale UP, 2000.

Sloane, Thomas O. ed. *Encyclopedia of Rhetoric*. Oxford: Oxford UP, 2001.

Smyth, Herbert Weir. *Greek Grammar*. Cambridge, MA: Harvard UP, 1920.

Sterrett, T. Norton. *How to Understand Your Bible*. Westmont, IL: Intervarsity Press, 2010.

Taylor, Warren. *Tudor Figures of Rhetoric*. Whitewater, WI: Language Press, 1972.

Welch, Charles H. *In Heavenly Places*. The Berean Publishing Trust: London, 2003.

Wierwille, Victor Paul. *Are the Dead Alive Now?* New Knoxville, OH: American Christian Press, 1971.

Williams, Gordon. *Figures of Thought in Roman Poetry*. New Haven: Yale UP, 1980.

Winokur, Jon. *The Big Book of Irony*. New York: St. Martin's Press, 2007.

Zuck, Roy B. *Basic Bible Interpretation*. Wheaton, IL: Victor Books, 1991.

ARTICLES

Black, David Alan. "New Testament Semitisms." *The Bible Translator* 39:2 (Apr 1988): 215-223.

Edgeworth, Robert J. "Darkness Visible" *The Classical Journal*. 79:2 (1983-84): 97-99.

Leigh, James H. "The Use of Figures of Speech in Print Ad Headlines." *Journal of Advertising* 23: 2 (Jun 1994): 17-33.

Marlowe, Michael D. Ed. "New Testament Semitisms." *The Bible Translator* 39:2 (Apr 1988): 215-223.

ALSO BY JULIA B. HANS....

Take the mystery out of Bible history and customs....

$15.00 + s/h

and help kids understand what the Bible means when it speaks in unfamiliar words describing ancient people, places, and things.

This comprehensive guide, designed for teachers and students, covers the full spectrum of life in Bible times, including

➤ **Dwellings**—read about nomadic life then make a mini Bedouin tent
➤ **Food**—learn about food customs and cook some authentic Middle Eastern favorites
➤ **Clothing**—see how people dressed and then make your own costumes
➤ **Education**—read how students in Bible times learned about God
➤ **Family and marriage**—appreciate marriage customs and see how families lived
➤ **Trades and professions**—build understanding of jobs and commerce in the ancient world
➤ **Music, recreation, and games**—play some games of ancient Israel

MORE THAN 70 classroom-tested CRAFTS AND ACTIVITES FOR BIBLE LESSONS!
✓ How to make a "goatskin" bottle out of burlap
✓ How to tie a turban using strips of muslin
✓ How to make a phylactery out of cotton strips
✓ How to make an "animal skin" scroll out of canvas

To order: visit www.baystatebiblefellowhip.org and click on resources

INDEX

INDEX

CPSIA information can be obtained
at www.ICGtesting.com
Printed in the USA
LVHW112337040822
725258LV00004B/305